D0217627

Literary Sisters

Literary Sisters

Dorothy West and Her Circle

A BIOGRAPHY OF THE
HARLEM RENAISSANCE

VERNER D. MITCHELL
AND CYNTHIA DAVIS

RUTGERS UNIVERSITY PRESS
New Brunswick, New Jersey, and London

Library of Congress Cataloging-in-Publication Data

Mitchell, Verner D., 1957–

Literary sisters : Dorothy West and her circle, a biography of the Harlem
Renaissance / Verner D. Mitchell and Cynthia Davis.
    p.   cm.
  Includes bibliographical references and index.
  ISBN 978–0–8135–5145–6 (hardcover : alk. paper)
  ISBN 978–0–8135–5146–3 (pbk. : alk. paper)
  1. American literature—African American authors—History and criticism.
  2. American literature—Women authors—History and criticism.
  3. West, Dorothy, 1907–1998—Criticism and interpretation.
  4. African American women—Intellectual life.   5. African American women
in literature.   6. Harlem (New York, N.Y.)—Intellectual life—20th century.
  7. African American arts—New York (State)—New York.
  8. Harlem Renaissance.   I. Davis, Cynthia, 1946–   II. Title.
  PS153.N5M58 2012
  813'.5209896073—dc22
      2011001039

A British Cataloging-in-Publication record for this book is available from the
British Library.

Copyright © 2012 by Verner D. Mitchell and Cynthia Davis

All rights reserved

No part of this book may be reproduced or utilized in any form or by any means,
electronic or mechanical, or by any information storage and retrieval system, without written permission from the publisher. Please contact Rutgers University
Press, 100 Joyce Kilmer Avenue, Piscataway, NJ 08854–8099. The only exception
to this prohibition is "fair use" as defined by U.S. copyright law.

Visit our Web site: http://rutgerspress.rutgers.edu

Manufactured in the United States of America

For Jared, Courtney, Dylan, Jack, Caroline, and Sofia

Contents

ACKNOWLEDGMENTS

THIS BIOGRAPHY took root in April 1997 at the Fifty-seventh Annual College Language Association Convention in Atlanta, Georgia. The conference was hosted by Spelman College, the historic black college for women, founded in 1881. We appeared on a panel focused on women writers of the Harlem Renaissance and presented papers on first cousins Helene Johnson and Dorothy West. Since then we have collaborated on presentations, scholarly articles, and two books. The current project is the culmination of this work and the final part of a trilogy on the intellectual, emotional, and literary relationships of Dorothy West, Helene Johnson, and their circle.

A number of very important persons deserve credit for making this book possible. First we thank the family of Dorothy West and Helene Johnson. Their enthusiasm for and pleasure in the project were matched only by our own. Abigail McGrath generously opened her homes to us in New York and on Martha's Vineyard, provided access to hitherto unpublished material on the two writers, and shared her memories of her mother, Helene Johnson, and of Edna and Lloyd Thomas and Olivia Wyndham. Abigail also introduced us to World War II veteran John Johnson, the writers' first cousin and the last surviving family member of that generation. Johnson enthusiastically shared his memories of his mother, the Reverend Scotter Benson Johnson, and of several other family members. We were especially fortunate in establishing warm relationships with the late Barbara Franklin and her daughter, Courtney Franklin, and we thank them for hosting us in New Haven, Connecticut, and for providing vintage family photographs and valuable perspectives on the two writers. Tom Wirth shared his memories of Richard Bruce Nugent and provided important photographs from the 1920s.

We thank Dr. Carol-Rae Sodano, dean of the School of Adult and Continuing Education, Barry University; Dr. Eric Link, chair of the

Department of English, University of Memphis; and Dr. Marie Cini, dean of the School of Undergraduate Studies at University of Maryland/ University College. Without their support and encouragement over the past years, we could not have traveled to the archives, libraries, and interviews that provided us with primary sources.

Several friends and colleagues also gave crucial support. We extend special thanks to Cheryl A. Wall, whose pioneering work on black women writers provided the inspiration for work on West and Johnson. Cherene Sherrard-Johnson, initially an anonymous reader, has our heartfelt thanks for her cogent commentary and early, pivotal support. Our colleagues DoVeanna Fulton Minor and Ladrica Menson-Furr read the entire manuscript and offered prudent, immensely helpful feedback. Patricia Feito, Linda DiDesidero, Reginald Martin, and Lisa Beth Hill offered valuable perspectives on women's writing and African American history. Sincere thanks to our graduate assistants, Jervette Ward-Ellis and Jennifer Weber, whom we wish much success as they begin to pursue their own scholarship. We are also indebted to Adelaide Cromwell and the late Isabel Washington Powell, who gave generously of their time and memories in personal interviews.

The unsung heroes of academic research are, of course, librarians, and we were fortunate in working with some of the very best. We gratefully acknowledge Beth Madison Howse of Franklin Library, Fisk University; Ruth Caruth and Graham Sherriff of Beinecke Rare Book and Manuscript Library, Yale University; Janet Sims-Wood of Moorland-Spingarn Research Center, Howard University; Karen Jefferson and Cathy Lynn Mundale of Atlanta University Center Archives; JC Johnson of Mugar Memorial Library, Boston University; Brenda B. Square and Shannon Burrell of Amistad Research Center, Tulane University; Ellen Shea and Diana Carey of Schlesinger Library, Radcliffe Institute, Harvard University; Perida A. Mitchell of Thomas County (Georgia) Public Library; Dave Proulx of Family History Center, Plantation, Florida; Elspeth Healey of Harry Ransom Center, University of Texas; Julia Gardner of Special Collections Research Center, University of Chicago; Vicki Catozza of Western Reserve Historical Society, Cleveland, Ohio; and the staff of the Library of Congress, Manuscript Division, WPA Federal Writers' Project Collection. Barb Mann of University of Maryland/ University College has provided unstinting and enthusiastic support and valuable suggestions for using the materials in the University of Maryland Library System.

Much gratitude goes to the staff of Rutgers University Press for their commitment to African American literature and for their consummate professionalism. Kathryn Gohl provided outstanding copyediting assistance. Our sponsoring editor, Leslie Mitchner, believed in the project from the very beginning and provided unwavering enthusiasm and wise counsel.

Finally, for their inspiration and many acts of kindness, we thank our families and friends: most especially our parents, without whose love and support none of it would have been possible; our children and their generations, Jared, Courtney, Renee, and Matthew; and as always, Veronica and Robert, to whom this book is offered with love.

Literary Sisters

Prologue

As an American cultural phenomenon, the Harlem Renaissance extends far beyond the geographical boundaries of New York. Artists from all over the United States, including New Mexico, Texas, Utah, Kansas, and California, contributed to the movement. The work of Renaissance writers Langston Hughes and Claude McKay, among others, was translated and was well known in Europe and the Soviet Union. In recent years, the steady stream of anthologies, memoirs, criticism, biographies, social commentary, and collections of letters from the period attests to the popular and academic interest in the Harlem Renaissance. Indeed, since the Renaissance's zenith in 1926, interest in the field has never been keener.

Dorothy West (1907–1998) and Helene Johnson (1906–1995) were the youngest of the Harlem Renaissance writers. The cousins were also unique because their social and professional connections were not limited to literature but encompassed theater, dance, film, graphic arts, music, politics, high society, academia, and artistic bohemia. West studied writing at Columbia University with John Erskine, Dorothy Scarborough, and Blanche Colton Williams. In 1929 she performed in the Theatre Guild's production of *Porgy*. A few years later she and Langston Hughes went to Russia with a group of African American artists and intellectuals to make a film on American racism. In 1948 her satirical first novel about Boston's elite African American aristocracy was reviewed and praised in newspapers across the United States. Although West initially received more critical and popular attention than her cousin, particularly after her novel *The Wedding* (1995) was produced for television by Oprah Winfrey, Helene Johnson's literary reputation has expanded in recent years. In her February 27, 2000, *Washington Post* column, the Pulitzer Prize–winning poet Rita Dove proclaimed that "Helene Johnson proved herself a lyricist of utmost delicacy yet steely precision" (X12). Another recent admirer, also a Pulitzer Prize winner in poetry, is Yusef Komunyakaa. For him,

Johnson was "the youngest and most talented of the Harlem Renaissance poets." It may come as a surprise that Komunyakaa ranks Johnson ahead of better-known luminaries, yet decades earlier the Harlem Renaissance novelist and playwright Wallace Thurman had reached the same verdict. Writing in his 1928 essay "Negro Poets and Their Poetry," Thurman maintained that "Helene Johnson alone of all the younger group seems to have the 'makings' of a poet." Earlier, she had been praised by William Stanley Braithwaite, Robert Frost, and James Weldon Johnson. Frost, who served as a judge for the 1926 *Opportunity* contest, called Johnson's "The Road" the "finest" poem submitted.[1] The poem, which originally appeared in Alain Locke's *The New Negro* anthology, personifies nature as "A leaping clay hill lost among the trees, / . . . And stretched out in a single singing line of dusky song."[2] It is likely that Johnson's alluring nature verse, set in the woods and shores of her beloved New England, reminded Frost of his own approach to poetry.

Despite the two women's significant contributions to the Harlem Renaissance and the fact that they knew and corresponded with most of the luminaries of the period, no one has written a biography of Dorothy West and Helene Johnson. In telling the story of West, Johnson, their family, and their friends, this book takes a national, global, and multi-disciplinary approach to the Harlem Renaissance. West and Johnson were raised in the privileged atmosphere of Boston's African American society, whose forebears helped lead the abolitionist cause. As young women they left Boston for New York in order to write, and against many odds they succeeded. Johnson's poetry was published by Frank Crowninshield in *Vanity Fair*, while West published many short stories and contributed essays on African American culture to the Works Progress Administration (WPA). Later, with her intimate friend Marian Minus, West created a literary journal that was eventually taken over by Richard Wright. Her inaugural novel *The Living Is Easy* is an account of the spiritual decline of the black Bostonians from abolitionist idealism to banal materialism. West's second novel, *The Wedding,* takes place in Oak Bluffs, the exclusive African American summer resort on Martha's Vineyard; the book was edited by Jacqueline Kennedy Onassis and made into a film by Oprah Winfrey. West's and Johnson's work is now routinely included in courses on African American literature, American cultural history, women's studies, and ethnic studies.

Throughout the 1960s West, like her Harlem Renaissance contemporaries, was sidelined by the Black Arts Movement, which privileged a more militant and Afrocentric approach to literature. Interest in her work revived in the 1970s with the feminist movement and the impetus to recover forgotten African American texts. Several critical studies on women writers of the Harlem Renaissance explored her writing. With the resurgence of interest in the period, West, who was then living quietly on Martha's Vineyard, gave interviews about her cousin Helene and their relationships with Zora Neale Hurston, Langston Hughes, Wallace Thurman, Countee Cullen, and A'Lelia Walker. West also reminisced about Richard Wright, Richmond Barthé, Ralph Ellison, Claude McKay, and Bruce Nugent. Unfortunately, most of these accounts, including reports of several marriage proposals, contain factual and biographical errors, some promulgated by West herself and repeated without verification by subsequent scholars. We aim, therefore, to correct the record and to clarify some false perceptions and incorrect assumptions about members of the Harlem Renaissance and their work.

Since the 1970s scholars have interrogated the Harlem Renaissance through a number of approaches and perspectives. The feminist scholarship of Mary Helen Washington, Barbara Christian, Henry Louis Gates Jr., Nellie McKay, Cheryl A. Wall, Maureen Honey, and Deborah McDowell, among others, has recovered significant African American women's texts. Economic, political, and cultural perspectives on the period were explored by Cary Wintz and David Levering Lewis. The collected letters of Zora Neale Hurston, Jean Toomer, and Carl Van Vechten have provided new insights, while Tom Wirth's work on Bruce Nugent has initiated inquiry into the gay and lesbian subculture of the period. Several collections of photographs have enhanced our appreciation of the vitality and creativity of the Harlem Renaissance.

Literary Sisters draws on all of these approaches and combines them with the careful investigation of public documents. Too often birth records, death certificates, school and Social Security records, cemetery records, street directories, and census reports are not part of academic research. These sources are particularly important in the recovery of African American letters since many writers did not benefit from the book reviews, interviews, and other avenues of marketing and publicity offered to white authors. We have thus tried to capture what Cheryl Wall calls the "multidimensionality" of African American cultural identity and literature.[3]

Our intention is not to write a linear biography that traces a subject's life through specific dates. Instead, we set down a literary genealogy that focuses, recursively, on several key moments in the lives of West and Johnson. As such, *Literary Sisters* is somewhat akin to Langston Hughes's *The Big Sea*. In this work Hughes tells his life's story, beginning at age twenty-one, shortly after leaving Columbia University; he intersperses various travels and other experiences, and ends the work, still in his twenties, at the close of the Harlem Renaissance. Cheryl Wall's *Worrying the Line: Black Women Writers, Lineage, and Literary Tradition* (2005) provides a recent critical model. Wall explains that " 'worrying the line' is inevitably a trope for repetition with a difference," just as the four lines of a blues repeat key words and phrases with subtle but significant differences (16). In the absence of accurate information on Dorothy West's literary influences, and with virtually no word at all from Helene Johnson, we have woven the information gleaned from personal interviews, family stories, photographs, letters, diaries, memoirs of the period, and public documents into a literary genealogy based on both literary influences and social/cultural models, in order, as Wall expresses it, to "access and confront history" by filling in "the missing links in family genealogies" and reconnecting with the past (244). We have thus tried to demonstrate the ways in which "a confluence of social and historical events enabled the creation of 'the community of black women writing' that Hortense Spillers designated 'a vivid new fact of national life.' "[4]

We approach West and Johnson by contextualizing them in the milieu of women's support and networking and through their connections with the African American presence in literature. By positioning the cousins in their unique Bostonian milieu, one in which the influence of Pauline Hopkins is significant, and by exploring their experiences in New York and on Martha's Vineyard, we endeavor to bring out a private dimension that is currently unknown and, by extrapolation, to draw conclusions that illuminate their published texts.

The book's central argument is that in the absence of a literary establishment, such as those supporting white writers and to a certain extent black male writers (like Wright, Hughes, and Ellison), Dorothy West reached out to her sisters in other branches of the art world, including

theater, painting, film, and music. West and Johnson benefited from a network for mutual sustenance as well as for the promoting, marketing, publishing, and performing of their respective works. These relationships were
not only professional but often intimate, emotional, and sexual.

Literary Sisters focuses primarily on Dorothy West's relationships with
her sister Bostonians Pauline Hopkins (1856–1930) and Helene Johnson
(1906–1995), and with Zora Neale Hurston (1891–1960), social activist
and writer Marian Minus (1913–1972), and actress Edna Thomas (1885–
1974). Actress Fredi Washington, public relations expert Mollie Moon,
theater impresarios Elisabeth Marbury and Cheryl Crawford, and professors Blanche Colton Williams and Dorothy Scarborough also contributed
to West's and Johnson's literary output. The biography contextualizes
African American women's artistic expression with a discussion of Pauline
Hopkins and the inspiration she offered West through her lifestyle, creative
work, and editorial endeavors. Although research has been done on West,
Johnson, Hurston, and Hopkins, little has been written on either Marian
Minus or Edna Thomas, and, to our knowledge, no one has looked at the
strong influence of the theater on the work of West and Johnson.

The women's relationships reflected, to borrow from Gloria Hull, a
"kind of racial and sororal camaraderie."[5] Still, we do not want to suggest an uncomplicated, idyllic relationship, for there were conflicts and
disagreements among them. West, for example, accused Hurston of steal-
ing and pawning her Russian fur coat, while Hurston claimed that Johnson had lost a box of her papers. When West and Johnson boarded with
Edna Thomas and her husband, West objected to Lloyd Thomas's penchant for "drifting around the house in his bathrobe."[6] In January 1936,
a conflict, possibly over rent money, caused West to distance herself from
Edna, leading Claude McKay to chastise her in a note: "You ought to go
and see Edna Thomas and invite her down. She is very sweet and says she
loves you and you should not be pettish about a little situation that was
very difficult for her."[7]

Despite stresses and difficulties, theirs were enduring, vital friendships. They contrast sharply with Hurston's deeply problematic relationships with her white patrons, Charlotte Osgood Mason and Fannie
Hurst, and with the women's relationships with many contemporary
black male writers, such as Richard Wright, Langston Hughes, and
Countee Cullen. Wright published a hostile review of Hurston's novel

Their Eyes Were Watching God and wrested the literary magazine *New Challenge* away from Minus and West. Although Countee Cullen published several of Johnson's poems, he seldom, despite his many professions of devotion, offered West any practical professional assistance. Bruce Nugent and Langston Hughes remained similarly detached from the women writers of the Harlem Renaissance for whom they claimed to have so much affection and respect.

Mindful of the dearth of assistance from the literary establishment, Dorothy West and Marian Minus nevertheless fully intended to support themselves as writers. In addition to editing the journal *New Challenge*, they collaborated on at least one novel, *Jude*.[8] Although both published in the Harlem Renaissance journals (Minus in the *Crisis* and *Opportunity* and West in the *Messenger* and *Opportunity*), they were unable to break into the "slick" magazines, despite the efforts of the famous literary agent George Bye. Bye did get West a contract with the *New York Daily News* to write a weekly story, and Minus received an award from Simon and Schuster in 1946 for the partly completed manuscript of her novel *Time Is My Enemy*.[9] She also published seven short stories in *Woman's Day* magazine. Yet, a year after Minus's award, discouraged and in debt, and threatened with eviction, they separated. West returned to her mother on Martha's Vineyard and began writing *The Living Is Easy*. Minus and Helene Johnson stayed in New York, and both obtained jobs with Consumers Union.

————

Literary Sisters chronicles the professional, emotional, sexual, and literary relationships of women artists of the Harlem Renaissance. Chapter 1 begins in media res in 1929. It offers an overview of the book's central theme and introduces the people in Dorothy West and Helene Johnson's circle, who are discussed in greater detail in subsequent chapters. Chapter 2 introduces the mothers of Dorothy West and Helene Johnson—Ella Benson Johnson and Rachel Benson West. The rural, womanist environment in which they were raised comes into focus, as does the passion for art and education that they passed on to their daughters. Ella and Rachel moved from rural South Carolina to Boston in the late 1800s, in search of better opportunities. They eventually formed a communal, matriarchal household in which resources were pooled in order to give their daughters every educational and cultural advantage. This model of womanist support and cooperation would influence the cousins' life choices.

Chapter 3 links Rachel West's early life in Boston with the social and artistic milieu of Pauline Hopkins. The chapter highlights commonalities in the experiences of Dorothy West, Helene Johnson, and Pauline Hopkins in order to locate West and Johnson within a black womanist literary tradition of writing and editing. The chapter also provides a bio-critical review of the art, social activism, professional activities, and family background of Hopkins and her Boston milieu, and it contextualizes the history of literary friendships among the women writers and artists of the Harlem Renaissance. Chapter 4 focuses on the childhood and adolescence of West and Johnson, and on their early theater connections. The chapter discusses the ways in which Eugene Gordon, an editor on the *Boston Post* and founding president of the Saturday Evening Quill Club, nurtured the work of several young Boston women writers, including West and Johnson.

Chapter 5 follows the cousins through their early years in New York. It explores their connections in theater, dance, music, and art, and highlights their friendships with Edna Thomas, Fredi Washington, and Zora Neale Hurston. Lastly, it details the influence of academic women such as Blanche Colton Williams on the cousins' work. Chapter 6 documents West's warm friendship with Mollie Moon and their year-long sojourn in Russia, her important romances with Langston Hughes and Mildred Jones, and her partnership with Marian Minus in the 1930s and 1940s. The chapter concludes with West's writing of *The Living Is Easy* and her retreat to Martha's Vineyard, where she lived the remainder of her life.

In November 1970, *Black World* magazine published a special issue commemorating the Harlem Renaissance and included West's now widely anthologized essay "Elephant's Dance: A Memoir of Wallace Thurman." But she was not pleased. On the cover were pictures of five black male writers (Cullen, Hughes, McKay, Bontemps, and Sterling Brown) but no women. And upon opening the publication, she found that even the articles tended to exclude the Renaissance's female artists, including, to her dismay, her close friend Zora Neale Hurston. *Literary Sisters* strives to make clear, as Dorothy West and Helene Johnson well knew, that the women of the Harlem Renaissance survived by supporting and encouraging one another in their various arts.

CHAPTER 1

"Nothing So Broadening
as Travel"

Porgy, 1929

ON A WINTER NIGHT in 1929 Dorothy West, an aspiring twenty-one-year-old African American writer from Boston, waited backstage in the wings at the Republic Theatre on Forty-second Street for her entrance cue in the play *Porgy*, a naturalistic drama of Gullah life set in Charleston, South Carolina. Although Dorothy West's New England background was vastly different from that portrayed in the drama's Catfish Row, the play must have resonated with her. Her mother Rachel had emigrated from rural Camden, South Carolina, and twenty years later Dorothy borrowed from Gershwin's musical version of the play, *Porgy and Bess*, for the title of her first novel, *The Living Is Easy* (1948), in which she describes Rachel's journey from a South Carolina farm to an elegant home in Brookline, Massachusetts.

Dorothy West had not intended to be an actress; she and her cousin Helene Johnson had come to New York to study at the Columbia University Extension. An aspiring playwright, Dorothy had written a "charming letter" to Theresa Helburn, one of the few women theater executives and the producer of *Porgy*, offering to write a play. Helburn, who ran the prestigious Theatre Guild, said that the organization had no money to commission scripts but offered West a clerical position. Shortly thereafter Cheryl Crawford, assistant to director Rouben Mamoulian, hired Dorothy as a supernumerary in *Porgy*.[1]

Crawford, who would enjoy a brilliant career in the American theater, had also come to the Theatre Guild after begging Theresa Helburn for an opportunity to work there. She was a graduate of Smith College, where her "low voice and the ability to ape men . . . always won [her] male roles" in school plays.[2] Helburn hired her at a minimal salary, but Crawford supplemented her income playing high-stakes card games and manufacturing bootleg gin. Outwardly conventional, she masked her iconoclastic persona with a shy personality and a poker face. Crawford was acutely aware of discrimination toward women in the arts. Even her family in Akron, Ohio, had discouraged her desire to work in the theater: "The response couldn't have been greater if I had told them I was going to enter a brothel or a nunnery" (29). Undeterred, she moved to New York and "made the rounds from office to office looking for work as a stage manager. I was told there had been only one woman stage manager in the professional theater. No producer seemed interested in a female stage manager. . . . Or even a water girl" (31). Perhaps because of these experiences, Crawford was sensitive to the added challenges faced by African American actors. She maintained lifelong friendships with members of the African American theatrical community and provided employment opportunities whenever possible. With the more adventurous *Porgy* cast members, Georgette Harvey, Bruce Nugent, Ed Perry, and Wallace Thurman, Crawford frequented Harlem rent parties, drag shows, and all-night card games. She was a regular at speakeasies like Small's Paradise, and at the jazz clubs along Lenox Avenue. The young Dorothy West and Helene Johnson were excluded from these Harlem forays, but Crawford and her glamorous actress friends Edna Thomas, Rose McClendon, and Georgette Harvey watched over the two cousins and offered them the guidance they needed to begin a life in the arts.

Through Crawford, Thomas, McClendon and Harvey, West and Johnson met an international, interracial, sexually ambiguous group of artistic and creative women in New York. Most were from the theater, but some represented the other arts; in addition to actresses Thomas, Harvey, and McClendon, the group included Fredi and Isabel Washington, and Ethel Waters; theatrical agent Elisabeth Marbury and her partner, interior decorator Elsie de Wolfe; singer Alberta Hunter; and writers Zora Neale Hurston and Marian Minus. Together, members of this loosely affiliated group, all committed to equality in the arts and opposed to gender and racial discrimination, created a network of support and established the professional and personal relationships without which many of the women would never have prospered or even survived.

When West obtained her walk-on part in *Porgy*, Crawford had already hired Rose McClendon and Georgette Harvey. Crawford's memoir discreetly alludes to the lesbian orientation that she and Harvey shared. Rose McClendon, a striking woman with aquiline features who reminded people of Eleonora Duse, the bisexual Italian actress whose lovers included Isadora Duncan, was married and maintained an elegant home with her husband in Harlem.[3] The irrepressible Georgette Harvey was "an ample woman" who had managed a group of singers and dancers in pre-Revolutionary Russia, and who enjoyed telling people that the Russians dubbed her the "Queen of Spades" (54). Crawford's description corroborates Richard Bruce Nugent's sexually coded portrait of Harvey as an "excellent businesswoman" with a "deep—very deep—contralto voice" who "ruled with an iron hand" and "husbanded her girls, their energies and their talents—in more ways than one" through Russia and back to America.[4] When Crawford hired Harvey for *Porgy*, the latter insisted that her "girls" all be given roles as well. Edna Thomas, originally from Boston and a friend of Rachel West's, was hired later for the London company of *Porgy* and would chaperone Dorothy on that trip. Edna had worked as a social secretary to Madam C. J. Walker, the hair entrepreneur, and was a member of her daughter A'Lelia Walker's bohemian circle. She combined a marriage of convenience with Lloyd Thomas, a gay man and former manager of Madam Walker's flagship Harlem salon, with a discreet, long-term relationship with a British aristocrat named Olivia Wyndham. It was probably Edna who first encouraged West to contact Theresa Helburn at the Theatre Guild.

Thomas, Harvey, and McClendon were surely pleased to obtain steady work in *Porgy*. As they knew only too well, and as Dorothy West and Helene Johnson would soon learn, institutional support for creative African American women in New York in the 1920s, whether in the theater or in literature, was sparse. Of course, the Guggenheim, Harmon, and Rosenwald foundations did offer grants to African American artists; in fact, the mission of the two latter organizations was specifically focused on African American achievement in culture and the arts. Nevertheless, although Nella Larsen won a Harmon award, and Zora Neale Hurston obtained a Rosenwald and a Guggenheim, the three foundations supported men almost exclusively, and their assistance for women was often qualified. For example, Hurston's promised multiyear $3,000

Rosenwald fellowship for doctoral research was abruptly reduced to $700 for one semester, and her Guggenheim award for anthropological work was meager and grudgingly given. In fact, Nella Larsen was the only woman of the Harlem Renaissance who received a Guggenheim for creative writing. On the other hand, Walter White, Countee Cullen, Langston Hughes, and Richard Wright all received Guggenheims for their poetry and fiction, while James Weldon Johnson, Chester Himes, Arna Bontemps, Langston Hughes, W.E.B. Du Bois, Claude McKay, and Sterling Brown received Rosenwald fellowships, and Hughes and Cullen won Harmon awards. While all of these writers were indisputably talented and deserving, personal connections among male writers certainly played a part in their success with the foundations. Chester Himes, for example, obtained his Rosenwald through the influence of his cousin, Henry Moon, then publicity director of the NAACP. Henry's wife Mollie was a New York society hostess who specialized in public relations, and she attracted the Rockefellers and the Roosevelts to her interracial cultural events. Himes reciprocated by skewering the Moons and their circle in his satirical novel *Pinktoes*.[5] When it came to funding from foundations, Dorothy West, despite repeated efforts, never succeeded. In a letter to Countee Cullen, shortly before his death in 1945, West wrote that her application for a fellowship to write a novel had been rejected by the Rosenwald Foundation.[6] The reason, she felt, was that her work was not sufficiently "racial" in its tone and treatment of the upwardly mobile African American community in which she had been raised.

Nor did Dorothy West and Helene Johnson ever participate in the patronage system prevalent during the Harlem Renaissance in which wealthy individuals gave money for creative projects. For example, the cousins, although living on Nedick's hot dogs and orange soda, were often invited to the sumptuous home of the theatrical agent and artistic patron Elisabeth Marbury. Their Boston upbringing precluded even a hint to their hostess about their precarious circumstances, but the first time West brought Wallace Thurman to see Marbury, he departed with five hundred dollars for his novel *Infants of the Spring*.[7] Certainly, Zora Neale Hurston benefited from patronage, from novelist Fannie Hurst and particularly from the mysterious "godmother" (Mrs. Osgood Mason) who financed her trips to collect African American folk material in the South. Mason, however, held Hurston to more stringent requirements and required much more obsequious behavior from her than she did from Langston Hughes, Alain Locke, and the other male writers she assisted.

Perhaps even more important than patronage were the networking opportunities provided to male authors by literary agents, publishers, sponsors of writers' colonies, and well-connected individuals like Carl Van Vechten. Not only did Van Vechten secure the contract with Alfred A. Knopf for Langston Hughes's first book of poems, *The Weary Blues*, but he introduced the poet to Frank Crowninshield, the influential editor of *Vanity Fair* magazine, who published Hughes's early work and ensured his national recognition. Conversely, when Helene Johnson was interviewed by Crowninshield, probably through the intervention of Elisabeth Marbury, he made a crude pass at her. Like Langston Hughes, Chester Himes benefited from literary networking. Although he and Richard Wright were not close friends, they had an understanding that the more financially secure Wright would always help Himes; at a particularly desperate time, Wright secured for Himes an interest-free loan for five hundred dollars from the Authors' League Fund. Retreats, colonies, and writers' workshops such as Yaddo and McDowell also provided important support. African American writers were not invited to Yaddo until 1942, when Langston Hughes accepted a fellowship; although Yaddo welcomed white women writers like Carson McCullers, Katherine Anne Porter, and Patricia Highsmith, women of color were not included until many years later. Chester Himes followed Hughes to Yaddo in 1948, although the irrepressible Himes got drunk every day, pursued the mysterious Patricia Highsmith, and did very little writing.[8] Even Jessie Fauset, whose efforts as an editor of *Crisis* magazine from 1919 to 1926 inspired Langston Hughes to dub her the midwife of the Harlem Renaissance, was edged out of a leadership role in the literary movement by Alain Locke and her own mentor, W.E.B. Du Bois. Just as a midwife no longer commands interest once the child is born, Fauset found herself outside the network and unable to find a job in the publishing industry; she ended her career teaching French in a junior high school.

Without established avenues of support, there were, as Nellie McKay points out, few opportunities for African American women to display their work in mainstream (white) journals, and even fewer to publish a book.[9] The literary establishment insisted that novels by African Americans portray a hectic, sensationalized primitivism or a proletarian perspective, as in

Claude McKay's *Home to Harlem* or Richard Wright's *Native Son*, whereas the writing of African American women, as Cheryl Wall observes, "does not focus on the traumatic encounters of blacks and whites across the color line . . . [but] on those intimate relationships in which the most painful consequences of racism are played out."[10] Such were certainly the themes of Dorothy West's stories and novels, although some contemporary critics still misread West's purpose and misinterpret her satire of the black bourgeoisie. Both Jessie Fauset and Nella Larsen, stung by the impunity with which white writers like Carl Van Vechten and T. S. Stribling appropriated black themes and characters, published novels that challenged racial stereotypes, but it was only later that these novels received critical and popular acclaim. In general, only the race journals *Crisis*, *Opportunity*, and the *Messenger* encouraged the writing of African American women.

The theater was probably the most liberal and welcoming of the arts, but with the exception of a few women such as Rose McClendon, African American actresses found their careers were fraught with insecurity and substandard conditions. From the turn of the century through World War I, talented women like mezzo-soprano Belle Davis, dancers Ida Forsyne and Dora Dean, and opera soprano Sissieretta Jones lived a precarious existence on the road. They were universally appreciated in Europe but in the United States were often cheated by producers and managers on the syndicated vaudeville circuit. Few were able, like the Whitman Sisters, to maintain a lucrative thirty-year career on the stage, always under their own management, always able to promote and advertise their shows, and never at the mercy of unscrupulous producers.[11] Like their male counterparts, few African American actresses were allowed into the unions. There were no drama schools that taught aspiring black actors; most performers, such as Bill "Bojangles" Robinson, who toured with the Whitman Sisters, learned through an apprenticeship on the road. Except for the Theatre Owners Booking Association (TOBA, nicknamed "Tough on Black Actors"), which arranged tours on the vaudeville circuit up and down the East Coast, no agencies existed to promote African American talent. The TOBA performers traveled in special "colored" Pullman cars and played southern towns in which they could not stay in a decent hotel. Sometimes box office receipts were so small they did not get paid; other times theater managers had to hire armed guards to protect the actresses from the unwanted attentions of white men.[12] It is not surprising that when Edna Thomas began her career as an actress, her husband Lloyd vehemently opposed it, wanting to protect her from the humiliating conditions on the road. Even in the mid-1920s, Richard Bruce Nugent, touring with Wallace Thurman's play *Harlem*, wrote to Dorothy West that he was glad she was not with the show as she would be disillusioned by the racism in the Midwest.[13]

Thus, in the absence of institutional support or secure job opportunities, African American women in the arts depended on each other for jobs, advancement, and encouragement, as well as for emotional and sexual relationships. While all of Dorothy West's circle made contributions in their fields and under different circumstances would have been acclaimed for their art, they are perhaps best seen as having created a mosaic of interlocking artistic contributions in which the whole outshines the parts. With her participation in the cast of *Porgy*, Dorothy West and her cousin the poet Helene Johnson joined this unique milieu of artistic women.

Dorothy and Helene had moved to New York in 1926 upon winning prizes in a literary contest sponsored by *Opportunity* magazine. West split second prize in the short story contest with Zora Neale Hurston, while Helene won three honorable mentions for her poetry; her poem "Magula" was praised by Robert Frost, one of the judges, as a "macabresque fantasy mingled with living emotion."[14] The two young women lived first at the YWCA in Harlem and later sublet Zora Neale Hurston's apartment at 43 West Sixty-sixth Street.[15] In addition to studying at the Columbia University Extension, they supported themselves with odd jobs.

Zora Neale Hurston introduced the cousins to novelist Fannie Hurst, through whom they met the theatrical agent Elisabeth Marbury. Marbury came from an old New York family, and her forebears had developed Sutton Place. The independently wealthy, entrepreneurial, and very liberal Marbury devoted herself to promoting the new form of musical comedy and championing her protégées, such as African American bandleader James Europe and society dancers Vernon and Irene Castle. In fact, Marbury and Europe arranged for the Castles to receive lessons in African American popular dances like the Shimmy and the Texas Tommy, which they subsequently appropriated and "introduced" to New York society.[16] Dorothy West was always amused at Marbury's comment that the thing Marbury liked best about her (West thought it would be her writing) was the fact that she never asked Marbury for money. Marbury showed her support in other ways, however, when she persuaded the literary agent George Bye to add West to his "stable" of famous authors.

Zora Neale Hurston moved easily between the Park Avenue neighborhoods of wealthy whites like Hurst and Marbury, and the impromptu cocktail parties of the black avant-garde. She often brought Dorothy and Helene to these gatherings, and they soon knew everyone who would be associated with the Harlem Renaissance: Countee Cullen, Langston Hughes, Arna Bontemps, Gwendolyn Bennett, Harold Jackman, Ed Perry, Aaron Douglas, Nella Larsen, Jessie Fauset, Augusta Savage, Claude McKay, Richmond Barthé, Carl Van Vechten, and Wallace Thurman. Richard Bruce Nugent's novel *Gentleman Jigger* offers a firsthand account of the interracial dance parties, the witty conversations about literature, and the creation and consumption of exotic cocktails that the cousins would have observed. In the novel the defiantly effete Stuartt (Nugent) wears evening dress without socks, draws homoerotic pictures, cruises for rough trade in Harlem bars, and concocts drinks of anisette, champagne, gin, and codeine for his friends. Asked to describe a new cocktail, Rusty (Thurman) replies: "A Tom Collins when Stuartt makes it is a mixture of gin, anise, lemon juice, grenadine, and Vichy. A long, cool, pretty [pink] drink. . . . Did I ever tell you about the time in a low dive on . . . 133rd Street, when Stuartt decided he wanted a Tom Collins?"[17] Years later, remembering how Thurman and Nugent and their circle imitated F. Scott and Zelda Fitzgerald's self-destructive behavior, West said: "We were beautiful people. We were a beautiful young group. We supported each other. We drank too much, though. We drank too much."[18]

Porgy had played for two years in New York when the company went to London in 1929. Dorothy wrote excitedly to her mother: "Cheryl Crawford called me up this morning and told me I can go abroad . . . someone backed out at the last moment, and Cheryl immediately thought of me. . . . We are sailing the 26th. . . . Tommy [Edna Thomas] says earnestly that I must tell you that she will take really excellent care of me. And Cheryl will be along, too." In the same letter, Dorothy expresses regret that her cousin Helene cannot accompany them, although she would shortly join the road company of Wallace Thurman's musical *Harlem*.[19] Soon Dorothy would be traveling, living, and working with some of the most talented women in American theater, and she would observe firsthand how these sophisticated women created a safe space and a mutually supportive network that fulfilled them professionally, sexually, and emotionally.

Even before Dorothy's involvement with *Porgy*, the cousins had many connections to the theater. The Benson-West family summered on Martha's Vineyard, and their neighbors, the Shearers, ran a guesthouse frequented by New York show business people. Before she married, Dorothy's mother Rachel had intended to go on the stage herself. Frustrated in her own ambitions, she instilled in her daughter and her niece Helene a passion for the theater. The family spared no expense for dancing, singing, piano, and elocution lessons for Dorothy and Helene; they firmly believed that, given the cost and quota system of the professions, a theatrical career was one of the few realistic options for an intelligent and talented African American woman.[20]

The cousins subscribed to Edith Isaac's liberal *Theatre Arts Monthly*, which promoted African American performers and productions, and to *Theatre Magazine*, and they followed the careers of their favorite actresses: Irene Bordoni, Rose McClendon, Greta Garbo, and Tallulah Bankhead. After writing a fan letter to Bordoni, Helene and Dorothy corresponded with her, in French, for years.[21]

When Rachel learned that her daughter was invited to go to London, accompanied by her friend Edna, she was delighted. She believed in her daughter's talent and was ambitious for her success. For her part, Dorothy wrote Rachel detailed accounts of the culture, social life, fashion, food, and adventures of the trip. From the writing salon of the ocean liner *Bremen* she described the lifestyle of her lively companions: the steamer trunks of elegant clothes, the poker games that Edna and Cheryl always won, the free-flowing cocktails, and the luxurious shipboard meals.[22] Though several prominent male actors traveled with the group, they are never mentioned by West or Crawford; the women seem to have existed in a world of their own.

Rachel surely knew that her daughter's companions, Crawford, Thomas, and Harvey, lived discreetly variant lives. At the Shearers' she had met their friends Ethel Waters and Alberta Hunter, whose homosexuality was an open secret. In fact, the family believed that Rachel's first cottage on the island burned down after Ethel Waters tossed a careless cigarette under the porch during one of Rachel's all-female soirées.[23] Rachel was open-minded and advanced in her childrearing practices: Dorothy and Helene called all the adults in the family by their first names, and Rachel was determined to raise them free from racial anxieties or complexes, and definitely free from the restraints of heteronormative marriage. Though Rachel was anxious to be accepted by Boston's "blue-veined" aristocracy, she balked at the concomitant heterosexual imperative.[24]

Instead, Rachel admired contemporary women who rejected marriage in favor of a career. Prodigiously well read and well informed on popular culture and the arts, she followed the careers of Josephine Baker, Tallulah Bankhead, Ethel Waters, Greta Garbo, and A'Lelia Walker. These women opposed any constraints on their sexual, emotional, and economic freedom. They demanded equal access to whatever they wanted: careers, money, fame, power, or alcohol, drugs, sex, and adventure. Reported upon in both the tabloid press and the rotogravure society pages, they drew scathing criticism from the establishment as much as they fascinated and inspired the male novelists who popularized their antics: Evelyn Waugh, Aldous Huxley, Wallace Thurman, Michael Arlen, F. Scott Fitzgerald, Ernest Hemingway, and Anthony Powell.

Although women artists were often able to disregard social conventions, Rachel and Edna, as Bostonians, would have been well aware that most African American women in the arts dared not live as flamboyantly as Georgette Harvey, Zora Neale Hurston, Josephine Baker, or the male impersonator and entertainer Gladys Bentley. Particularly among the educated and aristocratic Talented Tenth, the group to which Rachel and Edna felt they belonged, "sex of any sort had to remain discreet, often was repressed [and was] frowned upon even as a topic of conversation." Georgia Douglas Johnson's literary salon in Washington, D.C., for example, included individuals of ambiguous sexuality such as Alice Dunbar-Nelson, Bruce Nugent, Angelina Grimké, Alain Locke, and Langston Hughes, yet the group carefully avoided scandal: "post-Victorian prudishness and a well-reinforced predilection to uphold . . . respectability . . . consumed the Negro upper class [and] even sophisticates like . . . W.E.B. Du Bois sometimes succumbed to homophobia." For example, Carrie Bond Day, a Radcliffe graduate and a drama teacher at Atlanta University, of whom Rachel probably knew through their mutual friends Bessie and Maud Trotter, saw marriage as "an opaque cloak that helped deflect probing inquiries . . . and allowed [her and her husband] space to conduct their

intimate behavior in non-traditional ways." In fact, Carrie Bond's marriage of convenience was probably similar to Edna Thomas's marriage to
Lloyd Thomas, a former manager of Madam Walker's hair salon in
Harlem. For women like Carrie and Edna, "even an unconsummated
marital partnership provided a cocoon of respectability so crucial to
upper-class Negroes who, because of white America's perverted perceptions, were vulnerable to . . . censure concerning their sexuality."[25]

Of course, white women also felt the grip of Victorian prudishness.
Rachel, who assiduously read the society pages, drew Dorothy's attention
to women from old abolitionist families who chose spinsterhood or
Boston marriages rather than submit to male authority, such as the
women in Henry James's novel *The Bostonians*. James examines the
repercussions of a life lived in defiance of male authority and reputedly
based the character of Olive Chancellor on one of the liberal, abolitionist Peabody sisters. Dorothy remembered Rachel calling her to watch
another famous Bostonian, Eleanora Sears, striding past their window.
Sears may have been training for her marathon walk of 108 miles, which
she completed in less than twenty hours. She was famous for walking
forty miles in a single day, along Washington Street, through Hyde Park,
and out to Dedham. A great great granddaughter of Thomas Jefferson
and a legendary beauty who never married, Sears was a society athlete
who played mixed doubles, squash, and polo, and raced horses, cars, and
motorboats.[26] Perhaps Sears's exploits reminded Rachel of her own adolescence when she mounted a thoroughbred horse and raced bareback
through the South Carolina woods.

Like Eleanora Sears, Edna, Rose, Cheryl, and Georgette led remark-
ably free private lives, protected by their friends and shielded by their
careers. Sometimes, as in Edna's case, they described their lovers as house-
guests or borders. Edna's interracial, international, and sexually variant
circle included the Carl Van Vechtens, the British choreographer Frederick
Ashton, the producer John Houseman, the writer Sybille Bedford, aristocrats such as Nancy Cunard and Olivia Wyndham, and wealthy socialites
such as A'Lelia Walker and her partner Mayme Wright, the daughter of a
Reconstruction-era congressman. Certainly, if anyone could show
Dorothy an alternative path to a fulfilling life it was Edna Thomas, who,
throughout her long theater career, negotiated the constraints of race and
gender and retained the respect and affection of all who knew her.

Nevertheless, despite their attendance at Van Vechten's interracial and flamboyantly bisexual soirées, and Wallace Thurman's predominantly gay cocktail parties, Dorothy and Helene were still naïve Bostonians who seemed unaware of sexual variance. The trip to England, however, appears to have opened Dorothy's eyes. "There is nothing so broadening," she wrote to her mother from London, with characteristic understatement, "as travel."[27] Indeed, in Dorothy's interview with Genii Guinier, her description of her "embarrassment," when, at dinner with Cheryl, Edna, Rose, and Georgette, she ordered milk instead of coffee while they all laughed merrily, sounds like a coded reference to her sexual awakening (151).

West seemed equally unaware of the private life of her friend Countee Cullen, with whom she often went dancing in Harlem. Cullen was also in London in 1929, after his brief marriage to Yolande Du Bois. In letters to her mother, West neither mentions his marriage nor seems aware of any connection between Cullen and Ed Perry, another member of the *Porgy* cast, with whom Cullen was probably sexually involved. At the end of June, Cullen went on to Paris on a Guggenheim fellowship, where he initiated a correspondence with West that lasted until his death in 1945. At first the relationship was flirtatious on both sides, but Cullen's tone cooled as Dorothy became more insistent that they marry. That Dorothy did become more sexually aware, perhaps as a result of the London trip, was clear when she passed through London a few years later with Mildred Jones, an artist with whom she was in love. Dorothy took Jones to see the apartment she and Edna had shared and cried when she found it was now a gentleman's club.[28]

During the run of *Porgy*, Edna and Dorothy shared an apartment, and Edna introduced her to the British and expatriate African American entertainment world. Edna's good friends the Paul Robesons were touring in England, after Paul's sold-out success at the Albert Hall, and Dorothy met them. She wrote Rachel excitedly that she had also met the entertainers Turner Layton and Tandy Johnstone, who were the darlings of café society and the British aristocracy, and George Dewey Washington, as well as the impresario John Payne. Payne, who had come to England in 1919 with clarinetist Sidney Bechet in Will Marion Cook's Southern Syncopated Orchestra, offered career advice, hospitality, and accommodations to many compatriots including Robeson, Marian

Anderson, and Roland Hayes. Payne's intimate friend, Lady Mary Cook, a descendant of Lord Nelson, assisted his protégés with money and public relations. She insisted everyone call her "Mother" and explained that she and Payne had been married in a previous life—except that she was then the husband and he the wife. It was probably through Payne's contacts at the BBC that Edna recorded some spirituals with Marian Anderson during the summer of 1929.[29]

To Helene, Dorothy wrote that she was having a "joyous time" in London and that Countee Cullen was "a charming comrade."[30] Cullen also wrote to Helene from London. She had been shy and reserved two years earlier when he asked her to contribute some poems to his forthcoming book *Caroling Dusk: An Anthology of Poems by Negro Writers*; she had neglected to send him a photograph of herself for the third *Opportunity* literary contest and had provided only the briefest biographical statements. But Cullen had published eight of her poems in his anthology, and Helene had apparently warmed to him. He told her that his poem "A Song of Praise" was published in the BBC Radio Times to accompany the spirituals sung by Edna Thomas and Marian Anderson. Helene wrote that she wished she could be in London with him and Dorothy and sent him good wishes.[31]

When *Porgy* closed, Edna also went to Paris to visit friends. Josephine Baker, and black culture in general, had taken Paris by storm, and the city was full of jazz clubs, dance clubs, and stage shows featuring African American performers. Countee Cullen, in a discreet compliment to her dark complexion, wrote to Dorothy, "Paris is lovelier than words just now, and you would be such a hit here."[32] Edna knew, of course, that Paris in the 1920s was "an oasis for talented women, offering both artistic and sexual freedom," but also a world without men since "most who had married were now divorced or widowed." Paris was the home of many famous couples such as Gertrude Stein and Alice B. Toklas, but "even those who . . . were not lesbian or bisexual cultivated strong emotional relationships with other women, supporting and inspiring one another in their work."[33] Edna may have met Natalie Barney and Gertrude Stein and Alice B. Toklas; all three women were close to Edna's good friend Carl Van Vechten.

Dorothy, however, did not accompany Edna Thomas to Paris; instead, she returned to the family's summer cottage on Martha's Vineyard where

Helene was waiting, recuperating from a leg injury suffered during the run of *Harlem*. On the Vineyard, the cousins slipped into the summer routine that had been theirs since childhood: they were now too big to catch the rings on the Flying Horses carousel, but they walked in the woods and on the beach, picked flowers and blueberries, and motored around the island with the artist Lois Mailou Jones, Adam Clayton Powell Jr., and the composer Harry T. Burleigh. In the evenings they attended band concerts and bonfires. For African American vacationers, Martha's Vineyard was a respite from discrimination and racism. As Adelaide Cromwell points out, "its combined advantages of isolation and northern liberalism made it most attractive," and the black, white, Native American, and Cape Verdean residents of the island mingled amiably.[34]

Unlike New York, with its frenetic pace, the Vineyard was an ideal environment in which to write. Now, as Helene sat alone by the ocean, writing poems of "defiant sensuality" such as "Vers de Société" (Outside Society) in which she "rejected bourgeois rituals of courtship" and the hypocrisy of conventional relationships, Dorothy began a novel about her London experiences.[35] Thurman, to whom she sent a draft, recognized portraits of Georgette Harvey, Cheryl Crawford, and Edna Thomas and encouraged her efforts, although he suggested she acquire some sexual experience in the interests of art.[36]

In fact, despite their talents and promise, their critical acclaim, and their supportive family, both women were somewhat adrift, and the summer of 1929 was a period of stock taking. The worldwide financial crisis was worsening, and neither had completed a degree or had a job, a permanent relationship, or a clear professional direction. Certainly, they felt limited not only by the social expectations of their Boston Brahmin background, but also by the general constraints of race, gender, and economics. On the other hand, their unconventional upbringing, their strong matriarchal family history, their friends among Boston's African American leaders in the arts and in civil rights, their connections to the theater, their openness to a womanist Zeitgeist, and their willingness to resist "the heterosexual imperative" certainly helped them to chart a future course not only for their art but also for their emotional and sexual fulfillment.

CHAPTER 2

The Benson Family
Comes to Boston

HELENE JOHNSON AND DOROTHY WEST were raised in a communal, matriarchal household in which women were encouraged, indeed expected, to excel in education, the social graces, and the arts. At home, where the Benson sisters ran the household and the only male was the shadowy figure of Dorothy's father, Isaac West, Helene and Dorothy learned that women create a powerful and self-sufficient network of financial and psychological support, and that such support could always be counted upon, even in a world in which the artistic careers of African American women were treated with indifference, if not hostility. The cousins were born in Boston almost exactly one year apart, on Saturday, July 7, 1906 (Helene), and Sunday, June 2, 1907 (Dorothy). Their cousin Eugenia Rickson was also born in 1907, and the three girls grew up as sisters.[1] The children's mothers, Ella, Rachel, and Minnie Benson, along with their sister Carrie and various other siblings, moved to Boston from Camden, South Carolina, as each graduated from grammar school.

The cousins' great grandparents had belonged to the relatively privileged group of house servants, although they strenuously resisted the depredations of slavery. West recalls that "Great-aunt Fanny hung herself in the hay loft where her master left her running blood after he gave her her first whipping for stepping on the tail of his valuable hunting hound," and Great Grandmother Patsy, who was scolded for burning a pan of biscuits, the first time she had ever done so in forty years, "walked out of that kitchen and down to the river . . . where they fished her out by her long black hair." Benjamin Benson, the father of Rachel, Ella, Carrie, and Minnie, also had long, straight hair and was described by one of his daughters as Indian.[2] This description is consistent with the family mythology promulgated by Rachel that the Bensons, despite fair skin and straight hair, were not part-Caucasian but instead descendents of a "white tribe of Indians." Dorothy West wrote several accounts of her mother's insistence that the family had no white blood.[3] If, as is likely, Benjamin Benson's white and black forebears had intermarried with Native Americans in South Carolina, the family story acquires some credibility, although its purpose, in Rachel's mind, was clearly to reinforce the children's self-esteem and to distance them from the horrors of slavery.

In fact, Benjamin and his future wife Helen were born in bondage, and both were children of their masters. Dorothy described her grandmother Helen Benson as a child with curly red hair, and Ella recalled, in a WPA interview with Dorothy in 1938, that "when my mother was a little girl and freedom had just been declared, she was dancing up and down and making a big noise outside in the yard. Her madam came to the door and said 'What is the matter with you, Helen? Are you crazy?' Mother said, 'No, I'm not crazy. I'm free, bless God, I'm free at last!' "[4] The stories of these strong and assertive foremothers were retold in the Benson family and provided models for West and Johnson as they pursued their artistic careers.

Helen and Benjamin married when she was sixteen and he nineteen. They lived in rural De Kalb County, near Kershaw, South Carolina, where Benjamin, a skilled carpenter, also worked at a sawmill. Although they were the working poor, Helen Benson was meticulous about her children's appearance; she dressed all of them in handmade lace-trimmed drawers. Unfortunately, Rachel invariably tore hers in tomboy pursuits. According to Ella, the Bensons lived in self-sufficient isolation and were not allowed to play with other children. This practice was not a manifestation of snobbishness but a cultural expectation of the time and place—that one relied on one's family for everything, including play. Nevertheless, Helen encouraged her children to shine in community activities: in 1938, Ella could still recite the long Victorian poem she memorized fifty years earlier for Children's Day at church.[5] Like Zora Neale Hurston's mother, Helen Benson saw a horizon of endless possibility for the first generation out of slavery and was determined that her children would succeed. She and her husband, despite enormous sacrifice, sent all nineteen children to a private grammar school.[6]

At the time there was no public education for African American children in South Carolina, although, according to Dorothy, "beginning

to spread across the state was a scattering of private academies, established by gentlewomen from the North, mostly New England spinsters
of means and selflessness, whose abolitionist background was their impetus." These schools, initiated by benevolent aid societies, employed well-
trained teachers, both black and white, with degrees from normal schools
and colleges. The curriculum, like that of northern public schools, was
challenging and included intensive preparation in grammar, elocution,
literature, history, geography, and basic mathematics. When Ella, Rachel,
Minnie, and Carrie left school after eighth grade, they possessed a solid
foundation of learning. "Sending her children to school," Dorothy West
wrote, "was my grandmother's greatest miracle, an enduring monument
to her memory. That she, who could neither read nor write, and could
have said easily that such adornments were of poor use to black folks . . .
could aspire to open the doors of their minds was the miracle that made
the generations that came after her more than mind creatures."[7]

In addition to providing schooling, Helen taught her daughters the
womanist skills of berrying, canning, and quilting. Two of Dorothy and
Helene's aunts, Mayme Reese and Emma Ayer, recalled the emotional
intimacy and economic support that rural women offered each other in
these domestic pursuits; the finished products and the pride the women
felt in their work reflect Alice Walker's belief that genius can be expressed
through domestic skills and that an unlettered woman, like Helen Benson, could become "an artist who left her mark in the only materials she
could afford, and in the only medium her position in society allowed her
to use."[8]

Both Ella and Rachel were extremely intelligent, although their
opportunities were circumscribed by race, gender, and economics. Ella,
known as "Daughter," was the first to emigrate to Massachusetts around
1890. This fact contradicts the events in West's novel in which Cleo
(Rachel) arrives first and sends for her sisters. Ella, who had a gift for
healing, hoped to study nursing. She may have gone first to Springfield,
Massachusetts, but eventually she moved to Boston because the only
nursing course then open to African American women was in Roxbury
at the New England Hospital for Women and Children, the same hospital where her daughter Helene was later born. According to her granddaughter, Abigail McGrath, Ella completed a course in practical nursing,
and she worked all her life in the nursing field; although she never com-

pleted her R.N. degree, she possessed a deep knowledge of herbal and homeopathic remedies. In a famous family story, Ella raced out of the house one night to the Gypsy camp on Martha's Vineyard to deliver a baby. She was rewarded with a promise of long life for her "three daughters."[9] Though Ella really had only one child, she helped support her two nieces, Dorothy and Eugenia, and the little girls did not know until they were five years old that they were really cousins.[10]

As the oldest girl in the family, Ella had helped care for her many siblings; she "had seen enough children to have seen them all, and none of us, including her own, had anything special to delight her."[11] Later, when the sisters and their families lived together, Ella quietly kept the family together and provided financial support, while Rachel took charge of household management and the girls' education and accomplishments. Ella ceded the title of "chief mother" to her sister Rachel, who enjoyed being the boss, although Ella always received the respect due her as the "senior sister." Ella, recalls West, "carried herself above reproach [and was] the soul of starched dignity. She never told lies and was a true Christian. She went to church rain or shine and visited the sick. She read the Bible and could quote it. She gave counsel when asked for it, and was never wrong. We were all in awe of her, even my irreverent mother" (172). Like Rachel, Ella spoke like a northerner and had eliminated all traces of her South Carolina "Geechee" accent. In 1938, she described her interests as religion and nature, and although work had consumed much of her life, Ella's artistic nature was emerging in her new hobby, photography.[12] Photographs of Ella through the years show a fashionably dressed, quietly self-assured woman.

Carrie (called Dolly by the family) and Minnie flanked Rachel in the family order. Carrie, who worked from a very young age and contributed to the household, always lived with her employers and rarely came home. She did not go out with men and never married or had children, but she was devoted to her three nieces, and she and Dorothy corresponded faithfully through the years. It was Carrie who saved her money and bought the cottage in Martha's Vineyard that became Rachel's (and later Dorothy's) home. Rachel, careless and improvident with money throughout her life, found herself in reduced circumstances after her husband's death and had to throw herself at the mercy of the practical and thrifty sister who had saved up a down payment for a retirement cottage. When Carrie suffered a stroke, Rachel and Dorothy cared for her, and Dorothy eventually inherited the property. Dorothy describes the prickly relationship between the elderly sisters living on the Vineyard in the short story "The Richer, the Poorer" and in her poignant novella *Where the Wild Grape Grows*.[13]

Minnie was very fair, and the family attributed her fragile health to her light skin, since most of Helen Benson's fair-skinned children died young. Dorothy West portrays her in *The Living Is Easy* as pathologically timid and subservient to Rachel, although Minnie's nephew John Johnson, who lived with her as a child, disagrees with this portrait. Minnie had moved north as part of Rachel's plan that they live together and pool resources in order to maximize their opportunities. Rachel then convinced Minnie to pass as Irish and to work for a family on Commonwealth Avenue; there she met her future husband, a handsome chauffeur named Eugene Rickson, who was also passing.[14] When Rickson proposed, Rachel forbade the marriage, but Minnie resisted Rachel's opposition, eloped with Rickson, and moved to Ohio, where his brother was a pharmacist. Some years later, Scotter Benson, another sister, and her family joined Minnie in Ohio, first in Cleveland and later in Oberlin, although by this time Eugene Rickson was no longer living with the family.[15] Eventually, Minnie and Rickson separated, and Minnie moved back with Rachel after her daughter Eugenia was born.

In reality, none of the family portraits in *The Living Is Easy* are accurate. According to Helene's daughter, even the wealth of West's father, a fruit wholesaler, was exaggerated in the book, and "all of the sisters (all nine of them) pitched in together in a communal way in order to maintain a lifestyle which had the façade of the real Boston Brahmins." West's book caused a "catastrophic uproar in the family"; incensed that their characters had been distorted and their contributions unrecognized, "most members stopped speaking to Dorothy."[16] Several of the aunts never forgave Rachel for allowing Dorothy to become a writer. Rachel, on the other hand, loved the book. Despite its portrait of herself as a ruthless, scheming egotist, the novel fulfilled her fantasy that she had established her nieces in Boston's aristocratic "blue vein" society.[17]

Other Benson family members settled in Camden and Charleston, South Carolina, or moved to other northern cities. Scotter Benson Johnson and her husband Charles, both of whom were preachers, lived first in Cleveland and later in Boston. By the early 1940s, Scotter and Charles were spending the summers in the cottage they had built on Martha's Vineyard. They founded a church, the Gospel Tabernacle, in their home and eventually built the small clapboard church in which they ministered to members of the island's African American community until the 1960s.[18] A brother, Benjamin Jr., moved to Worcester, Massachusetts, although he sent his daughters Katherine, Bessie, and Ruth to the Vineyard, where they spent the summers with Rachel and their cousins. Eugene moved to New York in the early 1930s. Emma (Ayer), whose daughter Mildred owned a beauty shop in Harlem, often visited the city, although she preferred her home in South Carolina. Sarah and Belton, two of the younger children, lived with Rachel and her husband in Boston in 1910.

Rachel was the sixth of the nineteen Benson children and the third girl. She was the dominant personality in the family: "spirited, fearless, sassy, and smart. . . . She walked at six months and talked at nine." She memorized the alphabet the first time she heard it.[19] Rachel was a beautiful child with golden skin, pink cheeks, gray-green eyes, and wavy dark hair. But she was an incorrigible trickster, rebellious, defiant, and resistant to authority. Corporal punishment had no effect on her behavior; years later, she boasted to her well-behaved daughter and nieces that "Mama lived on my behind but I had enough fun to make up for it." When she was a toddler her older brothers carried her around as a mascot and taught her "every cuss word that had ever been invented . . . and when well-intentioned souls came toward her [Rachel] let out a string of curses that could curl a sailor's hair" (184). She did not understand the words, but she loved the effect; even then she demanded an audience. From an early age she was clever and cynical enough to trick her sisters out of their money; she rejected southern superstition and once dressed as a ghost to terrify an elderly neighbor.

Rachel ruled her siblings and invented their games. When she was six, according to Dorothy, she took her father's shotgun and chased the others, shouting "Run, children, run, you massa's drunk and got a gun." The gun went off and the children scattered, with Rachel diving under the porch. Her long-suffering mother, horrified, called each child's name. Dorothy wrote: "she called my mother in a voice that reached under that porch and scooped [her] out like sand in a shovel. Mama didn't even bother to ask who . . . had stolen Papa's gun. She just lit into my poor mother as if all her other children had halos on their heads. My mother so often said that when she was a child she got everybody's beating. But mostly, I think she got her own" (185–186). Though Rachel loved her mother passionately, she constantly tested her.

Despite the family's remote location, they were aware of popular culture, since reviews of traveling minstrel shows, jubilee singers, and vaudeville acts were published in the black press. When Rachel was around ten, her handsome young uncle Gabriel, who lived with the family, taught her the latest dance steps as well as juke songs and blues tunes in which code words and double entendres veil sexual references. Rachel was a born performer; she later sketched herself dancing and singing:

> I went to the guard house on my knees:
> First thing I saw was a pan of peas.
> The peas so red and the meat so fat,
> I got stuck on the guard house just from that.

In the note accompanying the pictures she said she would never forget the dance that accompanied the words:

> I love that gal and I always will
> I'll love her till the seas run dry.
> And if I thought she didn't love me,
> Take morphine and die.[20]

Although these songs horrified her God-fearing parents, they gave Rachel a taste for performance. Her talent for singing, dancing, and mimicry, not to mention her contempt for social convention, inspired dreams of a stage career. It is possible she knew of the Hyers Sisters, African American artists who, beginning in 1876, toured the country for thirty years in musical reviews and stage shows. In 1890, the sisters' production of *Out of Bondage* was an important milestone, "signaling the transition from minstrelsy to black musical comedy."[21] Rachel undoubtedly read about or saw women on the vaudeville and burlesque circuits who performed "in lavish costumes, with showy high-stepping and international touring schedules"; unlike the models of modest womanhood offered by the God-fearing Benson family, these entertainers were "figures of self-gratification, not self-abjection and denial."[22] Although most African American women worked with a male partner with whom they performed the cakewalk and other dances, Rachel/Cleo envisioned a solo act for herself, without a partner's sweaty hands to mar her costume. She seems to have sensed the trend toward more female agency as performers like Belle Davis chose to work with troupes of talented African American children. The advantage of working with young performers, referred to in the vaudeville business as "picks" (from the word "pickaninny"), was that all of the audience's attention focused on the glamorous female star, who usually adopted a maternal persona toward the enthusiastic young performers. Others worked in girl groups or chorus lines in shows that were "smart and up-to-date in material and costumes . . . [made of] silk, satin, glitter, and gold" (93, 96). Rachel moved to Boston thinking her dreams would be fulfilled; she took singing lessons. When she was obligated to work in domestic service instead of on stage, she daydreamed about running away from her employer (leaving a sassy note) and finding a vaudeville show: "She was going to sing and dance. That would be wickeder than anything she had ever done, but almost as much fun as there had been in the Carolina woods."[23]

Rachel's best friend and companion in mischief was Josephine Kennedy, the daughter of an army general who was later made ambassador to China. Dorothy recalled that "my mother always talked about Josephine Kennedy with love. They were always equals."[24] In their intense connection, Rachel, in her will to dominate, alternated with "the tenderness she always felt toward those who had let her show herself the stronger." Eluding the constraints of race and gender, Rachel and Josephine shared "the wildness . . . the unrestrained joy, the desire to run to the edge of the world and fling [their] arms around the sun, and rise with it, through time and space, to the center of everywhere."[25] Certainly Rachel was difficult, but it is poignant to observe how the heritage of slavery must have affected such an intelligent and sensitive child. When she was thirteen, she and Josephine were separated by the racial boundaries of the South. Josephine put up her hair and moved into white society, while Rachel, whose parents had found her a kitchen job in a white household, took on a subservient position that she bitterly resented. Clearly, Rachel had inherited her spirit from the foremothers who resisted slavery with such determination.

Although West's novel captures the specific details of Rachel's girlhood, the novel attains universality as an African American bildungsroman. Many of West's images, tropes, episodes, and language are similar to those used by Zora Neale Hurston in her novel *Their Eyes Were Watching God* and in her autobiography *Dust Tracks on a Road*. West certainly read both of Hurston's books before *The Living Is Easy* was published, and Hurston's influence on her own work is undeniable. Hurston's protagonist in the novel, Janie, her own autobiographical persona of Zora, and West's Cleo (Rachel) share many characteristics. All three are golden-skinned women with long hair who challenge the tradition of the passive "tragic mulatta" found in earlier African American fiction, as they defy the boundaries of race, class, and gender. Janie, Zora, and Cleo all share a profound connection to nature and to animals. They are determined to enjoy "masculine" outdoor spaces instead of confining, interior "feminine" spaces, many of which, ironically, are more dangerous for unprotected women than the outdoors. Just as Janie prefers living on the "muck" (in the Everglades) with her man Tea Cake to visiting the home of the color-struck Mrs. Turner and her predatory brother, so Cleo avoids Miss Boorum's claustrophobic parlor and the predatory advances of her nephew. Nature is evoked in West's lyrical account of morning in South Carolina just as it is in Hurston's description of Eatonville's Spanish moss, lakes, and alligators. Even Cleo's desire to fling her arms around the sun recalls Hurston's mother's exhortation to her daughter to "jump at de sun."[26] The appropriation of thoroughbreds and saddle horses by young black women functions in both novels as a sign of resistance to white hegemony. Rachel's daring stunt of borrowing the General's fierce stallion and riding him bareback, while a true event, also evokes the episode in Hurston's autobiography in which she requests a horse for Christmas: " 'A saddle horse!' Papa exploded. 'It's a sin and a shame! Lemme tell you something right now, my young lady; you ain't white!' " (29).

Because Zora, Janie, and Rachel all defy social and racial codes, they are all compelled to leave the South. For Janie, the isolated migrant labor camps around Lake Okeechobee initially represent freedom from the laws and restrictive codes of white Florida, and the gendered expectations of Eatonville. Zora leaves Eatonville after battles with her stepmother make it impossible for her to remain, and Rachel, whose beauty and defiance make her too vulnerable in South Carolina, is sent north. According to West, she moved to Springfield, Massachusetts, where her sister Ella may already have been living and where, unbeknown to her, her future husband was already established in a fruit and ice cream business.[27]

At some point in the early 1890s at least four of the Benson sisters were living in Boston. Rachel, domineering and ambitious, insisted they pool their resources and live in upscale Roxbury Highlands, probably on

Harrishof Street. Roxbury Highlands was a square mile bounded by Dudley Street and Olmstead's Franklin Park on the north and south and by Washington Street and Blue Hill Avenue on the east and west. Steeped in the abolitionist tradition, the Highlands was one of Boston's most historic neighborhoods. The Reverend John Eliot, the "apostle to the Indians," preached at the Unitarian church on the town green in 1631, and in 1635 he founded Roxbury Latin School, the oldest private school in the United States. Dr. Joseph Warren, the Bunker Hill hero and co-conspirator with Paul Revere, once lived near the school. William Lloyd Garrison had lived on Highland Street, and when Rachel and her sisters moved to Harrishof Street, many of the old abolitionist families still resided in the area, although they had already begun the move out of the city toward the northern and western suburbs.

The culturally rich Highlands boasted a number of institutions such as the Fellows Athenaeum, a private library built in 1873, a lyceum that offered lectures to the public, and a number of aristocratic social clubs. When Rachel and her sisters lived on Harrishof Street, the neighborhood was still prestigious, although almost 50 percent of the residents were foreign born. As historian Sam Warner points out, "the old Protestant families only slowly moved away and for many years their places were taken by new families of different ethnic but similar economic standing."[28]

In addition to private residences, the Highlands boasted premium rental units that were larger and more attractive than elsewhere in Boston and brought higher prices. Upper-middle-class Irish, Jewish, and African American families, attracted by the housing and the easy commute to downtown, established themselves in the Highlands throughout the 1890s and founded social organizations and places of worship. Saint Peter's Catholic Church was built in 1880, and the first Jewish temples, Agudas Achem and Mishkan Tefila, were built in 1894 and 1898. In 1900, William Garrison's house on Highland Street became the Saint Monica Home for Elderly African American Women. The Saint Monica Home was the favorite charity of the Woman's Era Club, the social and political organization founded in 1890 by the distinguished Josephine St. Pierre Ruffin. Benson family lore maintains that Rachel met the daughter of an aristocratic African American family at this time and enjoyed a romantic interlude with her, similar to the relationship described by Pauline Hopkins in her novel *Contending Forces*. It was this individual who probably introduced Rachel to the social and cultural clubs of the "blue vein society."

Rachel's decision to move to Harrishof Street was probably motivated as much by her desire for self-improvement and education as by her social ambitions. Like her sister Ella, she had come North in the hope of further education, perhaps even college. Boston's free public education and night schools motivated many southern families like the Bensons to emigrate. Rachel and Ella would have seen themselves as members of "the better quality of immigrants from the South [who] came to Boston especially to take advantage of the superior opportunities for . . . education. A great many young Negroes, whom the necessity of working prevents from going to school in the daytime, attend the evening grammar and high schools. In these evening classes are enrolled . . . Negroes of all ages . . . all eagerly taking advantage of the instruction offered, from learning to read and write up to mastering higher mathematics."[29] In addition to the public schools, the YMCA offered night classes. Seventy-five African Americans belonged to the Boston Y at the turn of the century, and all of the suburban branches included members of the race.

Additional programs, classes, and social activities were provided by philanthropic organizations such as Cambridge House, Hale House, and Morgan Chapel in the South End. Mary Antin, the Russian immigrant to Boston whose chronicle of upward mobility is similar in many ways to West's novel *The Living Is Easy*, lived in the mixed African American and immigrant South End. Like Rachel's contemporaries from the South, she relied heavily on the social programs sponsored by the settlement houses, to which members of Boston society contributed their talents: "all the children of the neighborhood, except for the most rowdyish, flocked to Morgan Chapel at least once a week. . . . On Saturday evening a free entertainment was given, consisting of music, recitations, and other parlor accomplishments. . . . We hung upon the lips of the beautiful ladies who read or sang to us. . . . Sometimes [they] were accompanied by ravishing little girls who stood up in a glory of golden curls, frilled petticoats, and silk stockings to recite pathetic or comic pieces, with trained expression and practised gestures that seemed to us the perfection of the elocutionary art."[30]

The most integrated organization was Shaw House, which West satirizes as "Thaw House" in *The Living Is Easy*. The organization was founded by Mrs. Quincy Shaw, a relative by marriage of Col. Robert Gould Shaw. Maria Baldwin and other prominent members of the race served on its board and oversaw its strict policy of nondiscrimination. Shaw House employed a number of black social workers and was dedicated to "the removal of civil, political and industrial disabilities and the promotion of a just and amicable relation between the white and colored people."[31] African American society women also founded their own charitable and cultural institutions, such as the Harriet Tubman House on Holyoke Street in the South End. The mission of Tubman House, which Tubman herself often visited, was to offer counsel and accommodation for single African American women newly arrived in Boston; it later merged with the South End Settlement House.

Since before the Civil War, the educational success of African Americans in Boston was well known, and Rachel was certainly aware of their accomplishments. Maria Baldwin, the principal of the prestigious Agassiz School in Cambridge, graduated from Cambridge English in 1881, as did her friend Charlotte Hawkins Brown, who later led the Palmer Memorial Institute in Sedalia, North Carolina. Pauline Hopkins, whose life and work would be a model for Dorothy West and Helene Johnson, graduated from Boston's Girls' High School in 1875. Alberta Scott graduated with distinction from Cambridge Latin in 1894 and was the first black graduate of Radcliffe. Upon graduation, a number of Bostonians, like Maria Baldwin, were employed in education. Seven African American teachers in the Boston schools in 1910 were graduates of the Boston Normal School (now the University of Massachusetts Boston), where Helene Johnson enrolled before moving to New York.

Unlike these other individuals, Rachel did not have a family able to support her studies and was thus unable to complete her education. She became a passionate autodidact, however, who loved opera and the theater and who, according to her daughter, could recite passages of Shakespeare by heart. Rachel surely took full advantage of the fact that in Boston public institutions such as libraries, museums, lecture halls, and concert venues were open to all. The sociologist and recorder of African American life in Boston, John Daniels, remarks that he never went to the main library in Copley Square or the Boston Museum or to a public lecture without seeing African American patrons studying, taking notes, or enjoying the cultural experience (190).

The Benson sisters were joined by their father, Benjamin Benson, around this time. A skilled carpenter, Benson may have come to Massachusetts to work for a family with property on Martha's Vineyard since he eventually bought a summer cottage on the island. The *Boston City*

Directory lists a Ben Benson as a janitor between 1906 and 1908. If this is Dorothy's grandfather, he likely inspired the protagonist in "An Unimportant Man," a janitor whose dreams of success in Boston have not materialized. Benjamin Benson died when West was about fifteen, and she describes his death in the poignant story "Funeral."[32]

The Bensons' first communal home dissolved around 1897. Both Ella and Minnie left Boston, and for the next several years Rachel worked in service since in 1900 she is listed in the census as a servant with a family at 200 Warren Street in Roxbury Highlands.[33] According to Abigail McGrath, Ella went to an estate in New Hampshire where she worked as a nurse for an elderly man. She later moved to Chicago and married a policeman named George William Johnson. Johnson's real name, according to his granddaughter, was George Xanthoudakis; he was born in Imbros, Greece, but his swarthy complexion and foreign accent subjected him to insults and discrimination. Once married to Ella, George "passed" as a light-skinned black gentleman with a vaguely New Orleans accent and "good" hair. The marriage was not successful, and Ella, pregnant with Helene, returned to Boston for her daughter's birth.[34]

Many years later, Rachel returned to Harrishof Street when her husband moved to Brooklyn, New York. At this time Rachel was joined by her sister Scotter Benson Johnson and her four sons, and although the idea was that the family would again pool resources, Rachel spent most of her time in bed listening to radio soap operas. Her nephew John Johnson recalls that "her feet never hit the sidewalk."[35]

Rachel met her future husband, Isaac West, around 1900. Dorothy wrote at least three accounts of their meeting and, although the social class of the Rachel figure varies, they all involve a beautiful, independent young woman, a successful older man, and a bicycle. Bicycle riding, which swept Boston in the 1890s, and which would certainly have interested an athletic young woman like Rachel, represented speed, independence, and modernity. In addition to being a sport, cycling was associated with suffragettes and the women's movement. Women in their special "bloomers" were ridiculed in the popular press, doubtless because both the sport and the costume suggested not only freedom but also androgyny and variant sexuality. Marcel Proust made this connection explicit in *Remembrance of Things Past* when the effete narrator sees Albertine and her "little band" of boyish girls arrogantly wheeling their bicycles at a seaside resort.[36] In fact,

Proust's description of Albertine, in coded language that suggests racial mixing, strikingly resembles the young Rachel. In the novel, Albertine, with her "straight nose and dark complexion . . . like an Arabian king in a Renaissance picture of the Epiphany . . . [and her] brilliant, laughing eyes and plump, matt cheeks . . . [is] pushing a bicycle with an uninhibited swing of her hips, and using slang terms" (850). The bicycle craze was also reflected in African American vaudeville shows such as *Oriental America* (1896), which Rachel would certainly have seen. In this production the voluptuous singers and comediennes, Belle Davis and Dora Dean, along with Mattie Wilkes and Ollie Bourgoyne, "formed a quartet of cycling girls in bloomers" to the enthusiastic cheers of the audience.[37]

In Boston, a contemporary of Rachel's recalled, "bicycles were the vogue and clubs were formed everywhere. . . . On holidays long trips were taken and sometimes as many as eighty miles had to be accomplished in one day."[38] Normally, only men participated in these rides. Walter Stevens, however, a member of Boston's brown Brahmin society, remembered a woman named Kate Knox, a "luscious female" with a "wonderful figure" like Lillian Russell's. Knox, who lived near Stevens in the West End, shocked the neighborhood when she rode with these all-male clubs, although she ignored the gossip since she was "fifty years ahead of the times" (35–36). Whether Kate Knox, like Eleanora Sears, was a Boston personality known to Rachel, it is interesting that in West's *The Living Is Easy,* Cleo (Rachel) imitates Knox when she rides alone out to Norumbega Park, a resort twelve miles west of Boston and a popular destination for cyclists. West thus depicts Rachel as a quintessential "new woman" for whom, as for Proust's Albertine, the limitations of time, space, gender, class, and race do not apply.

In West's first published piece about her parents' meeting, "Prologue to a Life" (1926), Lily Bemis (Rachel Benson), a servant, trips over a bicycle left at the back door by Matt Kane (Ike West), a successful caterer on a delivery. He takes her in his arms to comfort her and is immediately smitten by her long hair and golden skin. Like Dorothy's father, Matt is dark brown with unusual blue eyes. As the story develops, it becomes clear that the unhappy marriage that follows is the result of Matt's choice of hegemonic standards of beauty instead of compatibility or shared values. In another account of her parents' meeting, in *The Living Is Easy,* Cleo (Rachel) Jericho has moved up the social scale and is not a servant like Lily but a "companion" to an elderly spinster whose dishonorable nephew tries to woo Cleo with a bicycle. Cleo jumps on her bicycle and rides to Norumbega Park, where she collides with her future husband, Bart Judson, a successful wholesaler in the Faneuil Hall market. Like Matt, Bart falls in love immediately and rescues Cleo from an imminent assault on her virtue. In the novel, West blames the couple's unhappy marriage on Cleo's difficult personality, but the husband is also culpable, as he is in the stories "Hannah Byde," "An Unimportant Man," and "Prologue to a Life," for choosing a light-skinned wife for superficial reasons.[39]

The third version of her parents' meeting appears in an unpublished novel about Dorothy's father. Jude Crumb (Ike West), a fruit wholesaler in Faneuil Hall market, goes to meet Lila, the upper-class daughter of a businessman, in the Boston Garden. Jude has already met her socially, although he is from a lesser rung of society, and plans to take her to an elegant dinner and to the theater. He is now chagrined to see her disembark from the Swan Boats, pushing a bicycle and dressed in bloomers and a middy blouse, her hair in a childish braid. Lila's androgyny is reinforced by her conversation; when Jude objects to her outfit she replies that she could have met him on horseback wearing "Papa's pants." She wants to leave home and go on the stage, the only career possible "because I'm a girl. I should have been a boy. Then I'd have gone to college and been a doctor [or] a lawyer . . . something in a man's world anyway."[40] When Jude, already smitten, tries to propose, Lila jumps up and orders him to her bicycle: " 'Get on,' she said sharply. 'Get on and peddle. I'll help you balance. I'm strong as anything. I'm just like a boy' " (60).

Jude is also athletic, with "rippling muscles in his strong black arms," and he quickly gets the hang of the machine (62). They take turns doing tricks on the bicycle, "Lila laughing uproariously," and end the day "on either side of the bicycle smiling at each other. Their look was frank and filled with comradeship." But in envisioning a future, each completely misreads the other. Lila anticipates "the active things they would do together. . . . She would teach him to play, and that would prolong her play period, too. . . . This man was her own kind. With him she could stay out of stuffy parlors and roam the limits of her world without the impediments of stays and sweeping dresses" (60–61). Lila, despite her "blue vein" lineage, is not color-struck or snobbish. She is sexually naïve, however, and supremely egocentric, and she marries Jude in the mistaken belief that he will allow her an androgynous life. Lila mistakes Jude's tolerance of her boyish behavior for unconventionality and does not realize that he will insist on completely conventional behavior in his wife.

Jude, on the other hand, sees Lila as she would least want to be seen: a projection of his image as a successful businessman, a sexual conquest, and a mother. She is "inexperienced [but] he would be gentle with Lila. . . . [He] thought of the soft-haired son she would bear him." Jude wants to see "passers-by admiring his taste in women." He anticipates bringing Lila to his workplace "and thought with satisfaction of how Miss McGinty would gape with envy at the beautiful girl who was going to be his bride, and then wondered worriedly if Miss McGinty would think he was a cradle robber." After inviting Lila to his office he asks anxiously, "What you going to wear?" (61–62). Lila misses the warning of Jude's conventional expectations. The relationships between Jude and Lila and Matt and Lily explain much of the tension between Cleo and Mr. Judson in *The Living Is Easy*, and taken together give an accurate picture of the complicated relationship between West's parents, Rachel and Isaac.

Isaac West, nineteen years Rachel's senior, was in real life a successful wholesaler for the Boston Fruit Company (later United Fruit) in Faneuil Hall market. He was born on a plantation in Henrico County, Virginia, in 1860. After the Civil War his mother, Mary, an accomplished cook, moved her five sons to Richmond and started a catering business. Isaac, a born entrepreneur, opened his first bank account at the Freedman's Bank in Richmond at the age of eleven. His parents were deeply religious "shouting Baptists," and his father may have been a preacher. According to West, Mary's "mattress was lined with money and she spent most of her spare time on her knees, thanking God for His generosity."[41] Isaac himself underwent a dramatic religious conversion as a teenager; the language and imagery in West's description evokes James Joyce's account of the Jesuit retreat attended by Stephen Dedalus in *Portrait of the Artist as a Young Man*. Isaac apparently had both healing powers and clairvoyance. The husband in "Prologue to a Life" literally brings his wife back from death through a laying on of hands, and in *The Living Is Easy*, Bart makes a fortune in the wholesale market when he dreams correctly that a ship laden with bananas has sunk en route from Port Antonio, Jamaica. In 1898, coincidentally the year that Isaac opened his own business, a steamer operated by the Boston Fruit Company was wrecked near

Gay Head on Martha's Vineyard, and the whole cargo of bananas lost. Isaac's clairvoyance and quick thinking on this occasion may well have given him the stake to move from a clerk, as he was then listed in the *Boston City Directory*, to the proprietor of his own business.[42]

Rachel and Isaac married and moved to Holyoke Street, near the Back Bay Station in the South End. Next door, at 23 Holyoke Street, lived Susie King Taylor, the Civil War nurse and advocate for black veterans, whose 1902 memoir encouraged many southerners to emigrate to Boston. The Harriet Tubman House, a charitable organization founded by a group of prominent African American women, was located at 25 Holyoke.[43] The neighborhood was still respectable, although most of the once-elegant brownstones and brick bow-fronted townhouses had been divided into flats and boardinghouses. According to John Daniels, black families "of the better class took up their residence here soon after that area was taken from the water and made into land in the late sixties" (148). The South End had been planned and laid out by Charles Bullfinch in the 1830s on seventy-three acres of new land claimed from Boston Harbor. The community boasted bow-fronted brick townhouses and little squares, and green spaces enclosed with decorative wrought iron gates and palings. Originally Boston Brahmins bought the homes, but, as William Dean Howells shows in *The Rise of Silas Lapham,* postbellum industrial million-aires like Lapham began to move in, and the old Yankees quickly decamped to the even newer Back Bay. The South End maintained its prestige until the depression of 1873, when banks collapsed and some of the elegant buildings were converted to flats and boardinghouses. Mean-while, African Americans had abandoned the old buildings of the West End for the cleaner, more attractive South End. When the Back Bay Station was built in 1897, many black families were paid for the land and bought houses in the suburbs. Around 1907 the area around the station began to deteriorate into a "sporting" zone, and Rachel probably insisted on the move to Cedar Street, farther south in Roxbury Highlands.[44]

The Cedar Street house, where Isaac and Rachel rented a large apart-ment, is described by West as "a fine old brownstone dwelling." Since West is usually accurate about these details in her work, it seems likely that the house was in a predominantly white neighborhood and was owned by an elderly African American lady who had lived there for forty years and to whom it had been left by her former employer. "It was this bizarre bequest . . . that had started the exodus of well-to-do whites from this particular street. At the time of this mass removal, there was a scattering of Negro householders on neighboring streets. But they were moneyed people whose progeny went to white Sunday schools and played decorously in next-door yards."[45] The Turner sisters, society women whose father owned a livery stable near what is now Boston University, lived nearby, as did the Trotter family. When Mr. Turner's business failed with the advent of automobiles, his daughters were reduced to eking out a living as governesses for the children of upwardly mobile people like the Wests. In *The Living Is Easy*, Althea Binney is Judy's etiquette teacher; her story, a poignant one of the demise of black businesses due to undercapitalization, combines elements of the Turner, Trotter, Lewis, and West families. As the wealthier black and white families left Roxbury Highlands, Rachel too decided it was time to move to Brookline.

In West's novel, it is the Brookline Avenue house in which Rachel gathers her family, although that move did not take place till 1914. In fact, the 1910 census found Isaac, Rachel, Dorothy, Ella, Helene, Carrie, and younger siblings Sarah and Belton all living at 30 Cedar Street.[46] The *Boston City Directory* of 1911 lists Eugene Rickson, a chauffeur, as a boarder at Cedar Street, as are, presumably, his wife Minnie and daughter Eugenia. From 1912 Rickson, still listed as a chauffeur, boarded at various other addresses before disappearing from the directory after 1914.[47]

The family's move to Brookline in 1914 was the culmination of Rachel's ambition and a testimony to her determination to avoid Boston's imminent de facto segregation. In the novel, Cleo/Rachel is determined to leave Boston because in the South End and Roxbury Highlands "the once fine houses of the rich were fast emptying of middle-class whites and filling up with lower-class blacks" (37). Rachel sees that her race is being squeezed into a narrow strip bounded by Columbus Avenue and Washington, Dartmouth, and Dudley Streets, and she wants her daughter and nieces to attend better schools and live in more genteel surroundings. On Brookline Avenue, between 1914 and 1924, the year that Isaac West lost his business and moved to Brooklyn, New York, Dorothy West and Helene Johnson were being groomed by Rachel and her sisters to take their places in the world of art and culture.

CHAPTER 3

Pauline Hopkins and African American Literature in New England

THE CHALLENGE in tracing literary precursors of Dorothy West and Helene Johnson, particularly African American models and influences, is that Dorothy West never acknowledged the work of other writers, aside from vague references to Dostoyevsky and F. Scott Fitzgerald, and Helene Johnson never wrote or spoke publicly about her poetry. For example, despite the best efforts of interviewers to get West to claim connections to Nella Larsen and Jessie Fauset, she always insisted she never knew them, although, in the case of Fauset, she "could have" known her because of their similar family backgrounds. Nor did West ever mention African American writers of the previous generation such as Charles Chesnutt, William Wells Brown, Frances E. W. Harper, and Pauline Hopkins. In her letters and interviews West freely discussed such prominent contemporaries as Countee Cullen, Langston Hughes, Claude McKay, Wallace Thurman, Gwendolyn Bennett, Zora Neale Hurston, Henry Moon, James Weldon Johnson, Alfred Mendes, Bruce Nugent, Ralph Ellison, and Richard Wright, but her comments were always personal or social, never literary. She told more than one interviewer that Cullen, Hughes, and Moon were in love with her, that McKay and Johnson dispensed fatherly advice, that Thurman was brilliant but alcoholic and undisciplined, that Hurston cast Voodoo spells on people, that Mendes had charming British manners, that Richard Wright was "timid and afraid of white people," that the Chicago South Side Writers' Group members were "Communists," and that Ellison was a government spy, but she never admitted the influence of their work on her own. West did admire the writing of her close friend Marian Minus, who was originally a member of the South Side Writers' Group, although that was primarily because Minus had the good taste to appreciate West's own work. Although West praised Helene's writing, called her a genius, and described her poetry as beautiful and glorious, she was vague about any influence even Helene may have had on her fiction; in fact, she routinely obscured the fact that Helene was originally the more critically acclaimed writer.[1]

Given her reluctance to acknowledge literary influences or forebears, particularly in African American letters, it is not surprising that West never mentions literary Bostonians such as Phillis Wheatley, William Stanley Braithwaite, and Pauline Hopkins. The lack of reference to Hopkins is particularly odd since the two women clearly share many personal, historical, and literary commonalities through their origins in African American Boston. At the very least, West's familiarity with Hopkins's work is evident in her plots and characters, in themes of passing and color consciousness, and in her use of Gothic elements such as ghoulish family secrets and paranormal phenomena.

Pauline Elizabeth Hopkins (1856–1930) was, like West, a journalist, magazine editor, playwright, actress, essayist, and novelist. She moved in the same cultural circles as Dorothy's mother Rachel, although Hopkins could truly claim the kinship with Boston's old African American families to which Rachel only aspired. Rachel and Pauline certainly knew of each other through Maud and Bessie Trotter, the sisters of journalist Monroe Trotter. Maud was Dorothy's godmother and the founder of a literary society to which Rachel belonged and at which Hopkins frequently spoke. In fact, Rachel may have heard Hopkins speak publicly on a number of occasions, such as the time she extolled her grandfather, who "signed the papers with Garrison at Philadelphia," at the William Lloyd Garrison Centenary Celebration at Boston's Faneuil Hall in 1905.[2] Isaac West's fruit wholesale business was located next to Faneuil Hall, and such an event would certainly have attracted the city's African American business community. Furthermore Rachel, a newcomer to Boston, anxious to win acceptance in Brahmin circles, probably read Hopkins's women's magazine the *Colored American*, since its emphasis on race uplift, the arts, fashion, and culture reflected her own values and interests.

Although the Wests lived in Boston and Hopkins in Cambridge, the families may even have met at church. For reasons of social rather than spiritual advancement, Rachel encouraged Dorothy, Helene, and Eugenia to cross the Charles River and attend "the colored church in Cambridge." This was the fashionable Episcopal congregation to which Hopkins belonged between 1896 and 1930. The Bensons and Wests were Southern Baptists, but since that denomination was not a marker of upward mobility, Rachel encouraged the family toward the Episcopal fold. Of the three cousins, Eugenia particularly liked attending the Cambridge church; she was bored in the white church, where people stared at her multihued family, whereas in Hopkins's church frequented by "all the nice colored families . . . everybody stared at [her] because she was beautiful."[3]

Like Dorothy West and Helene Johnson, Hopkins was an only child raised with cousins in an extended family that valued music, literature, and the arts. Both West and Hopkins were precocious children who won prizes for their writing at an early age, and both drew heavily on family history for the plots and incidents in their work. West, Johnson, and Hopkins enjoyed a similar, privileged upbringing and shared a pride in their unique situations as brown Bostonians. Despite their elevated status, all three were socially conscious and wrote about racial inequities and issues of discrimination and prejudice. Johnson penned only poetry, but West and Hopkins worked in various genres, although they are best known for their novels and journalism. Their creative expression was not limited to writing, and all three performed on stage. Johnson danced, West acted, and Hopkins sang and acted. In fact, Hopkins's stage career was the one that Rachel West would have liked to emulate, had she not married Isaac West.

Although neither West nor Hopkins married or had a family, children were important to the three women. Helene married briefly and bore a daughter to whom she dedicated the rest of her life, but West and Hopkins lived discreet, sexually ambiguous lives, and never apparently pursued serious heterosexual relationships. All three women wrote about children and youth, and felt it was a communal responsibility to provide love and security for them. "It is not right to take a child's joy away and give him hunger," West maintained during the depths of the Great Depression, as "bread should not be bigger than a boy."[4] In their novels, West and Hopkins often contrast the innocence of children with the hypocrisy and corruption of the adult world. West's childhood persona, a little girl named Judy, appears in *The Living Is Easy* and in several of her short stories. Just as Winona and Judah innocently offer hospitality to a vicious slave-catcher in Hopkins's *Winona*, Judy instinctively behaves with a kindness and sensitivity that is lacking in her mother and other adults. When, in *The Living Is Easy*, Cleo indifferently informs her elderly landlady that they are moving to a better address, Judy sees her distress: " 'I'll miss you,' she said gently, and laced the gnarled fingers in her own" (89). West never lost her love for children; she saw their vulnerability and the ways in which they became pawns for unscrupulous adults. She and Hopkins were both fascinated by power relationships, particularly those in families, and West often said that her best writing was about children and the elderly. Blythe Coleman, the granddaughter of West's childhood friend, Jamie Coleman, and the model for one of the little girls in West's novel *The Wedding*, fondly recalls her beloved godmother: "She was my mentor and my friend, and she left me with the gift of love."[5]

West and Hopkins were quintessential Bostonians, and the history and geography of the city play important roles in their work. Hopkins grew up on the north side of historic Beacon Hill, near the West End. Joy Street, a key thoroughfare in the neighborhood, extended from the State House and Boston Common on the south, to Cambridge Street and the AME Zion Church on the north. Although whites lived primarily on the hill's southern slope and blacks on the north, the races existed in close proximity, and Beacon Hill was an address claimed by such noted abolitionists, pro-race activists, and literary figures as David Walker, Maria W. Stewart, Judge George and Mrs. Josephine Ruffin, Colonel Robert Gould Shaw, Masonic leader Prince Hall, Louisa May Alcott, Ralph Waldo Emerson, and James Russell Lowell. In January 1832, William Lloyd Garrison had traveled to the African Baptist Church (also known as the African Meeting House) on Joy Street and organized the New England Anti-Slavery Society. Six years earlier, the community's Masonic order, led by William Guion Nell and David Walker, established the Massachusetts General Colored Association, the country's first black antislavery society.

Both West and Hopkins created fictional portraits of famous Bostonians and prominent visitors to the city, such as Monroe Trotter, John Brown, Booker T. Washington, and W.E.B. Du Bois. The latter appears as Will Smith in Hopkins's *Contending Forces*, while Washington inspires both Dr. Lewis in *Contending Forces* and Dean Galloway in *The Living Is Easy*. Like Hopkins and most African Americans of their social circle, West recognized serious flaws in the Tuskegee model, but she also followed

Hopkins's lead and ignored prevailing opinion in order to create a sympathetic Booker T. Washington character in her novel. Paralleling the Washington–Du Bois truce in *Contending Forces*, West constructs Washington and his outspoken rival, the newspaper editor Monroe Trotter, as allies. When, in *The Living Is Easy*, Dean Galloway visits Boston on a fundraising trip for his southern college, Cleo hosts an elaborate reception. In an impassioned speech, Galloway urges Simeon Binney (Monroe Trotter), editor of the *Clarion* newspaper, to publicize the South's routine killing of blacks: "I and my school can be here only in spirit, but we will be waiting for Dr. Binney's flaming words to light the torch with which we will burn out one of the South's evils" (259). West acknowledged that her intent was to make Galloway a comical figure, since she didn't subscribe "to any of the things [Washington] believed in," but as she was writing, the character took over and came out "dignified."[6] Dean Galloway, like Hopkins's Dr. Lewis, is an admirable individual with a passionate interest in justice and racial uplift.

In their novels, West and Hopkins chronicle the upward mobility and changing geographic patterns of Boston's black community. West was a generation younger than Hopkins; by her time the once-elegant houses of the West End had decayed, and the city's middle-class African American population had dispersed toward newer homes in Roxbury Highlands and the South End. West obviously knew that the old buildings had become gambling dens and sites of other illegal activities, since she places the gaming house of the enigmatic "Duchess" in the West End, albeit with a fictional street name. Hopkins and West carefully delineate the neighborhoods of their characters; in *Contending Forces* the Smith family lives "in a respectable part of the South End of Boston," as do Cleo and Bart Judson in *The Living Is Easy*.[7]

In a period when Boston's reputation as a haven for racial tolerance was slowly eroding, and in keeping with Monroe Trotter's exhortation that Boston's African American citizens must assert their rights to public places, both West and Hopkins establish an African American presence in the city. Boston was a city in which people of color were sometimes invisible, but West and Hopkins claim Boston for their characters, who take full advantage of its amenities. Just as Cleo introduces her sisters to streetcar travel and cultural sights, so the Smiths escort Sappho Clark, newly arrived from the South, to Saint Monica's Hospital, the Boston

Common, Tremont Temple, and Faneuil Hall, "ancient landmarks of peculiar interest to the colored people" (129). West precisely describes the public transportation system as her characters ride the trolleys that rattle along Huntington Avenue, past Symphony Hall and the Christian Science church, and across the bridge to Cambridge. She sets one of her stories at the Swan Boats in Boston Garden. Another takes place in Norumbega, a family resort in suburban Newton, close to the banks of the Charles River where the boating accident occurs in Hopkins's *Of One Blood*. In the same novel the protagonist, Dr. Reuel Briggs, lives in a modest rooming house near Harvard Square but visits the homes of his wealthy friends near Mount Auburn Cemetery. The black-owned businesses in *Living* are dotted about the city on major thoroughfares such as Washington Street and Commonwealth Avenue. No section of Boston is off-limits to the characters in West's and Hopkins's novels, although the city's eventual de facto segregation was already beginning.

West, Johnson, and Hopkins were all products of Boston's excellent free education system. Before moving to Cambridge, Hopkins matriculated at the city's prestigious Girls' High School. With their similar educations at elite Boston schools, it is not surprising that West, Johnson, and Hopkins were solidly grounded in the canon of English, American, and European literature. According to Helene Johnson's daughter, the cousins knew Shakespeare by heart and read classics in the original French and German. Hopkins favored Shakespeare, Milton, and the great American abolitionist writers. Hopkins, particularly, was cognizant of her position in a matrilineal tradition that extended back to Boston's earlier black woman writer, Phillis Wheatley. Brought from Africa as a child and enslaved in Boston, Wheatley defied all odds and made history in September 1773 with *Poems on Various Subjects, Religious and Moral*. The book, published in London after being rejected in Boston, was the first by an African American and won her acclaim on both sides of the Atlantic.

In 1902 Hopkins published a biographical profile of Wheatley, noting that the story of her life "is common history with all classes of people, yet, we love to rehearse it, renewing our courage, as it were, for the struggle of life, with live coals from the altar of her genius." In the same essay she provided "a short sketch of the labors of Frances Ellen Watkins Harper," whose 1892 novel *Iola Leroy* was long thought the first published by an African American woman.[8] Although West does not acknowledge

Wheatley or Harper, the character of Cleo suggests that she read *Iola Leroy* and was influenced by the strong, independent black women in Harper's work. Hopkins was more open regarding her sources; she consciously rewrote the final pages of *Iola Leroy* by ending *Contending Forces* with double marriages. In the novel's penultimate chapter, Dr. Arthur Lewis, head of "a large industrial school" in the South that recalls Tuskegee Institute, marries Dora Smith (123). The newlyweds then journey back to the South, to labor on behalf of the race: "In the last beautiful days of October Dora became the wife of Doctor Lewis, and went with him to his far-off Southern home to assist him in the upbuilding of their race" (381).

Despite the conventional relationship she depicts between Dora and Lewis, Hopkins, like West, was a severe critic of the ways in which heterosexual marriage hindered women's artistic expression. Her fiction is replete with coded homosexual behavior, cross-dressing, and homoerotic relationships, and West follows her example. This is perhaps most apparent in their inaugural novels, *Contending Forces* and *The Living Is Easy*, though similar treatments of androgyny and sexual variance run throughout their fiction. For example, Hopkins's 1902 novel *Winona: A Tale of Negro Life in the South and Southwest* features the cross-dressing character Allen Pinks, who Warren Maxwell thinks is "the prettiest specimen of boyhood he had ever met."[9] Maxwell, accused of "aiding slaves to run away and depart from their master's service," is sentenced to death and dragged to a prison, where, like Paul D in Morrison's *Beloved*, he witnesses a series of sexual assaults (383). When the "heart-rending cries com[ing] from the [prison's] lower room" are more excruciating than usual, he hurries "to the stove-hole," "gazed one moment and then fell fainting with terror and nausea upon the floor. He had seen a Negro undergoing the shameful outrage, so denounced in the Scriptures, and which must not be described in the interests of decency and humanity" (385). Maxwell becomes delirious and another prisoner, Allen Pinks, is summoned to nurse him back to health: "Bending over the sick man . . . there was a light touch on his hair; a tear fell on his cheek; the nurse had kissed the patient!" (387). Perhaps because it was too dangerous to describe homosexual rape or to have one man kiss another, Hopkins later discloses that Allen Pinks (a play on her own name) is really Winona disguised as a man.

Hopkins employs a similar strategy in *Contending Forces*, exploring at length an intimate relationship between two women, only to undercut the lesbian undertones when the women eventually marry men. When Sappho Clark moves to Boston, she rents a room in Ma Smith's boardinghouse, run by Will and Dora Smith and their recently widowed mother. Sappho has a terrible secret, having "suffered so much at the hands of selfish men" (396). In Boston she is pursued simultaneously by Dora and Will, but it is Dora, who thinks her "the prettiest creature I ever saw," with whom she develops a particularly close friendship (89). Dora enters "Sappho's lonely self-suppressed life . . . like a healthful, strengthening breeze," and the women quickly become inseparable (114). Their most intimate encounter occurs during a snowstorm, when they lock themselves in Sappho's room and spend the day laughing, cuddling, talking, and eating little pink ham sandwiches. "By eleven o'clock they had locked the door . . . to keep out all intruders, had mended the fire until the little stove gave out a delicious warmth, and had drawn the window curtains close to keep out stray currents of air" (117). In drawing the curtains, mending the fire, and locking the door, they create their own secluded, private space, free from the heterosexual gaze. The locked door, a powerful marker of erotic tension, holds back even as it invites.

Dorothy West's repetition of the tropes of tongues and locked doors in an erotic encounter between Cleo Judson and the Duchess, the elegant blond proprietor of a West End gambling house, suggests that she was familiar with Hopkins's novel. Cleo's susceptibility to feminine beauty and her low opinion of males are established when she visits her husband's business and reflects that the blond good looks of his Scandinavian employee "were wasted on anything as lowly as a man" (73). Cleo avoids any marital intimacy: her husband brushes "her cheek with his lips [since] he knew that she did not like to be kissed on the mouth" (346). Moreover, after ten years of marriage, Bart can "count on one hand, and have fingers to spare, the number of times that Cleo had let him approach her" (75). Cleo's coldness and abrasiveness with Bart stands in sharp relief to her gentleness and passion with the Duchess: "Her voice was tender and persuasive. The Duchess felt her warm sympathy, and was drawn to it. And Cleo's sympathy was real. In this moment she wanted nothing more than to know about this lovely woman. Her whole intensity was directed to that end. The power of her personality was like a tongue of fire that ignored locked doors and penetrated whatever reticences might stand in the way of her passion to probe the lives of other women" (104).

Cleo's burning desire "to know" the Duchess is the first in a series of erotic metaphors. The probing, penetrating "tongue of fire that ignored locked doors," for example, is an explicit, poetic expression of lesbian love. Several critics have also noted that Hopkins uses fire imagery to suggest passion; Sappho's little stove gives "out a delicious warmth," and her name is an obvious connection to the Greek poet. During their encounter in Sappho's room, Dora reveals that she gets "tired of a man so soon," while Sappho acknowledges thinking of remaining a "bachelor-maid to the end" (121).[10] In the end, however, they both marry men, just as Cleo remains married to Bart. Though West never acknowledges a model for her exploration of intense relationships between women, it is highly likely that Hopkins provided just such a paradigm.

In addition to her sexual and political influence on West's work, Hopkins seems also to have shaped her style. Like Hopkins, West adopts a wry, ironic tone to convey an interest in nature, paranormal phenomenon, and the dispossessed, and she experiments with repetition, sophisticated vocabulary and syntax, extended metaphors, and the personification of abstract qualities. For example, in "The Mystery within Us," Hopkins describes wisdom as guardian angels: "the clouds, tinged with the gold of an exquisite sunset were, for a moment, radiant angel forms, clad in celestial garments."[11] Similarly, in *The Living Is Easy* West personifies and allegorizes beauty as "the white-gold moon [riding] the summer sky" (144). Both writers were innovative artists who persevered in the face of limited venues for black women writers, and their enduring legacy is a distinguished body of literature.

Hopkins was truly an old New Englander. She could trace her family tree back four generations to her maternal great great grandparents, Lovey Rollins (1768–1832) and Caesar Nero Paul (1741–1823). Lovey Paul was a white woman from Exeter, New Hampshire, whereas her husband, Caesar, was originally an enslaved African. Caesar Paul fought in the French and Indian War and later lived as a free man in Exeter. The Pauls were the parents of at least six children, the most famous of whom was the Reverend Thomas Paul, founding minister in 1806 of Boston's First African Baptist Church. Lovey and Caesar's daughter Nancy, described by Hopkins as "the only sister of the five brothers Paul," was her great grandmother.[12] Nancy Paul married Joseph Whitfield Sr., a farmer, hunter, and escaped slave who was born in Virginia in 1762. The couple settled in Exeter and had three children: the celebrated poet James Monroe Whitfield, the Civil War sutler (or supply officer) Joseph Paul Whitfield, and Hopkins's grandmother, Elizabeth Whitfield.

Elizabeth Whitfield married Jesse Allen, a native of Bermuda, and they eventually settled in Charlestown, across the harbor from Boston. Hopkins gives special attention to Elizabeth and her husband Jesse in *Contending Forces*. The novel, which even borrows their surname, cele- brates their courtship and marriage and offers further clues to her grand- parents' history. In a riveting scene in chapter 4, sixteen-year-old Jesse escapes from slavery in North Carolina and flees north to Boston and then to Exeter, New Hampshire:

> When he left Boston he was directed to see Mr. Whitfield, a Negro in Exeter, who could and would help the fugitive. . . . Mrs. Whitfield thought him a white man come on business with her husband. "A handsome lad," she thought. Jesse seated himself; and then as the child continued to cry, said: "Shall I rock the cradle for you ma'am? The child seems fretful." Fifteen years later Jesse married Elizabeth Whitfield, the baby he had rocked to sleep the first night of his arrival in Exeter. By her he had a large family.   (78–79)

Between 1827 and 1848 Elizabeth gave birth to three sons and seven daughters, including twin daughters born in Exeter in 1834, Sarah A. and Annie Pauline. Annie (1834–1901) was a gifted pianist and singer; she married Joseph Pindell of Boston in 1853 and in 1860 moved with him to California, where, notes Hopkins, "for thirty years her magnificent organ was celebrated on the Pacific coast."[13]

In the late 1840s, Elizabeth's brother, James Monroe Whitfield, moved from Exeter to Buffalo, New York, where he worked as a barber and associated with a group of young antislavery activists that included Frederick Douglass. Believing that blacks could not expect to be treated fairly in America, he joined Martin Delany and Mary Ann Shadd Cary in calling for black emigration to Canada and Central and South Amer- ica. Whitfield held that "the American government, the American churches, and the American people are all engaged in one great conspir- acy to crush us." Emigration was desirable, he insisted, because God "helps those who help themselves." Douglass, by contrast, favored inte- gration and assimilation and supported remaining in the United States.

"The question is," he asked, "can the white and colored people of this country be blended into a common nationality, and enjoy together in the same country, under the same flag, the inestimable blessings of life, liberty, and the pursuit of happiness, as neighborly citizens of a common country? I answer most unhesitatingly, I believe they can."[14] He and Whitfield debated the merits of emigration throughout the 1850s. Despite their political disagreement, Douglass published several of Whitfield's poems in his newspapers, the *North Star* and *Frederick Douglass' Paper*. The poems were well received and culminated with the publication of *"America" and Other Poems* in 1853. "America," the 160-line verse that gives the book its title, is representative of Whitfield's skill and his uncompromising critique of slavery: "America, it is to thee, / Thou boasted land of liberty,—/ It is to thee I raise my song, / Thou land of blood, and crime, and wrong. / It is to thee, my native land."[15] Later, Hopkins paid homage to her great-uncle by quoting his verse in her novels.

Pauline Hopkins was aware of the political and artistic contributions of several other ancestors, on both her father's and her mother's sides of the family, as she makes clear in her December 1905 "Address at the Citizens' William Lloyd Garrison Centenary." Her 1914 essay on Mark De Mortie (1829–1914), an Underground Railroad conductor who migrated from Virginia to Massachusetts before the Civil War, hails him "a race man of distinct individuality." He and his friend Joseph Paul Whitfield, a "New England black man, who had located in Buffalo, New York, and accumulated about sixty thousand dollars in money and real estate," had been the sutlers of the 54th Massachusetts Colored Troops, commanded by Col. Robert Gould Shaw.[16] In her essay, Hopkins omits the fact that Joseph Whitfield was her great-uncle and James Monroe Whitfield's younger brother. She is less reticent with regard to her links to their sister, Elizabeth Whitfield, her maternal grandmother.

There is much confusion about the identity of Pauline's father, partly because, like Dorothy West, Hopkins deliberately obscured unpleasant facts about her family. Hopkins's illegitimate birth and her parents' dysfunctional marriage and acrimonious divorce in staid Boston undoubtedly account for Pauline's silence about her early years. Pauline's mother Sarah, unlike her twin sister, Annie Pauline, lived her entire life in New England. She gave birth to her only child, Pauline Elizabeth, in August of 1856 in Portland, Maine. Sarah named Pauline for her sister Annie Pauline

Allen-Pindell and their mother, Elizabeth Whitfield Allen. Pauline's father is often incorrectly identified as Northrup Hopkins, a Virginian who moved to New England before the Civil War. On June 16, 1857, however, in Boston, Sarah wed Pauline's father, Benjamin Northrup. Northrup was "a member of one of the most politically active and established African American families in Providence, Rhode Island."[17] Six years later, Sarah filed for divorce, alleging infidelity. She was granted permission to resume using her maiden name and given custody of the couple's minor child, Pauline Elizabeth. This surprising discovery by literary scholar Lois Brown clears up much of the confusion surrounding Pauline's early years. For example, as a fifteen-year-old schoolgirl she won a prize of ten dollars in gold for her essay "The Evils of Intemperance and Their Remedy." She signed the manuscript "Pauline E. Allen," which many had assumed was a pen name. Her school records show that she would continue using Allen into her twenties, when she took the surname of her stepfather, William A. Hopkins. Interestingly, Dorothy West, as a teenager, would also win cash prizes for her writing.

Pauline Hopkins's stepfather, William, originally from Alexandria, Virginia, arrived in Boston in 1857 and lived at 31 Garden Street, in the heart of historic Beacon Hill. The 1860 directory lists him as a hairdresser living at 189 Grove Street, a boardinghouse near the church Pauline and Sarah attended, the Twelfth Baptist Church, which was then on the corner of Phillips and Grove streets. Hopkins and the first pastor of the church, the Reverend Leonard Grimes, had both emigrated to Boston from Virginia before the Civil War, and it is possible that Hopkins met Sarah Allen at the church. In May 1860, Hopkins enlisted in the U.S. Navy; he served for two years, first on the USS *North Carolina* and then on the USS *Niagara*. After battling Confederate forces in Charleston, Pensacola, Mobile Bay, and New Orleans, he was honorably discharged in June 1862.[18] Upon his return to Boston, he rented a room at 42 Grove Street and resumed work as a barber. On Christmas Day 1864, young Pauline watched as Grimes married her mother and William A. Hopkins. The Christmas wedding was twenty-eight-year-old William Hopkins's first marriage and thirty-year-old Sarah Allen's second. William Hopkins, "a kindly man who was protective and indulgent of both Sarah and her daughter, Pauline," would play a pivotal role in his stepdaughter's life.[19]

Evidence suggests that Pauline and her real father initially remained in contact, although she eventually wrote him out of her biography. Like Dorothy West, Hopkins freely edited her family history to conform to the public image she wished to project. In an autobiographical sketch published years later in the *Colored American Magazine*, no mention is made of Northrup, and she claims William Hopkins as her father:

> Pauline E. Hopkins of North Cambridge, Mass., was born in Portland, Me., but came to Boston when an infant; subsequently she was raised a Boston girl, educated in the Boston public schools, and finally graduated from the famous Girls' High School of that city.
>
> Her father, the late William A. Hopkins, a G.A.R. [Grand Army of the Republic] veteran of the Civil War, is a native of Alexandria, Va. He is a nephew of the late John T. Waugh of Providence, R. I., and a first cousin of the late Mrs. Anna Warrick Jarvis of Washington, D. C.
>
> By her mother Miss Hopkins is a direct descendant of the famous Paul brothers, all black men, educated abroad for the Baptist ministry, the best known of whom was Thomas Paul, who founded St. Paul Baptist Church, Joy Street, Boston, Mass., the first colored church in this section of the United States. Susan Paul, a niece of these brothers, was a famous colored woman, long and intimately associated with William Lloyd Garrison in the anti-slavery movement. Miss Hopkins is also a grandniece of the late James Whitfield, the California poet, who was associated with Frederick Douglass in politics and literature.[20]

Here she omits the fact that in 1864, father and daughter lived a block apart on Beacon Hill: Benjamin Northrup resided at 150 Russell Street, while eight-year-old Pauline lived at 67 Joy Street, with her mother and stepfather.[21] Thus, although carefully crafted and edited, Hopkins's statement captures her literary heritage and her family's distinguished record of activism, racial uplift, and patriotism, aspects of her personal narrative of which she was especially proud.

Still extant, Twelfth Baptist is a direct descendent of the First African Baptist Church, founded in 1805 on Belknap (now Joy) Street by Pauline Hopkins's great granduncle, the Reverend Thomas Paul. In August 1826, the community convened at the African Baptist Church and watched as Paul joined James W. Stewart and Maria W. Stewart in marriage. City records show that the couple resided at 25 Belknap Street. Through her geographic location, Hopkins was therefore firmly linked to the intellectual, transcendentalist, New England tradition of civil disobedience and social justice. She would draw on this history for several scenes in her novels and short fiction.[22]

After Rev. Thomas Paul's death, family members eventually joined Twelfth Baptist, which was established in 1848 by a group of parishioners who had separated from First Baptist. Rev. Leonard Grimes, then living in New Bedford, Connecticut, was chosen as the church's first pastor. He served until his death in 1874; the membership, observes Hopkins, had grown from its original twenty-three to over six hundred. Hopkins documents the connection between her family and their minister in her essay "Men of Vision: II. Rev. Leonard A. Grimes." She reveals that during the antebellum period, Twelfth Baptist was known as the Church of the Fugitive Slave. Among its members were the celebrated fugitives Shadrach Minkins, Thomas Sims, and Anthony Burns. After the passage of the Fugitive Slave Law of 1850, Burns and Sims were arrested and returned to slavery. Minkins and over forty others, with Grimes's help, escaped to Canada. He then "collected money and bought the members of his church out of slavery that they might return to the United States without fear."[23] After the Civil War the church counted among its members the pioneering physician and lawyer John Swett Rock; the legendary abolitionists Lewis and Harriet Hayden; Judge George L. Ruffin, the first African American graduate of Harvard Law School; and the civil rights activist and clubwoman Josephine St. Pierre Ruffin, Hopkins's girlhood Sunday school teacher.[24] Unlike Dorothy West, who embraced the youthful defiance and excesses of the 1920s, Hopkins would continue to center her life on religion, social justice, and spirituality. At the age of fifteen, she won an essay contest; years later she revealed that her "first effort was made at the age of fifteen, when the Congregational Publishing Society, Boston, offered a prize of ten dollars in gold, through Dr. William Wells Brown, for the best essay on the 'Evils of Intemperance and Their Remedies,' to the colored youth of Boston High Schools." She "won the prize, and received a warm letter of encouragement."[25]

In addition to her family and her church, Hopkins was strongly influenced by the schools she attended: Wells Primary, Wells Grammar, and Girls' High. The latter, a highly selective institution, was established

in 1852 to provide girls an "English classical education."[26] Pauline's stepfather stressed the importance of education and introduced her to a
socially progressive artistic community. In 1866 the family moved six
blocks west, to a house at 1 Allen Place, near the Massachusetts General
Hospital. Ten-year-old Pauline apparently remained enrolled in the Wells
Primary School, a coeducational facility on Blossom Street in Beacon
Hill; she later transferred to the all-girl Wells Grammar School. Black
children had been attending Boston's public schools since 1855, but by
1865 there were only five enrolled in the high schools. Because the
numbers were somewhat better at the lower levels, with 103 in the
grammar schools and 263 in the primary schools, Pauline likely benefited from having a critical mass of African American classmates. She
excelled in her studies and in the spring of 1872 passed a rigorous exam-
ination that won her admission to Girls' High School; it was then the
female counterpart of English High and Boys' Latin, since Girls' Latin
(which Dorothy West and Helene Johnson attended) would not be
established until 1878. The four-part exam tested mastery of arithmetic,
grammar, geography, and history, and included tasks such as "Extract the
cube root of 27054035008"; "What does the past tense of the potential
mood express"; and "Describe the overland route from London to Bom-
bay, stopping at Malta and Alexandria."[27]

School records show that she enrolled at Girls' High on Monday
morning, September 2, 1872, under the name Pauline E. Allen. Her age
was sixteen years and one month.[28] William A. Hopkins, a barber, is listed
as her parent, and their residence is 1 Allen Place. The school, an impressive five-story brick building situated on a lot extending from West Newton Street to Pembroke Street, offered a three-year curriculum. Pauline
studied algebra, botany, chemistry, drawing, English literature, Latin, and
rhetoric her first year; chemistry, drawing, English literature, French, history, Latin, and physiology her middle year; and physics, history, astron-
omy, Shakespeare, drawing, ethics, and music her senior year. As might be
expected, she generally fared best in the humanities, with a 95 in English literature, a 95 in drawing, a 91 in rhetoric, and an 89 in Shakespeare,
though she also received a 95 in chemistry. She graduated in September
1875, at age nineteen, and made her professional debut as a singer with
the group the Progressive Musical Union. The following year the family
moved to a building at 15 State Street, where William worked as a jani-

tor. Pauline was still living with her parents and using the surname Allen when she returned to Girls' High in 1878 and completed a six-month course, perhaps in stenography.

Like Rachel, her daughter Dorothy, and her nieces Helene and Eugenia, Pauline Hopkins had a passion for the theater. She was more fortunate than Rachel in that she actually enjoyed a stage career. It is not surprising, considering that her mother and her aunt were singers and her stepfather a guitarist and vocalist, that Pauline began performing at an early age. Even before completing her studies at Girls' High, she had begun her forays into artistic life and the public sphere. During her senior year in March 1875, she sang with the Progressive Musical Union, a group organized by her cousin Elijah William Smith Jr., a grandson of Rev. Thomas Paul. Smith's daughters, Anne Smith Simms and Harriet Smith Burrell, were among Pauline's closest friends. Two years later in March 1877, she played a leading role in the musical *Pauline; or, The Belle of Saratoga*, performed at Boston's Parker Memorial Hall. An advertisement promised that the play would be performed "with elaborate costumes and full scenic effects" and that it would be judged "the most amusing and interesting entertainment of the season."[29] Pauline's relatives Elijah William Smith and William Hopkins helped produce the play and served on the Committee of Arrangements.

Judging from press accounts, the performances were well received and bolstered Pauline's reputation as a singer and actress. In fact by 1882 when she turned twenty-six, she was known as "Boston's Favorite Colored Soprano."[30] But her "great desire," she later revealed, "was to become a playwright."[31] While in her twenties she authored at least three plays: *Aristocracy—A Musical Drama in Three Acts* (1877), *Winona*, a five-act play copyrighted in 1878, and the musical *Slaves' Escape; or, The Underground Railroad, a Musical Drama in Four Acts* (1879), which she later titled *Peculiar Sam; or, The Underground Railroad*.[32]

An additional work, "One Scene from the Drama of Early Days," is frequently labeled juvenilia and a play, but it is actually an 800-word essay, written when she was living at 15 State Street, and still using the name Pauline Allen. Hopkins begins the account of Daniel in the lion's den by urging dramatists to survey the Bible as a powerful source for their art and to "draw inspiration from the hero, who uplifted on the cross, breathed His blessing upon us." Enacting her theory, she shows

King Darius sentencing an unrepentant Daniel "into the den of lions."
When the scene changes to the following morning, "a mighty shout
bursts from the assembled multitude, as the beloved of the Lord steps
forth, unharmed."[33] The piece captures Hopkins's early love of drama as
well as her lifelong belief that just as God saved Daniel, he was willing
and able to save blacks living in the "American lion den."

Of her three plays, only *Peculiar Sam* has survived. Program folders
show that Hopkins and her parents performed in the play in July 1880
at Boston's Oakland Garden, as members of the Hopkins Colored Troubadours, a family group organized by her stepfather. William, Pauline,
and her mother, Sarah, formed the nucleus of the group, and they were
frequently joined by Annie Parks, James Freeman, James Henry, and
George Tolliver, all singers, and Carrie Alden, a popular vocalist and pianist.
Sarah and Pauline sang, while William sang, played the guitar, and handled
most of the advertising and travel arrangements. Between 1879 and the
late 1880s when the group disbanded, the Troubadours were well known
in regional musical circles; they gave concerts as far north as Ayer, Massachusetts, and as far south as Providence, Rhode Island. In January 1882, a
reporter for the *Malden Press* announced that "despite the unfavorable
weather the Hopkins Colored Troubadours had a very good audience at
the City Hall last Sunday evening. The programme was an appropriate
one, and excellent in all respects, consisting of solos, duets, piano and guitar renderings, and chorus singing by the entire company. The company
has left behind a very good impression, and will be heartily welcomed
whenever they choose to visit our city again." James A. Roberts, a
Bostonian who hired the ensemble several times, recommended them to
societies, since "no meeting of this kind is complete without good music."
He singled out "Miss Pauline Hopkins, the soprano," noting that she "has
a sweet voice, and is a favorite wherever she sings."[34]

Hopkins's accomplishments as a singer, actress, and playwright have
received little attention from scholars, although contemporary press
accounts show she was quite popular and reached a wide audience. *Peculiar Sam* "catapulted her to the forefront of nineteenth-century African
American theater culture." During 1879 and 1880 an eleven-person acting company took *Peculiar Sam* on a national tour, performing "in major
cities of the Northeast and Midwest such as Boston, Buffalo, Chicago,
Minneapolis, Milwaukee, and St. Paul. In addition, the company 'combed

the Midwest exhaustively, moving through New York, Illinois, Minnesota, Wisconsin, Michigan, Iowa, Kansas, and Missouri, playing one- and two-night stands in any place that offered accommodations, and returning by request for repeat performances to St. Paul, Chicago, and some of the larger towns.' "[35] Sam Lucas (1850–1916), the veteran actor, singer, and songwriter, starred as Peculiar Sam; the famous Hyers sisters, Anna Madah and Emma Louise, played the leading female roles. Hopkins held the sisters in high regard and wrote that they were Californians who made their debut at Sacramento's Metropolitan Theatre in April 1867. "Never," she observed, "until undertaken by these ladies, was it thought possible for Negroes to appear in the legitimate drama, albeit soubrette parts were the characters they portrayed."[36] Given Rachel West's passionate interest in the theater, it is likely that she saw Hopkins in one of her productions.

As a member of the Hopkins Colored Troubadours, Pauline starred in *Peculiar Sam*, singing soprano and playing the role of Virginia. As a result she became, as Lois Brown notes, "the first American woman to perform publicly in her own play" (140). It is ironic that a groundbreaking play so popular in its own day, at the end of the nineteenth century, should be virtually unknown in ours. Much of the difficulty undoubtedly comes from Hopkins's jarring and ultimately unsuccessful use of southern black vernacular. Zora Neale Hurston, commenting on Richard Wright's similarly vexing use of black vernacular, termed his writing "puzzling" and "tone deaf."[37] Unlike Wright and Hurston, however, who were born and reared in the South, Hopkins was a daughter of New England. In fact, evidence suggests that the farthest south she ever traveled was New York City. Dorothy West and Helene Johnson, much like their Boston predecessor, lived their entire lives in Massachusetts and New York; they too would have fared better forgoing southern black vernacular speech. Johnson's poem "Goin' No'th," for example, features a lad who tires of life "down south pickin' cotton—/ Allus jes' pickin' cotton." As he is leaving home, in search of opportunity in the North, he says, unconvincingly, "Goodbye, mammy, at de cabin do' / Goin' no'th, won't see you no mo.' "[38] At bottom, *Peculiar Sam*'s linguistic challenges prove a major impediment to students and scholars alike, often preventing them from moving beyond the play's dialect to its underlying themes and arguments.

By the 1890s, as Pauline Hopkins entered her fourth decade, changes were occurring in the private and public spheres that affected the Hopkins family. With the dissolution of the Hopkins Colored Troubadours in the late 1880s, as an aging William dealt with old war injuries, Pauline lost her primary source of income. To support herself, she took a hiatus from writing and, beginning in 1892, worked as a stenographer, first for Massachusetts state representatives Henry Parkman and Alpheus Sanford, and from 1895 to 1899 for the Massachusetts Bureau of Statistics. In part because she was no longer singing or acting, the 1890s would prove her most active decade as a public orator. Many of the speeches resulted from her activities with the women's club movement; other invitations came from church groups; and others, such as a Memorial Day address in 1892 to the Robert A. Bell Post 134, G.A.R., stemmed from her stepfather's membership in the Grand Army of the Republic and other veterans' organizations. As a naval veteran of the Civil War, William Hopkins was both civic minded and well connected, and he was able to introduce Pauline to luminaries from the entertainment, political, veterans, and literary communities.[39]

During the 1890s, Hopkins's work as a public speaker coincided with a spike in racial tension as Jim Crow laws, vigilantism, lynching, and mob violence spread across the South. She protested the state of affairs in her preface to *Contending Forces*: "In these days of mob violence, when lynch-law is raising its head like a venomous monster, more particularly in the southern portion of the great American republic, the retrospective mind will dwell upon this history of the past, seeking there a solution of these monstrous outbreaks" (14). The violence was likely precipitated by the Compromise of 1877, which awarded Republican Rutherford B. Hayes the presidency in exchange for the removal federal troops from the South, thereby restoring "home rule" to the region. The Compromise effectively ended Reconstruction and all federal protection for the four million former slaves and slave descendents living in the South. In the wake of the Compromise, the Ku Klux Klan and other southern-based hate groups rapidly increased in popularity. Determined to reassert white dominance, southern mobs lynched 85 blacks in 1890, 113 in 1891, and "an all-time high of 161 in 1892."[40] In response to the lawlessness, poet Paul Laurence Dunbar opined, "Ah, Douglass, we have fall'n on evil days, / Such days as thou, not even thou didst know."[41] In Memphis, journalist Ida B. Wells reacted to the March 1892 shooting and hanging of her friend Thomas Moss and his business partners Calvin

McDowell and Henry Stewart by launching a nationwide anti-lynching campaign. She described the incident in her newspaper the *Memphis Free Speech and Headlight,* explaining that the men, "three of the best specimens of young since-the-war Afro-American manhood," were murdered "in a shockingly brutal manner" because a white grocer considered their flourishing grocery business too profitable and damaging to his.[42] She applauded those blacks who denounced the lynching and left Memphis "by thousands, bringing about great stagnation to every branch of business," and she urged all others to follow, since "the appeal to the white man's pocket has ever been more effectual than all the appeals ever made to his conscience" (68–69). Whites reacted by burning her newspaper office and threatening to kill her if she ever returned to Memphis, which resulted in her relocating permanently to Chicago.

For Hopkins, no reformer of the nineteenth century "stands more powerful than Mrs. Ida B. Wells-Barnett."[43] Both women, prompted by increased discrimination in the North, the wave of violence sweeping the South, and a passionate desire to uplift the race, became active participants in the black women's club movement. After moving to Chicago, Wells continued her crusade against lynching. Crisscrossing the country, she spoke at numerous rallies and established anti-lynching societies from California to New York. She also edited the *Chicago Conservator* newspaper and in 1893 founded a Chicago women's club organized for "civic and social betterment," later renamed the Ida B. Wells Woman's Club in her honor. Wells's anti-lynching campaign provided the impetus for the founding of the National Association of Colored Women (NACW), initiated in Boston in July 1895. When Missouri journalist James W. Jacks wrote a letter attacking Wells and asserting that most black women were "prostitutes, thieves, and liars," Josephine Ruffin, president of Boston's Woman's Era Club, summoned women's groups from across the country to Boston.[44] Over one hundred delegates from fourteen states convened at Boston's Berkeley Hall on July 29, 1895. Hopkins was a member of the host committee and observed seven years later that "this great Association is now of powerful growth, adding yearly to its roll of membership Federations from every Southern State."[45]

Although she did not rise through the hierarchy and play as prominent a role in the club movement as Wells or Ruffin, Hopkins was an active, dedicated participant. She served as secretary of the Woman's Era

Club and as vice president of the Women's Auxiliary of the Young Men's Congregational Club.[46] Ira Dworkin adds, in *Daughter of the Revolution*, that in 1898 she represented the Woman's Era Club "at the Annual Convention of New England Federation of Woman's Clubs" (xvi). A year later she relinquished her civil service job with the Massachusetts Bureau of Statistics and accepted an editorial position with the *Colored American Magazine*. As literary editor of the magazine, she could devote more time to creative writing while continuing her social reform work with groups like the Women's Relief Corps, the Woman's Era Club, and the Congregational Club. Apparently she had already been at work on a novel and a number of short stories. She published her first story, "The Mystery within Us," in the magazine's premier issue in May 1900. The September 1900 issue contained a two-page advertisement for her novel *Contending Forces*, scheduled for publication in October. Readers were informed that "Miss Hopkins presented this work before the Woman's Era Club of Boston on November 15, 1899, with instant success" and that she would be glad "to give readings before women's clubs in any section of the country" (196).

The *Colored American Magazine* afforded Hopkins a nationwide audience, largely of women, and an ideal forum in which to combine her political and literary passions. Agents from all over the United States, including New Jersey, Florida, Missouri, Wisconsin, Louisiana, Colorado, and Texas, sold subscriptions. The periodical was owned and published by the Boston-based Colored Co-operative Publishing Company. The company's president, G.A.R. veteran William Dupree, described it as "an organization founded by Colored men and women, who put into it what money they could spare because they believed the time had come for the publication of a high class magazine, which should take up and discuss the great questions that interest the colored people, and which should give the world some idea of the progress we have made . . . since the abolition of slavery." In addition, the magazine was intended to show "that the colored people can advance on all the lines of progress known to other races . . . that they can attain to eminence (both the men and women among them) as thinkers, as writers, as doctors, as lawyers, as clergymen, as singers, musicians, artists, actors, and also as successful businessmen, in the conduct of enterprises of importance."[47]

That Hopkins embraced this philosophy is evident in the columns, short stories, essays, and three serialized novels she published during her four-year stint with the magazine, May 1900 to March 1904. Her dozens of biographical sketches of prominent African Americans are carefully designed to reinscribe black Americans in the national consciousness. Through stories such as "Talma Gordon" and "A Dash for Liberty" she argued against pernicious racialist theories. In her novels she eschewed the stereotypes of minstrelsy and urban poverty, which, in any case, were not representative of her own family background, and she placed her articulate, witty, and well-educated characters in professional occupations and genteel surroundings. She further gave them complex, ethically grounded lives of adventure and fulfillment.

Although Hopkins was too skilled a writer to produce mere polemics, her convoluted, unbelievable, coincidence-ridden plots and simplistic characterizations have bound and dated her fiction within the writing conventions of Victorian women's magazines. Recent scholars have argued that she consciously problematized and subverted these conventions. We maintain that Hopkins was uninterested in rewriting literary conventions and instead used the media available to her, the popular magazine, to reinscribe the black community intellectually in the rapidly shifting culture and geography of late nineteenth- and early twentieth-century Boston.

Until the 1890s, black Bostonians moved freely through the city, living anywhere they chose and enjoying the many leisure and cultural amenities. Like their white counterparts, they attended the legitimate theaters on Tremont Street and vaudeville at the Old Howard in Scollay Square; they ice-skated on Boston Common, rode the Swan Boats in Boston Public Garden, and enjoyed the rides at Norumbega Amusement Park. Although the more established families lived first on the north side of Beacon Hill, and later in the South End, African Americans had always been dispersed throughout greater Boston in Chelsea, Charlestown, Medford, Brookline, and Everett.

In 1896, Pauline Hopkins moved from the historic African American community on Beacon Hill across the Charles River to Cambridge. She purchased a house at 53 Clifton Street, North Cambridge. Hopkins seems to have enjoyed an unusually close relationship with her parents, with whom she lived on Clifton Street until their deaths. After her stepfather's passing in 1906 and her mother's in 1914, she sold the Clifton Street house and moved in 1916 to a boardinghouse at 19 Jay Street, a

few blocks southeast of Harvard. Her diminished circumstances are suggested by the description of the threadbare furnishings of the "third-rate
lodging house near Harvard Square" in which Reuel Briggs lives in her
novel *Of One Blood*.[48] Though her much-loved aunt and namesake,
Annie Pauline Allen-Pindell, had died in Los Angeles in 1901, it seems
likely that Hattie, the youngest of the seven Allen sisters, traveled to
Cambridge to support Pauline at her mother's passing.

The seventh of the ten Allen siblings, Harriet "Hattie" Allen was born
in Charlestown in 1840. After graduating from the Charlestown grammar
school, she was denied admission to the city's segregated high school.
Margaret Badger, however, the principal of the Charlestown Female Seminary and later Hopkins's teacher at Girls' High, intervened and admitted
her to the seminary. "On the day of graduation, three years from the time
of entrance," notes Hopkins, "Miss Allen was one of eight to receive a
diploma, and as a special mark of favor, the colored girl was the valedic-
torian of her class."[49] After her graduation, the school hired her as an
instructor, a clear sign of the high regard in which she was held. She later
taught in Canada and in Oakland, California, where she lived until her
retirement.[50] Hattie Allen never married, had children, or showed interest in heterosexual relationships. She was an independent longtime educator, and she provided a domestic model that would influence Pauline.

In 1914, Dorothy West and her family moved from the Roxbury
section of Boston to suburban Brookline. Hopkins and Dorothy West's
mother, Rachel, shared a love of music, literature, and the theater, and the
two families moved in overlapping progressive and artistic circles. Both
were closely aligned with the Ruffins, Pindells, and Trotters, all leading
families in black Boston. The Trotter family patriarch, James Monroe
(1842–1892), was among the first African American commissioned officers in the Fifty-fifth Massachusetts Infantry. After the Civil War he held
a supervisory position at the Boston post office, and in 1887 President
Grover Cleveland appointed him Recorder of Deeds for the District of
Columbia, a position previously held by Frederick Douglass. James Trotter and his wife Virginia were the parents of three children, William
Monroe, an 1895 Phi Beta Kappa graduate of Harvard College; Maud
Trotter Steward, wife of the prominent Boston dentist Charles Steward;
and Elizabeth "Bessie" Trotter Craft, who married a grandson of the celebrated fugitive slaves Henry and Ellen Craft.

Maud Trotter, Dorothy West's godmother and the sister of Rachel's best friend, was founding president of the Saint Mark Musical and Literary Union, organized in spring 1902 in an effort to enhance "the moral and intellectual improvement of the community."[51] She was also an executive board member of the Boston Literary and Historical Association, cofounded in 1901 by her brother Monroe and his friend Archibald Grimké (father of the Harlem Renaissance poet Angelina Weld Grimké). These were the city's most important black cultural groups, and at Maud's invitation, Pauline Hopkins spoke at both organizations. Her well-received lectures "helped to consolidate her place in New England's anti–[Booker T.] Washington circles." She appeared before the Literary and Historical Association on Monday, March 9, 1903, and the Musical and Literary Union on Sunday afternoon, November 19, 1905.[52] Given her passion for self-improvement and the arts, and her connection with the Trotter sisters, Rachel West certainly attended the lectures and recitals sponsored by these groups.

Monroe Trotter was also a close friend and a trusted confidant of both Pauline Hopkins and Rachel West. He published at least one of Hopkins's speeches in his influential newspaper and a few of Helene Johnson's early poems.[53] Monroe and his sisters are major characters in *The Living Is Easy,* and while the encounter between Trotter and Booker T. Washington did not take place in Rachel's home, she must have either observed their interaction or heard about it firsthand in order for West to describe it in such detail. When Trotter and his sisters disrupted Washington's speech at the Columbus Avenue African Methodist Episcopal Zion Church in Roxbury, Rachel may well have been in the audience.

In June of 1899, four years after leaving Harvard, Trotter married twenty-six-year-old Geraldine ("Deenie") Pindell, whom W.E.B. Du Bois had also pursued in the 1890s while a student at Harvard. In 1853 Deenie's relative, Joseph J. Pindell, married the pianist and singer Annie Pauline Allen, Pauline Hopkins's maternal aunt. By all accounts, the marriage of Monroe Trotter and Deenie Pindell was strong and supportive. When Trotter began publishing his weekly newspaper the *Guardian* in 1901, largely to oppose Booker T. Washington's accommodationist policies by offering a divergent plan for the advancement of the black masses, one based on active protest, Deenie joined him as associate editor. Together they became leaders of Boston's "anti-Washington" camp, a group that included George Washington Forbes, Josephine St. Pierre Ruffin, Archibald Grimké, Du Bois, concert pianist and playwright Maud Cuney Hare, and Pauline Hopkins. In an April 1905 letter to Trotter, Hopkins described her shock upon discovering that Washington had paid an operative to bribe her "to give up my race work and principles and adopt the plans of the South for the domination of the Blacks."[54] Decades later, seventy-year-old Dorothy West recalled that she and her family had "always despised Booker T. Washington, because Monroe Trotter was a family friend. And in those days, Booker T. Washington and Monroe used to have debates."[55]

Although Washington succeeded in buying out the *Colored American Magazine* and forcing Hopkins to resign her position as editor, he could not break her spirit. She continued writing and creating and in December 1904 began contributing regularly to the Atlanta-based *Voice of the Negro*. The following year, she launched her own publishing company and published *A Primer of Facts Pertaining to the Early Greatness of the African Race and the Possibility of Restoration by Its Descendants*. Eleven years later, in February and March 1916, Hopkins published her final five works: essays on the Reverend Leonard Grimes and Mark Réné De Mortie (a member of the Fifth-fourth Massachusetts Colored Troops), the unfinished novel "Topsy Templeton," and the lighthearted stories "As Told over the Telephone" and "Converting Fanny." All appeared in the short-lived *New Era Magazine*, which Hopkins, then age fifty-nine, edited.

On Independence Day 1901, the recently published novelist Pauline Hopkins joined her Woman's Era Club sisters on a forty-mile pilgrimage, north from Boston, along the winding Merrimack River, to Amesbury, Massachusetts. They were journeying on this sunny Fourth of July morning to the Friend Street home of the late John Greenleaf Whittier, "High Priest of the Anti-Slavery Party," in Hopkins's gracious phrase. She would later write that upon entering the joint sitting room and study, lined with majestic old books, a fine group-portrait of the original Fisk Jubilee Singers, and the very mahogany desk upon which so many antislavery poems had been written, "the spirit of the poet was upon us."[56]

"The spirit of the hour was still strong upon us," she later adds, now toward the end of their stay, "as we stood on the greensward of the garden, and sat beneath the old apple trees where Mr. Whittier was wont to sit with Charles Sumner and Mr. Garrison planning measures which should sway a nation" (253). Standing in the midst of the emerald garden, club president Josephine St. Pierre Ruffin led the party, as was their custom, in a brief memorial service. Ellen Taylor read Whittier's "Barbara Frietchie," prayer was offered by Agnes Adams, and Hopkins gave a brief sketch of the poet's life—beginning with his birth in 1807, progressing to his work as secretary of the American Anti-Slavery Society, decrying the mob attack on his Pennsylvania Freeman printing office, and ending with one of his more famous declarations: "I set a higher value on my name as appended to the Anti-Slavery Declaration of 1833, than on the title-page of any book" (255).

Hopkins's essay on Whittier, published two months after the trip to Amesbury, captures her talent as a creative writer, her commitment to racial justice, and her desire to be taken seriously as a New England intellectual, in the vein of Henry David Thoreau, Ralph Waldo Emerson, W.E.B. Du Bois, and William James. Her fiction is replete with references to Whittier and Emerson, and Du Bois is in part the model for one of her best-known characters. In *Contending Forces*, Hopkins writes of Will Smith/Will Du Bois: "Emerson's words on character were an apt description of the strong personality of this man: 'A reserved force which acted directly by its presence, and without (apparent) means'" (168). As a daughter of New England, she was always especially proud of the region's lengthy, distinguished record of antislavery activism, and she saw herself as a direct descendent of these earlier activist-intellectuals.

The Amesbury trip nicely contextualizes Hopkins's life work by situating her within multiple traditions: New England intellectualism, radical abolitionism, and black feminism. It also gives insight into one of her key circles of friends, the Woman's Era Club. Organized in 1873 by Josephine St. Pierre Ruffin, the club took its name from the *Woman's Era*, edited by Ruffin and her daughter Florida and the country's first newspaper devoted to the interests of African American women. By 1902, the club had one hundred members and met twice monthly in Boston's Tremont Temple; one meeting was devoted "to business and the other to literary pursuits, lectures and similar educational features."[57] Mrs. Ruffin, whose husband Judge George L. Ruffin served on the Municipal Court of Charlestown and in the Massachusetts House of

Representatives, is likely the model for *Contending Forces'* Mrs. Willis, "the brilliant widow of a bright Negro politician." Mrs. Willis had been instrumental "in the formation of clubs of colored women banded together for charity, for study, for every reason under God's glorious heavens that can better the condition of mankind" (143, 147). Literary scholar Hanna Wallinger speculates that because she "had neither an influential husband nor a family background of great wealth . . . Hopkins never became a very prominent member of the Woman's Era Club, nor did she ever publish in the *Woman's Era*, the club's journal."[58]

While Hopkins frequently gave readings before women's clubs, she believed her work received little support from influential men of letters, such as William Dean Howells, Charles Chesnutt, Du Bois, Oliver Wendell Holmes, and Francis Jackson Garrison. They were, however, certainly aware of her career. Francis Garrison was president of the wealthy publishing house Houghton, Mifflin and Company and a son of abolitionist William Lloyd Garrison. In December 1905, Hopkins spoke at a William Lloyd Garrison centenary celebration and shared the platform with Francis Garrison and other luminaries. Du Bois knew of Hopkins's "efforts to oppose Booker T. Washington, was well familiar with the *Colored American Magazine*, and had moved in some of the same Boston circles," yet during her entire lifetime he failed to publicly acknowledge her career.[59]

Hopkins's sister writer Frances E. W. Harper (1825–1911), who launched her career during the years of abolitionist fervor, fared much better. In fact, William Lloyd Garrison penned the preface for Harper's first book, *Poems on Miscellaneous Subjects*, published in Boston in 1854. The situation had changed by the time Hopkins began her career. As Dorothy West shows in *The Living Is Easy*, the descendents of the old abolitionists had turned their backs on Boston's black community and moved out of the city to the North Shore. Hopkins had noted the change in the post–Civil War political climate in Boston and realized that it was up to her own community to resist discrimination and to reinscribe itself in the intellectual and physical space of Boston. Although she was an excellent classical singer and performed with the Hopkins Colored Troubadours, she eventually chose the pen as the tool with which she would delineate black space in Boston. That she recognized the extent of this challenge can be seen in her selection of the pseudonym Shirley Shadrach, with which she signed six of her publications. The name refers, of course to the three brave Hebrews, Shadrach, Meshach, and Abednego, who were thrown into a fiery furnace by King Nebuchadnezzar because they refused to renounce their faith (Daniel 3:25).[60]

Despite overt sexism and a hostile post-Reconstruction political climate, Hopkins persevered. She wrote through "hardships, disappointments, and with very little encouragement." Yet she was determined to "stick at it," particularly since her ultimate goal as a writer of fiction, she explained, was to detail "the wrongs of [my] race . . . so as to enlist the sympathy of all classes of citizens."[61] Her solution, and one that Dorothy West was to follow, was to single-handedly create her own audience, primarily of women, through intellectual relationships, literary and artistic organizations, and the two magazines she edited, the *Colored American Magazine* (1900–1904) and *New Era Magazine* (1916). West undoubtedly admired Hopkins's courage and her struggles to keep the *Colored American Magazine* going, and that may well have influenced her own decision to edit a literary journal, *Challenge*, many years later.

Like Dorothy West, Hopkins left no direct descendants, but she lived a long, productive life and she contributed to the race not only through her art, but also through the black philanthropic and social organizations to which she belonged. Through her lifestyle, creative works, and editorial endeavors, Hopkins offered inspiration to Dorothy West and Helene Johnson and future generations of black women writers.

CHAPTER 4

Boston Girlhoods,
1910–1925

WHEN ABIGAIL MCGRATH, the daughter of Helene Johnson, first read *Little Women,* she imagined Alcott's characters with the faces of Helene, Dorothy, and Eugenia. A fourth child in the family rounded out the similarity to Alcott's characters: Melvin Jackson, a younger cousin, was raised with the three girls; he is the "little blond boy" often mentioned by Dorothy in interviews, and the child on whom she based Tim in *The Living Is Easy.* McGrath's association of Alcott's novel with the Bensons is understandable, given the similarities between the two matriarchal Boston families. Not only does Alcott's book validate artistic careers for women but, beneath its veneer of Victorian propriety, it offers an alternative to the heteronormative family. Like the March women, the matrilineal Bensons reached across generations to offer each other support and encouragement in an environment in which men were mostly absent or marginal. This foundation supported Helene and Dorothy as they built their literary careers. Like the powerful Aunt March in *Little Women,* Rachel dominated the household and decided everyone's future. Although she was determined that the cousins rise socially in Boston's African American aristocracy, the lessons in deportment, elocution, and music, upon which she insisted, were probably intended less to help the cousins marry into a "blue-veined" Boston family and more to prepare them, as talented African American women, to confront an indifferent and possibly hostile world. Thus, in addition to their parlor accomplishments, the girls were given every opportunity for artistic expression through exposure to Boston's rich cultural environment. In this respect, West's novel is corroborated by Helene's account of her childhood: according to her daughter, the three girls "went to the theatre, joined writing clubs, and did all the cultural things that young ladies of privilege did."[1]

It would be difficult to envision a better atmosphere than early twentieth-century Boston in which to raise independent, artistic young African American women. As journalist Henry Moon said in a 1948 review of *The Living Is Easy* in *Crisis* magazine, "Boston . . . is more a state of mind than a geographic location . . . [for] the striving Negro community."[2] Even given the depredations of the city's subtle racism and economic discrimination, Boston's illustrious African American past and abolitionist tradition offered particular encouragement to ambitious women of color. In the careers of Phillis Wheatley, Louisa May Alcott, Pauline Hopkins, and Harriet Beecher Stowe (who reportedly began *Uncle Tom's Cabin* in William Garrison's office in Scollay Square), Dorothy and Helene would have noted that in Boston women could command respect, if not always financial remuneration, for their writing. Reading novels such as Henry James's *The Bostonians* and Hopkins's *Of One Blood,* they would also have observed examples of committed relationships between women, or Boston marriages, that were not unlike some relationships in their own family circle. Not only would the cousins have recognized in the accomplishments of Josephine St. Pierre Ruffin and her daughter, Florida Ruffin Ridley, the ways in which women could create new paradigms of social justice, but in the encouragement of enlightened men of letters like Eugene Gordon and William Stanley Braithwaite, they would have found support for their literary aspirations. Boston's affirmation of black artists is corroborated in accounts by other African American writers from the city such as Braithwaite, Gordon, Ruffin Ridley, Adelaide Cromwell, and Walter Stevens.

Although West's portrait of Boston is accurate in many ways, the autobiographical elements of her work must be approached with caution since she took artistic license when it suited her, particularly in respect to the family finances. Her fictional family borrows elements not only from the Bensons but also from other families she knew in Boston. According to McGrath, the Benson's Brahmin lifestyle was not supported exclusively by Isaac West's fruit business, as Dorothy claimed; instead, it was maintained by the pooled wages of the Benson sisters, all of whom worked in domestic service. In addition, boarders and relatives in transit contributed to the household budget, a detail revealed in short stories like "The Five Dollar Bill" and "The Roomer," but not in the novel. The fact that money was never as plentiful as Dorothy implied is evident in her accounts of the cash prizes she won for her short stories. At the time, the *Boston Post* offered weekly prizes of $2, $5, and $10. West recalled that "I received the ten-dollar prize with commendable regularity. It added to the family income, and I was proud of my contribution. When I got the five-dollar prize I was embarrassed that my contribution was cut in half" since the ten dollars "meant something to my family."[3] In fact, when she got a lesser prize, "everybody in the family was indignant because they were so used to my winning the $10 prize."[4] One cannot help wondering why, if Isaac was as financially secure as West claimed, her first fictional creations are sad, lower-class, middle-aged men who have not met their own or their families' expectations. In "The Typewriter," "An Unimportant Man," and "Hannah Byde," all written before West was twenty, the protagonists are bullied by their employers, nagged by their dissatisfied wives, and disrespected by their children. Helene Johnson's poignant poem "Regalia," written at the same time as West's early stories, corroborates her cousin's depiction of an emigrant from the South whose dreams of success are thwarted by racism and poverty. "Regalia," which seems to have been inspired by West's father Isaac, features Big Sam, a janitor in a large apartment house who tires of "Stokin' stoves, / Emptin' garbage, / Answerin' a million calls." But he persists, since his wife no longer has "To go out to do day's work," and his only child can attend school and learn "readin' and writin.' "[5] Why would anyone, Johnson seems to ask, view with disdain or have a need to ridicule such men? Her poems provide powerful models of manhood and also speak to the importance of black cultural pride.

When asked about her father, many years after the publication of these stories, Dorothy certainly revised his history. She always placed him on a par with such wealthy African American Bostonians as Henry C. Turner (1852–1919), father of her friends Marie and Grace Turner, and the owner of a livery stable on Commonwealth Avenue; John H. Lewis, a "bespoke" tailor who paid $10,000 a year for his premises on Summer Street; and Joseph Lee, a descendent of Robert E. Lee and a proprietor of two hotels near suburban Norumbega Park. These gentlemen, along with the couturier Phoebe Whitehurst Glover, who employed thirty-five seamstresses in her atelier on Newbury Street, did business with white clientele at the best commercial addresses in the city.[6] By the time she wrote *The Living Is Easy* West had changed the portrait of Isaac from the earlier stories, and she reinforced this description in interviews. She claimed that he was known as the Black Banana King and that he routinely brought home wads of money which he would lay on her pillow and ask her to "bless."[7] She told interviewers that the city gave him two solid gold charms, one of a banana and one of a pineapple, in appreciation of his contribution to Boston's commerce. She also insisted that Isaac's financial assets earned him a place in the Dun and Bradstreet index, although the only documentation of his business appears in the *Boston City Directory.* The directory identifies Isaac as a clerk at 71 Market St. from 1898 to 1912. In 1913, he became a distributor for the United Fruit Company and incorporated as Isaac West and Co. Fruit.[8] Born in slavery in Henrico County, Virginia, Isaac overcame enormous odds and certainly achieved middle-class status, although he did not quite reach the heights on which his daughter placed him. By all accounts, however, Isaac was a kind and loving family man. With the exception of his sharp-tongued wife, he was adored by all the women in the family, including his sisters-in-law. His nieces, Helene and Eugenia, always stayed in touch with him, visited him, and looked out for him when he was living in Brooklyn. When he died while Dorothy was in Russia, even Rachel felt bereaved and wrote to her daughter: "you and I have lost the best friend we ever had."[9]

Up until 1913 Isaac, Rachel, and Dorothy lived with various Benson relatives in Roxbury and the South End. In 1910, the household at 30 Cedar Street consisted of Isaac, Rachel, two-year-old Dorothy, Aunt Ella, three-year-old Helene, Aunt Carrie, and the teenaged Benson siblings, Sarah and Belton. The following year Eugenia and her father, Eugene Rickson, joined the family, while Aunt Minnie lived in with her employers.[10] It is likely that during these years Isaac supplemented the family income by performing janitorial duties in their rented houses as described in West's and Johnson's stories and poems.

In 1914, the family's fortunes improved, and with Isaac's new wholesale fruit business under way, Rachel convinced the family to leave Roxbury and the South End and to rent a substantial brick house in what she thought was the prestigious city of Brookline. To her disappointment, however, the family still lived in Boston; Brookline addresses began on the opposite side of the street. The area was still quasi-rural; a photograph of the newly built Children's Hospital shows cows grazing on the front lawn. Next to the house was an open field where the Boston Fire Department kept its horses. Just across the street was the Fens, the romantically wild urban parkland designed by Frederick Law Olmsted as part of the "emerald necklace" of greenery surrounding the city. The natural beauty of the Fens undoubtedly inspired Helene, who describes a winter's day in the neighborhood in her poem "Worship": "There is a church / Two blocks down between the baker's and the new hospital. / . . . The trees are like white holyroods, wind-riven" (54). In the poem, the narrator seems to contrast the restrictions and hypocrisies of organized religion with the worship of nature, although she does not quite dare to break with convention completely. Although some of the events described in *The Living Is Easy* took place before the family moved to Brookline Avenue, West sets the novel in this location, thus suggesting that the family's fortunes improved a few years sooner than they actually did.

Rachel had learned of the house on Brookline Avenue through her friend Bessie Trotter, whose brother Monroe edited Boston's African American newspaper, the *Guardian*. The owner, a scion of a distinguished abolitionist family, wished to rent to people of color in order to thwart the advances of the Irish into the neighborhood. Although startled by his prejudice, Rachel moved quickly to secure the house. She knew that in the South End the "once fine houses of the rich were fast emptying of middle-class whites and filling up with lower-class blacks. The street was becoming another big road, with rough-looking loungers leaning in the doorways of decaying houses and dingy stores."[11] Like Cleo in the novel, Rachel resented the fact that her race was being squeezed into a narrow corridor bounded by Columbus Avenue and Washington, Dartmouth, and Dudley streets, and she refused to allow de facto segregation to limit her ambitions for the family. Of course, Rachel's goals were not merely material; with her passion for education she recognized that the schools in the South End were deteriorating. Along with the Irish ascendancy in Boston came "nouveau Jim Crow" as the Irish, still smarting from anti-Catholic bias and from signs on work sites proclaiming "No Irish Need Apply," pulled their children from the city schools and established their own diocesan institutions. They soon acquired the political power to divert public resources to the parochial system, leaving the public schools in Roxbury and the South End (with the exception of the famous college-preparatory Boston Latin and Boston English) bereft of educational resources, well-maintained buildings, and qualified teachers, and thus setting the stage for Louise Day Hicks and the virulent opposition to school desegregation of the 1960s.[12]

Fortified by her belief in education and upward mobility, and despite Isaac's protests that they were living comfortably within their means in the South End, Rachel marshaled her sisters, much as she had done upon first arriving in Boston, and organized the move to Brookline Avenue. A major difference between West's novel and the family's real circumstances was that Rachel did not rescue her sisters and their children from lives of backwoods poverty in the South, since the siblings had been working in the North for almost fifteen years. Unfortunately, Dorothy's decision in the novel to delete her aunts' financial contributions in order to enhance her father's image as a prosperous businessman created great resentment in the family. According to McGrath, "to this day many family members still don't speak to one another as a direct result of that book." What is left out of the book "is that all of the sisters (all nine of them) pitched in together . . . to maintain a lifestyle which had the façade of real Boston Brahmins."[13]

Although West may have revised family history to suit the theme of her novel, she writes accurately about the sociological aspects of black Boston and shows the economic fragility of the African American elite. Major changes in America's commercial and credit system, discriminatory lending practices, mechanization, World War I, and the rise of the department and chain store ruined the prospects of several prominent African American businessmen. The automobile put Henry Turner's livery stable on Commonwealth Avenue out of business at the same time that Boston gentlemen rejected J. H. Lewis's bespoke tailoring for ready-made suits from Filene's department store. Ironically, Filene's was built on the location of Lewis's tailoring establishment. By the mid-1920s, Isaac's business, perhaps due to credit restrictions and his reluctance to join a supermarket chain, had deteriorated. Isaac moved to Brooklyn, New York, where Rachel occasionally visited him, and he continued to support Rachel and Dorothy until his death in 1933. By the time Helene's daughter Abigail was born in 1940, the family had moved from Brookline Avenue back to Roxbury and had become "shabby gentility at best."[14]

In the golden period between 1910 and 1925, however, Isaac, Rachel, and the Benson sisters experienced the dream of the southern emigrant. Even before they moved to Brookline Avenue, the family had always lived in desirable neighborhoods, and the cousins were raised within a few miles of the homes of the prominent African American women who led the community in the arts and in social action. Rachel, Isaac, and baby Dorothy first lived at 21 Holyoke Street, which is still a tree-shaded street of brownstones behind Back Bay Station. Next door, at 23, lived the elderly Susie King Taylor, the Civil War nurse and veterans' activist. King had written a memoir about leaving the South in which she included names and addresses of Bostonians willing to help other southern emigrants. Taylor's neighbor at number 25 was Julia O. Henson, a charter member of Boston's NAACP, who, with Josephine St. Pierre Ruffin, founded the African American Northeastern Federation of Women's Clubs.[15] Henson, encouraged by Harriet Tubman, subsequently donated her Holyoke Street home to the Harriet Tubman House, for many years the only residence for single African American women in Boston. Rachel may well have met Tubman on one of her frequent visits to Holyoke Street. A few blocks away on Routledge Street lived Mary Evans Wilson, who, like Julia Henson, was a founder of the NAACP and an active clubwoman. In fact, Henson, Ruffin, and Wilson were active in competing organizations. The League of Women for Community Service and the Women's Service Club were both formed around the turn of the century, but they took on a new mission as they sought to assist African American troops during World War I. Both occupied imposing mansions near Holyoke Street on Massachusetts Avenue. Maria L. Baldwin, the master (principal) of the prestigious Agassiz High School in Cambridge, had founded the League of Women for Community Service and, during World War I, persuaded Ruffin and Henson to help her establish a Soldier's Comfort Unit. The Women's Service Club, initiated by Wilson, also ministered to soldiers and "is generally credited with rendering effective service, entertaining soldiers, supplying the needs of servicemen, and educating and stimulating a war-depressed community."[16]

Rachel's connections with Boston's elite, initiated with the Trotter sisters when she first arrived in Roxbury, solidified with the women she met living on Holyoke Street. Josephine St. Pierre Ruffin, about whom Rachel wrote fondly in letters to Dorothy, lived in the West End but frequently visited the Hensons. Mrs. Ruffin's daughter, Florida, was a writer and journalist who later participated in a literary club with Dorothy and Helene. Another artistic friend of Rachel's from the South End was Maud Cuney Hare, the concert pianist and journalist. Maud attended the Boston Conservatory of Music and was briefly engaged to W.E.B. Du Bois while he was a student at Harvard. She was also a playwright and theatrical producer; she founded the Allied Arts Center and a children's theater. In 1929 she commissioned Dorothy to write a play, saying, "now I am quite in earnest about the play you are to do for us."[17]

Such prominent Boston women as Bessie Trotter and Maud Trotter Steward, their sister-in-law Geraldine Pindell Trotter (a relative of Pauline Hopkins), Maud Cuney Hare, Julia Henson, Mary Wilson, Josephine St. Pierre Ruffin, Florida Ruffin Ridley, Maria Baldwin, and Pauline Hopkins, among whom Rachel Benson West established herself, were all linked by ties of kinship, intellect, and commitment to social justice. They belonged to overlapping circles of women's clubs, civic organizations, and artistic and literary societies. As West shows in her novel, these dynamic and artistic women knew Rachel, included her in their activities, left visiting cards at the Brookline Avenue house, and attended her parties, thus forming a network of mentors and role models for the young cousins. In a rare interview in 1987, Helene Johnson acknowledged that Bessie Trotter and Maud Trotter Stewart were important sources of inspiration and informal education.[18]

In addition to observing Rachel's social life and discovering role models among the women who were her friends, the cousins filled their days with foreign language study, dancing school, recitals, and family theatricals. Rachel would call them to the drawing room and make them practice a "musical laugh" as she played scales.[19] West recalled that "in those days you had to have a parlor accomplishment," and children, though normally unseen and unheard, were summoned before adults to display their talents. Eugenia played the violin while Helene recited poetry. Dorothy's talent was the piano, and Rachel paid for lessons, hoping that she would become a concert pianist like Maud Cuney Hare.[20] At the age of five or six, Dorothy remembered, she listened to her teacher play and "lov[ed] the beauty of the music." Dorothy was also learning to read and write. One day she experienced a sort of epiphany or an intimation of her future as she recognized that words gave her even more satisfaction than music. Perhaps these parlor accomplishments, perfunctory as they might have been, laid the groundwork for Helene's and Dorothy's artistic careers. Although most of Rachel's circle expected their children to be doctors, lawyers, or cultivated homemakers, Rachel "believed in the arts" (up to a point) and encouraged Dorothy's, Helene's, and Eugenia's interest in literature.[21] All three of the girls wrote: Helene poems, Dorothy plays, and Eugenia stories. A favorite pastime was writing plays that they performed for the entire family. At the same time, Rachel was determined that all three should be self-supporting, and she had very definite ideas on their future careers.

Like Rachel, Dorothy was "a born actress" in a theatrical family in which a "circus" atmosphere prevailed on a daily basis.[22] In fact, much of her acting skill went into the portrayal of a perfectly behaved little girl whose demure demeanor hid her competitive nature and powerful ambition. Her story "Funeral" demonstrates a precocious self-awareness and a driving desire to succeed as a writer. Although at first reluctant to view her grandfather's body in the casket, the young protagonist "remembered that she meant to be a great writer and must welcome every experience."[23] Later, "the egotism that at all times swayed her was compelling her to store up impressions. She knew . . . that when she was older . . . the events of this day would . . . find release through her own particular medium of words" (66). West's parents encouraged her ambition. When she was seven she wrote a story that her proud father carried around with him for years. Confident in his ability to support his daughter's vocation, and fully expecting to leave a legacy that would enable her to be independent, Isaac told her: "Your little head is for making books, writing books, mine is for buying and selling bananas." Rachel also encouraged her daughter's artistic interests: "my mother had the foresight to see . . . [that] if you write books, maybe even if you don't sell them, there they are on bookshelves."[24]

Perhaps because Eugenia and Helene did not have active fathers to support their artistic aspirations, Rachel decided that they should earn their living in more conventional ways. Eugenia, despite her talents, was the "problem child." She was vivacious and rebellious, and had inherited Rachel's talent for mimicry; her speech was sprinkled with Irish expressions picked up from the neighborhood children. Although she enjoyed writing stories, she disliked school, and Rachel had no illusions about her academic success. Eugenia, the most beautiful but the least intellectual of the three girls, made it through school only because her cousins did her homework. Although Dorothy admitted later that she was jealous of her cousin's looks, Rachel worried constantly about Eugenia, fearing that "beauty was a dangerous asset without brains."[25] Her attempts to discipline her headstrong niece were futile; when the girls were about seven Dorothy wrote sadly to Aunt Carrie that "Eugenia is as bad as ever."[26] Abigail McGrath recalls stories of a teenage Eugenia sneaking into the house at night and slipping into her own bed into which Rachel had sprinkled hot pepper.

West offers two portraits of Eugenia in the stories "An Unimportant Man" and "The Black Dress." In the former, she is the pert, disrespectful Esther. When her grandmother warns, "You keep on, now. You jus' spoilin' for a spankin,'" Esther retorts rudely, "Yah, yah, yah! You just try it."[27] Later, she reduces her mother to tears and says coldly: "I hate women, Papa . . . they're sissies" (148). Esther's determination to go onto the stage upsets her family, although, as she explains to her sympathetic father, "I told Gramma dancin 'cause I didn't know how else to put it. I'd just as lief sing. I'd just as lief do anything . . . beautiful." Her father gently suggests that "it's hard . . . for colored girls to do things that are beautiful, like acting in plays, or singing in op'ra, or dancing in ballets," but he cannot shake Esther's ambition (150).

Esther's mother and grandmother felt that she "exhibited no talent for anything except kicking her heels when the gramophone whirled," and Rachel felt the same about Eugenia. Esther's family, like Rachel, feared that "some rotten man would ruin her before she got out of the chorus" (156). Ironically, Rachel herself had probably been sent North by her parents because they feared exactly the same fate for her. Now Rachel decided that Eugenia, instead of entering show business, would train for "sobering settlement work" at the Robert Gould Shaw House. West, who later did social work in New York, satirizes the organization as "Thaw House" in *The Living Is Easy*. The Rachel character thinks: "such refined white people lived and worked at Thaw House. And they were beginning to include a colored face in their personnel. True, [Windsor Street] was in the South End, but the address could have a distinguished sound when it was possible to add that you ate and slept there with better-class whites, and were paid to treat the Negroes in the neighborhood as inferiors" (220). As West demonstrates in the novel, social work had become a respectable profession for the daughters of Boston's blue-veined families of diminished fortunes. In the book, Miss Eleanor Elliot is "an auburn-haired social worker, the first of her race at Thaw House—though hardly representative—[and is] also distinguished as a Wellesley graduate who had no inclination to pass because her family name was honor enough" (244).

Despite Rachel's ideas for Eugenia's social and professional advancement, her niece had other plans. "She was going to be a great dancer. She could dance better than anybody in dancing school. But she wanted to dance by herself. She was sick of being encircled by a boy's arm. She wanted to go on the stage. . . . And she would not have to wait until she was eighteen. . . . By the time she was fifteen, she would look old enough to run away to New York."[28] Chafing under Rachel's supervision, Eugenia left Boston for a career on the stage. She married several times, once to a boxer named Tiger McVee, and eventually lived in New York, where she worked on the fringes of the arts and show business.[29]

West's story "The Black Dress" takes up Eugenia's life a few years after *The Living Is Easy* ends. The protagonist, Margaret Johnson, is an actress with a "hard, beautiful face." She is estranged from a "bigoted" father who opposed her career in show business. Since the characters West based on Isaac West are always sensitive and sympathetic to their daughters' artistic dreams, this hostile parent was probably inspired by Eugenia's own father, Eugene Rickson. West also alludes to Rachel's opposition to Eugenia's career, writing that Margaret had "always seemed hard to the home folks" and that she "had to fight the whole community, beginning with her father, to make them accept the theatre as a legitimate profession. . . . The neighbors had taken his side." The story's narrator and Margaret "had been like sisters all our growing years. I suppose she loved me more than she loved anyone else." Despite their childhood connection, the two women have not seen each other for twelve years although Margaret occasionally sends telegrams of "extravagant endearment" and "generous checks." For her part, the narrator truly believes that Margaret's coldness toward the family is a façade and that "it is only I who know she is not hard." The story opens as Margaret, "between shows and husbands," acquiesces to the narrator's plea that she visit her dying father. Margaret's cynical and unforgiving behavior, however, shocks her loyal friend, who realizes, as the two women prepare for bed, that "for the first time in my life I was going to sleep with a stranger."[30]

Helene's personality was very different from Eugenia's. She was witty and had a dry sense of humor but was also painfully shy. Like Eugenia, Helene was restless and high-spirited, but she "could be sobered and inspired by the simple act of opening a book. She turned pages tenderly, not wanting to break the ebony thread that wove itself into a wonderful pattern of words."[31] Although she loved to write, she was obsessively private about her work. In school, "when she was called upon to read one of her works she habitually denied authorship and ascribed the pieces to . . . Dorothy." Years later, she recalled that "it 'almost killed' her 'for somebody to recognize something' she wrote."[32] Though moody, solitary, and eccentric, she was "the family genius," who, according to Dorothy, had "an IQ of one hundred fifty something." At home, Dorothy's bedroom, warmed by the little pot-bellied stove that she tended carefully, was "the hub of the house" where the aunts gathered to chat. In contrast, Helene discouraged visitors to her room: "she let her fire go out, flung open her window, and shut her door against intruders."[33] Even within the family, Helene made her privacy inviolate.

Because Helene, like her mother, Ella, was so intelligent, Rachel decided she would be a teacher. Upon graduating from high school, Helene studied at Boston Teachers College and Boston University, and she later took extension courses at Columbia University, but she did not obtain a degree, perhaps because of financial constraints or perhaps because, as a single working mother, she chose to devote all of her time to her daughter, Abigail.

Dorothy always thought that Helene, with her intelligence and uncompromising character, was most like Rachel, and that her mother preferred Helene to herself and Eugenia. It was Helene, however, who seems to have suffered most from the family's communal arrangements and Rachel's dominating personality. Eugenia's father lived with the family periodically and Isaac was always around, but Helene's parents had separated shortly after her birth and she never knew her father. She hated to see her mother go off to the practical nursing jobs from which she would not return for weeks at a time. Helene "would watch her until she disappeared into the horizon. Then she would turn from the window to find that she was left alone with Rachel. When you were left with

Rachel, you were alone with no one on your side."[34] Helene's resentment and feelings of abandonment may have contributed to her solitary
and reserved nature. She was unconventional; unlike her cousins and
Rachel, she was uninterested in clothes or material possessions. When
Eugenia and Dorothy daydreamed of glamorous lives in New York,
Helene said she wanted to "run away and roam the whole world . . . she
was wild and free, and afraid of nothing. She would sleep in the woods
sometimes or in barns. . . . And she would write poems about everything
she saw and send them to her cousins."[35] Helene loved the outdoors, and
her precise observation of nature is evident in poems like "Trees at
Night," "The Road," and "Metamorphism."

Although the three girls were very different, they shared a passion
for dancing. At Rachel's insistence they, like other upper-class Bostonian
children, white and black, were given dancing lessons at an early age.
Cleveland Amory, in his satirical exposé of Boston high society, quotes
the *Boston Globe*'s perfectly serious assertion that "if you send your
daughter to the wrong dancing school at the age of six, you don't recover
for three generations."[36] Walter Stevens, who was a few years older than
the cousins, and who traced his ancestry back to Crispus Attucks,
attended Mrs. George Lewis's Dancing School. The Stevens family lived
in the old West End of Boston but crossed the Charles River to Cambridge for social activities. In his memoir of life in African American
Boston, Stevens recalls that "for dignified fun there was not a more desirable place for a boy or girl. This school was chaperoned and run by the
lovely, well-known Mrs. George Lewis of Parker Street, Cambridge. The
social standards of the school were very high and to have attended one
of its functions was to have obtained the very heights of social achievement, like the Cotillion Club in Baltimore. Each boy and girl was on his
best behavior and attired in his best clothes. We children danced the
waltz, the quadrille, the minuet and the polka to the accompaniment of
a delightful orchestra."[37]

Mrs. Lewis's competitor was Georgina Glover Brown, daughter of the
dress designer Phoebe Whitehurst Glover, who herself had been a leader
of society in the previous generation. Mrs. Brown directed the social life
of the "younger Negro elite" for almost fifty years. It is evident, from
West's descriptions, that the cousins attended her dancing school along
with "forty of Boston's best children."[38] Although Mrs. Brown's school

was held in a decaying South End neighborhood where the homes were being converted to flats and boardinghouses, Boston's African American parents eagerly sought places for their children, for "not to be known by Mrs. Brown was not to be an acceptable part of the Boston upper-class structure, and, conversely, admission into one of her classes in music or dancing was prima facie evidence of social acceptance."[39] At the Saturday dancing class, "a hand-picked collection of little boys in white gloves and little girls in best dresses formed a double line and made their bows and curtsies." In the novel, the Bessie Trotter character (Thea Binney) proposes the cousins' names for the class, just as it was probably Maud or Bessie Trotter who ensured the acceptance of the cousins into this elite group. Helene and Eugenia blended in easily, but the intraracial prejudice West experienced still rankled seventy years later. She remembered the watching mothers asking, "What is that little dark girl doing here?" West eventually got her own back: "I wrote the book, *The Living Is Easy*, and I made gentle—not cruel—I made gentle fun of that dancing class, [that] little dancing school that had forty children."[40]

Rachel and her sisters must have felt their ambitions for the girls were realized when they were not only accepted as pupils by Mrs. Brown but also, in the case of Helene and Dorothy, admitted to the prestigious Girls' Latin School. The school, founded in 1878 "to meet the demand that girls be provided with the same opportunities to fit for college that had long been enjoyed by boys," was originally a division of the non-college-prep Girls' High School located on West Newton Street in the South End.[41] The school moved to Copley Square in 1898 and, in 1907, to the Boston Teachers College on Huntington Avenue, just a few blocks from the Benson-West home on Brookline Avenue.

Although the average age of the incoming class was twelve, Dorothy, a precocious child, was accepted at the age of ten. Rachel's pride in her daughter is evident in a sketch she drew of herself and Dorothy as they walked to school. Dorothy wears a white dotted-Swiss frock trimmed with black ribbons, white silk hose, and a matching black tam. Rachel had paid ten dollars for the dress and always recalled it as one of her favorites. In the sketch Dorothy asks to be dropped off near the school but Rachel, perhaps wishing to protect her from comments by the rough Irish children of the neighborhood, replies: "Come on, Dorothy, I know what I'm doing."[42] Dorothy and her cousins had often been teased about being "colored" when they walked to the local elementary school, although both Helene and Eugenia fought back with impunity. Now Rachel reassured Dorothy that at Girls' Latin it would be different since "people of proper background never made fun of other people because of conditions over which they had no control, like being ten, like being small for ten, like being colored."[43] And indeed the students at Girls' Latin always treated the cousins politely, although Dorothy recalled that "there was a subtle prejudice there. . . . They were the kind of young people who were very nice to you in school. But if they saw you on the street, they got very busy looking in the window." If the girls complained about social slights to Rachel she was unsympathetic: "You're going to school to learn. What do you care? You come home and play with each other." Although they were "a very self-contained family," the cousins made some connections at school, including their lifelong friend Barbara Townes.[44] Oddly enough, despite the frequently published claim that Helene and Dorothy graduated from Girls' Latin, there is no record that they did so.[45] Dorothy's cousin Barbara Franklin recalled that the family was quarantined for illness and the girls missed too much school to continue at Girls' Latin, so they obtained their diplomas from Brighton High School. On an essay written by Dorothy in her senior year at Brighton High, she notes ruefully that her grade of "A" would have been at "C" at Girls' Latin.[46]

Every summer, as soon as school was dismissed, the family boarded the train from South Station to Woods Hole, from which they took the ferry to their cottage in Oak Bluffs, a town on the northeast shore of Martha's Vineyard. West recalls with gentle irony, "We were black Bostonians on a train full of white ones. Because we were obviously going the same way, laden as we were with all the equipment of a long holiday, children, luggage, last-minute things stuffed in paper bags, a protesting cat in a carton, in addition to the usual battery of disbelieving eyes, we were being subjected to intense speculation as to what people with our unimpressive ancestry were doing on a train that was carrying people with real credentials to a summer sojourn that was theirs by right of birth."[47] The first member of the family to come to the Vineyard was probably Rachel's father, a carpenter who worked for a wealthy family on the island.[48] Originally, the family rented a house, but when Rachel was twenty-one Isaac bought her a cottage: half of a duplex owned by the grandmother of artist Lois Mailou Jones. Rachel entertained her theatrical friends there, and it was this house that burned to the ground, perhaps victim of a carelessly tossed cigarette. Later Grandpa Benson bought the family cottage in which Dorothy, age five, wrote her first words: a note to her father in Boston requesting "a box . . . of rose ribbon . . . and some money in the box too."[49] Isaac rarely joined the family; he found the Vineyard social life and the beach boring and preferred to remain in the city and manage his business. West remembered that the family usually stayed on until September, and that the cousins were always late returning to school because "my mother could not bear to leave. Fall was so lovely . . . we lingered for those magic days until my father wrote, as he wrote every year, 'Come on home, there are no more flowers to pick.' "[50]

The cousins knew several African American families from Boston who summered on the island, including their lifelong friend Barbara Townes from Girls' Latin, the artists Grace Turner and Lois Mailou Jones, and Grace's sister Marie. Grace designed the graphics for Dorothy's literary journal *Challenge* in 1936. She and Marie had been raised as young ladies of privilege when their father's livery stable was thriving, but they trained as teachers as it became evident they would need to support themselves. The sisters, neither of whom married, were famous for their collection of international dolls, which they exhibited in libraries throughout New England.

A photograph of Lois Mailou Jones and the three cousins shows them on the beach, smiling gaily into the camera. Barbara Townes recalled that "I grew up with the writer Dorothy West and Lois Mailou Jones, the artist. We were very close friends. . . . We used to go in the Baptist Tabernacle in the Highlands and play hide and seek, do things that kids do." During their summers on the island, the young women met "a widening circle of African American intellectuals and artists who would influence [their] development."[51] The sculptor Meta Warrick Fuller and the composer Harry T. Burleigh were among the luminaries who encouraged the younger generation. Fuller, who had studied in Paris in 1899 under Rodin, urged Lois to follow her footsteps. In 1937 Jones won a fellowship to study and paint in Europe; she exhibited her work at the Salon de Printemps in Paris in 1938. Burleigh was a loyal supporter of Dorothy and Helene and, when the time came, certainly encouraged their mothers to allow them to move to New York. Burleigh was several generations older than the cousins; his New York was not the Harlem of the Renaissance but the area in the West Fifties known as Black Bohemia. There, around the turn of the century, Burleigh had frequented Jimmie Marshall's hotel on West Fifty-third Street, where he socialized with a glamorous, integrated, artistic group including poet Paul Laurence Dunbar, composers Will Marion Cook and W. C. Handy, bandleader James Europe, vaudeville stars Bert Williams and George Walker, producer Flo Ziegfeld, and actress Lillian Russell and her companion, the philanthropist and financier Diamond Jim Brady. West recalled that "he used to talk to us about New York and we called it 'the magic city.' "[52]

Back in Boston, the cousins took full advantage of the city's center as a major theatrical venue. Several of Rachel's friends were well-known actresses, including Edna Thomas, who performed in amateur theatricals, and Inez Clough. Clough, who started her career in the Broadway musical revue *Oriental America* in 1897, enjoyed a long career in both vaudeville and legitimate theater. Given her own interest in musical theater, Rachel undoubtedly took the cousins to one of Boston's "respectable" vaudeville houses such as the 1,700-seat Gaiety on Washington Street, which featured interracial casts and such important African American vaudevillians as George Walker, Bert Williams, and Sissle and Blake. In 1926 Josephine Baker performed at the Gaiety, and many years later Sammy Davis Jr. got his start there. The cousins would also have seen the important African American dramatic actors Charles Gilpin, Leigh Whipper, and Rose McClendon. Little did they guess that just a few years later Dorothy would appear on a Broadway stage with Whipper and McClendon in *Porgy*. The cousins subscribed to *Theatre Magazine* and kept abreast of current productions; they did not care for Mary Pickford, preferring Tallulah Bankhead, Greta Garbo, Helen Hayes, and Irene Bordoni. Bordoni, a popular French actress in musical comedies, whose eyes figured in Cole Porter's song "You're the Top," corresponded with Dorothy for many years, sent her a monogrammed handkerchief as a memento, and invited the cousins to join her in her private box for a performance.[53] A few years later, in her notebook for a theater class at Columbia University, West doodled the names "Irene Bordoni" and "Aunt Edna" (Edna Thomas), with whom Dorothy and Helene would live in New York.

Not surprisingly, given the cousins' passion for the theater, Dorothy's first serious creative ventures were plays modeled after her favorite playwrights, Eugene O'Neill, J. M. Barrie, and Cosmo Hamilton. In a high school essay she compared the play to the novel and concluded that although "books by well-versed authors preserve the keys to the world . . . no matter how vivid a novel may be it cannot compare with a play which to me offers the truest representation of life."[54] In 1925 Dorothy wrote a play called "The Emergence of Eleanor." She sent it to Sydney Rosenfeld, who advertised, in *Theatre Magazine*, his willingness to critique unpublished manuscripts for a fee of twenty-five dollars. Rosenfeld praised the dialogue and the atmosphere of the play but found the technical directions limited and the plot trite. Dorothy apparently disagreed but Rosenfeld held his ground, conceding only that the play was "a clever novelistic narrative."[55]

Both Dorothy and Helene began submitting their work for publication in the early 1920s. Perhaps discouraged by Rosenfeld's review of her play, Dorothy sent a story to the British playwright Cosmo Hamilton and received a positive response this time. She also sent stories to George Doran, publisher of the *Bookman* magazine. These may have been early versions of "The Typewriter," "Prologue to a Life," "An Unimportant Man," and "Funeral." Although West often gave the impression that her stories were published in the *Boston Post* when she was ten years old, it was probably at this time, when she was around sixteen, that they first appeared in print. Helene also published poems in the *Post* and in Monroe Trotter's newspaper, the *Guardian*. Interestingly, West always attributed the cousins' joint literary debut to an aunt's bringing home a copy of *Opportunity* in which the second (1926) contest was announced. She apparently forgot that Helene had sent "Trees at Night" to the 1925 contest, where it won an honorable mention. Johnson's poem is a spirited celebration of nature in which trees become "Slim Sentinels / Stretching lacy arms / About a slumbrous moon" (23).

Eugene Gordon, an editor and feature writer at the *Boston Post*, had noticed the cousins' work. He was responsible for three columns in the newspaper, including "The Observant Citizen," "Recipes," and "Short Stories"; in the latter column he published several of Dorothy's stories. In 1925 he organized a literary group called the Saturday Evening Quill Club. He invited the cousins to join what he described as "an organization of Boston writers," adding "most of these men and women are unprofessionals, and all, incidentally, are Negroes, although anybody who is eligible may become a member."[56] In fact, most of the members were women, and Gordon seemed particularly interested in encouraging women's writing. According to West, he had no idea the cousins were African American, and they did not know he was a member of the race. In July 1925, Dorothy and Helene traveled across the Charles River to Gordon's home in Cambridge for one of the club's meetings.

Gordon was always well known in African American literary circles. In 1926 Gwendolyn Bennett interviewed him in her column, "The Ebony Flute," in *Opportunity* magazine, where he reported on the Quill Club activities and announced that he was working on two novels. As the founding president of the Quill Club, he was the intellectual force behind an organization that offered a rare venue to African American women artists and writers such as Lois Mailou Jones (1905–1998), Edythe Mae Gordon (1897–1980), Gertrude Schalk, Dorothy West, and Helene Johnson.

That Gordon mentored West and influenced her work is clear from the writers' similar style and themes. Gordon's writing, like West's early stories, is naturalistic and geographically precise, and grounded in a gritty urbanism and a proletarian aesthetic. In the stories of both writers, streetcars rattle down Huntington Avenue, Albany Street, and other thoroughfares that divide Boston along ethnic and economic lines. Their protagonists aspire to the American dream but are thwarted by social and economic forces. Relationships between men and women are depicted as fraught, angry, and filled with resentment. Like Isaac West, Gordon appears to have selected a spouse based on a hegemonic definition of beauty. His stories, like Dorothy's, are bleak depictions of mismatched couples trapped by finances and social pressure. Both West and Gordon had firsthand experience with unhappy relationships: West's parents' marriage was dysfunctional to say the least, while Gordon's "interest in other women" caused the breakdown of his marriage to Edythe Mae; they separated in 1929 and divorced in 1940.[57] Although West concentrated more on the power relations among women and children in families, her male protagonists share with Gordon's a sense of the existential loneliness of the black man's confrontation with racism and prejudice. Both West and Gordon relieve tension in their work through subtle humor, although West's is more ironic and Gordon's more cynical and similar to that employed by Chester Himes in his novels and short stories.

Gordon, a Florida neighbor of Zora Neale Hurston's and a friend to Paul Robeson, Langston Hughes, and Richard Wright, was born November 23, 1891, in Oviedo, Florida, a few miles from Eatonville. He was the son of Elijah and Lillian Gordon. Like Hurston, he came from a religious background, and his father was a minister, although he may also have worked as a stevedore in New Orleans. Gordon's paternal grandfather owned a plantation in Georgia, but his childhood in the South seems to have been painful and unhappy. After high school he moved to Washington, D.C., where he worked as a janitor and, again like Hurston, studied English at Howard University.[58] During these years he met Edythe Mae Chapman, then a senior at Washington's famous M Street School (later Dunbar High), which she attended between 1912 and 1916. In fact, Edythe Chapman may have studied with the novelist Jessie Fauset and the poet Angelina Weld Grimké, both of whom were on the school's faculty. Although their marriage was not destined to be a happy one, the couple shared a love of literature and writing; they married in Alexandria, Virginia, on January 10, 1916, when Edythe was nineteen and Eugene twenty-four.[59]

Gordon, who wrote fiction and nonfiction and also painted, was in many ways a Renaissance man. He served in World War I as a second lieutenant with the 92nd Division and was awarded the Croix de Guerre by the French government for heroism in combat. His "first published story in a newspaper was an account of two daylight raids made by patrols he led behind the German lines on November 6 and 7, 1918, when he commanded a platoon of Company C, 367th Infantry."[60] West clearly drew on Gordon's military experience in "An Unimportant Man." The story, set in 1919, reflects Gordon's observations about African American participation in World War I. The protagonist is indignant that black soldiers "should be grouped in a separate regiment"; he eventually realizes that "they were going, poor fools, ironically enough, to fight for justice" (144).[61] In the March 17, 1945, edition of the *Daily Worker* Gordon published an article titled "Jimcrow Can't Inspire Men of the 92nd" in which he complained about the current conditions in the military, saying, "We Negro officers and men of the 92nd Division in 1918 used to say bitterly that a segregated outfit was an inferior outfit. . . . The men of that division today feel and say precisely the same thing."[62]

After he was demobilized, Eugene and Edythe moved to Cambridge, Massachusetts, and he joined the staff of the *Boston Post*. When Dorothy West and Helene Johnson met him he was publishing regularly in *American Mercury*, *Scribner's*, and the *Nation*. He held himself, and the race, to the strictest journalistic standards while refusing to be limited or stereotyped by color; in 1924 his frank articles in *Opportunity* on the mediocrity of the black press had touched a nerve and infuriated race leaders. Mainstream America also felt his censure: in an article in *Scribner's* (1930), he criticized whites for their facile stereotypes and indifference to black life. At the same time he complained that upper-middle-class African Americans replicated the very worst elements of white society: classism, materialism, snobbery, and social climbing. When he won an award in an *Opportunity* contest, his resentment of discrimination is reflected in his remark that "I was born colored in Oviedo, Florida, and have remained more or less so since. I honestly admit I am not proud of being known everywhere I go and by everything I do as a colored man. I [am] less annoyed in this respect, however, in Massachusetts than [in] Washington, D.C., or Oviedo, or New Orleans."[63]

Gordon set the bar high for his Quill Club, and West and Johnson undoubtedly benefited from his advice on publishing and his insistence on technical excellence. Eventually Dorothy would publish three stories in the club's annuals, "An Unimportant Man" (1928), "Prologue to a Life" (1929), and "Funeral" (1930). Seven of Helene's poems appeared in the second number, in 1929: "Regalia," "Worship," "Rustic Fantasy," "I Am Not Proud," "Remember Not," "Invocation," and "Why Do They Prate?"

Dorothy and Helene were the youngest Quill Club members; their friend Lois Mailou Jones, whose illustrations enhanced a number of poems in the annuals, was a few months older than Helene. Gordon, himself an accomplished artist, certainly encouraged Jones in her art as he did West and Johnson in their literary careers. Much like the cousins, Jones enjoyed a cultured Boston upbringing and had begun drawing, writing, and playing the piano as a young girl. Her father, like Zebediah Jenkins in West's story "An Unimportant Man," encouraged his daughter's artistic ambitions. Like Jenkins, Lois's father tried and failed three times to pass the Massachusetts Bar exam, although he was more successful financially than his fictional counterpart due to his real estate investments.

Jones went on to win international acclaim for her paintings and to enjoy a forty-seven-year career as a professor of art at Howard University. In 1980, President Carter invited her to the White House and honored her for outstanding achievements in the arts. She was also a favorite of the Clintons, who purchased her island painting *Breezy Day at Gay Head* for the White House. In spring 1996, ninety-year-old Lois Jones traveled to New York, where she was feted as the Studio Museum of Harlem's artist of the year. She remarked, to the cheering crowd's delight: "My friend Dorothy West tells people she's the last surviving writer from the Harlem Renaissance. Well, I'm the last artist."[64]

The Quill Club was thus an important venue in the artistic development of West, Johnson, and Jones. Guided by Gordon, they established supportive relationships with a number of progressive, artistic women, since most of the members were female. The most renowned was sixty-four-year-old Florida Ruffin Ridley (1861–1943), a friend of Pauline Hopkins's and the daughter of Josephine St. Pierre Ruffin and Charlestown Municipal Court Judge George Lewis Ruffin.[65] Florida, who followed in her trailblazing parents' footsteps, graduated from Boston Teachers College in 1880 and became the second African American school teacher in the Boston public schools. She taught at the Grant School until her 1888 marriage to Ulysses A. Ridley, a tailor in downtown Boston. In the 1890s she co-edited with her mother the *Woman's Era*, the country's first newspaper devoted to the interests of African American women. In July 1894, the *Boston Sunday Globe*, in a feature titled "Sets in Colored Society," explained that "the Ruffins and the Ridleys are the centers around which swell society at the West End revolves. . . . Mrs. Ridley presides over a very charming home on Charles St. She is a gracious woman and very pretty withal."

Ridley was not simply a society woman. Citing her active engagement "in welfare work," Eugene Gordon praised her in 1925 as "one of the few persons hereabouts, of any consequence, who was born in Massachusetts. She is imbued with this State's holy traditions—and much more."[66] Florida Ruffin Ridley contributed two stories, an essay, and a biographical sketch to the club's annuals. Her essay on her family's deep Massachusetts roots, "Other Bostonians," was inspired by the need to sort through an old trunk of her ancestors' memorabilia: deeds, receipts, Bibles, photographs, letters, and commendations, all of which testify to

the patriotism and the contributions of black Bostonians. Ridley maintains that the materials are important because they show "a Boston Negro
family, a family justifiably but modestly making its claim as 'Bostonian'
because of three generations born in Boston and free in Massachusetts: a
family which has its known beginning when a captured African escaped
from a trading vessel in the port of New Bedford, fled to the woods . . .
and took an Indian squaw as wife."[67] Ridley's genealogical research certainly encouraged West to investigate her own family's progress from
slavery to social and financial success in her novel *The Wedding*. West often
insisted that the point of the novel was to document the arduous journey
made by the forebears of the present-day African American elite.

Dorothy and Helene would have met the other professional women
in the organization who worked as teachers, playwrights, and journalists.
The club's secretary, Grace Vera Postles, was a teacher from Chester, Pennsylvania; she held degrees from Cheyney State, the nation's oldest black
college, and Boston's Emerson College of Oratory. Alvira Hazzard
(1899–1953) was a playwright and short story writer from Brookfield,
Massachusetts, while the poet Gertrude Parthenia McBrown (1902–1989),
originally from Charleston, South Carolina, was a graduate of Emerson
College and Boston University. Lois Jones's drawings occasionally accompanied McBrown's poems. The 1929 *Quill*, for instance, features Jones's
lively portrait of angels flying with lanterns beneath a star-sprinkled sky, as
two elves kneel on the ground below, quietly observing the scene. Beneath
the painting is McBrown's poem "Fire-Flies."

> When the tired day
> Smiles with the happy night,
> A thousand fireflies
> Flicker lanterns bright.
> Happy at their play;
> Flashing yellow lights,
> A thousand fireflies
> Shine with stars at nights.

The collaboration would continue into the 1930s, when Jones illustrated
McBrown's book of children's verse, *The Picture-Poetry Book* (1935).

Among the club's less well known members was Alice Chapman
Furlong, born in Albany, New York, and educated in the Cambridge,

Massachusetts, public schools. Her divorce around 1920 from Robert Furlong may account for the many poignant references to a broken heart in her poetry. In "Awaiting," for example, published in the 1929 *Quill*, the speaker reluctantly flees her occupied lover:

I shall be gone, my Love, before you find me,
So long, so long the day till dreams come true;
But I shall leave a blazoned trail behind me,
Clearly defined, to point the way for you.
And when the earthly things that now enthrall you
Unbind their clinging tendrils, one by one,
Then from some far off, lonely peak I'll call you
So you may climb to rest—when strife is done.

Rounding out the original club members were Gertrude "Toki" Schalk, editor of Boston's *Sunburst* literary magazine; Gordon's wife, Edythe, who published twelve poems and stories in the various issues of the annual; the poet Waring Cuney; and the theatrical producer Ralf Coleman. The attractive and vivacious Schalk became the society editor of the national African American newspaper the *Pittsburgh Courier* and often returned to Boston to cover social events. She remained active in journalism and in 1970 was elected president of the Women's Press Club of Pittsburgh.[68]

Cuney, along with West and Johnson, is the most frequently anthologized of the Quill Club writers. Three of his poems appeared in the initial *Saturday Evening Quill* and six in the second issue. In *The Big Sea*, Langston Hughes credits the Washington, D.C., native with recruiting him to Lincoln University. As Hughes tells it, "One day on a street car in Washington, I first met Waring Cuney . . . a student at Lincoln University, near Philadelphia. He told me it was a fine college, because you had plenty of time there to read and write. He said the tuition was cheaper than at Howard. So I sent for a catalogue . . . [and] at the mid-year I entered Lincoln."[69] In 1926 the young poets brought national attention to the school: Hughes received the Witter Bynner Prize for the best poetry submitted by an American undergraduate, and Cuney took the first prize in the 1926 *Opportunity* contest for his poem "No Images." The poem celebrates the beauty of an ordinary, urban black woman and remains the most influential of his lyrics:

She does not know
Her beauty,
She thinks her brown body
Has no glory.

If she could dance
Naked,
Under palm trees
And see her image in the river
She would know.

But there are no palm trees
On the street,
And dish water gives back no images.[70]

After graduating in 1927, Cuney moved to Boston, where he studied at the New England Conservatory of Music and, at Eugene Gordon's invitation, joined the Quill Club.

Another member of the club was Ralf Meshack Coleman, a stage actor, playwright, producer, and director who summered on Martha's Vineyard close to the cottages of the West and Jones families. Coleman first appeared in print in the *Saturday Evening Quill* with the poem, "Song of Youth"; in 1929 he contributed a play to the *Quill* and another in 1930. His big break came five years later in 1935 when he was appointed director of the Depression-era Federal Theatre Project's Boston Negro unit. Coleman proved extremely popular with Boston audiences. Between 1935 and 1939 he directed such works as *In Abraham's Bosom*, *Tambourines to Glory*, and an all-black version of *Macbeth*, which debuted in Boston in October 1935, six months before Orson Welles's *Voodoo Macbeth*. Coleman's younger brother Warren also dedicated his life to the theater: he played the character Crown in the 1935 Broadway version of *Porgy and Bess*, six years after West performed in the play.[71]

Gordon had managed to gather a virtual Who's Who among black Boston's artists and intellectuals into his club, including William Harrison, the editor of the *Boston Chronicle*, a weekly African American paper that the FBI claimed was sponsored by the Communist Party.[72] In 1925, Harrison published Helene Johnson's only known short story, "Respectability," in the *Boston Chronicle* after it won first prize in a contest sponsored by the paper. Eugene Gordon published three numbers of his club's annual, in 1928, 1929, and 1930. The 1928 issue, arguably the most successful, was favorably reviewed by the *Boston Herald*, the *Amsterdam News*, and *Commonweal*, and it was praised by both W.E.B. Du Bois, who deemed it the best of the black literary journals, and Alice Dunbar Nelson, who appreciated its judicious editing and "seventy-two pages of very excellent material."[73]

Despite his dedication to African American women artists, Gordon was a complicated and mysterious man. Between the mid-1930s and the 1960s, he was relentlessly investigated by the FBI and accused of pro-communist sympathies. At the time of the Quill Club, he and Edythe frequently attended theatrical performances at the Ford Forum on Beacon Hill, an organization founded in 1908 by George Coleman, a businessman and member of the Boston Baptist Social Union. The group invited controversial speakers on issues of social justice, including Margaret Sanger (after Mayor James Curley forbade her to speak publicly about birth control), W.E.B. Du Bois, and, many years later, Malcolm X. By the mid-1920s, however, the lecture series was linked with radical political issues, and the Baptist church dissociated itself from the organization. The earnest members of the Quill Club would probably have been surprised to know that they, like the members of the Ford Forum, belonged to an organization deemed by the FBI to be "Communist-infiltrated"; in the case of the Quill Club, the infiltrator was identified as William Harrison, with whom Gordon kept in touch for many years.[74] On December 16, 1944, the *Boston Chronicle* published Gordon's article "Equal Justice" in which he identifies himself as a writer for the *Daily Worker*. He describes the case of a group of white men accused of raping an African American woman in Alabama; Gordon went to Birmingham and elicited a promise from the governor to investigate the case.[75]

In 1954, Edythe Chapman Gordon, who had since remarried a man named Kelley, "cooperated" with the FBI and gave several interviews about her life with Eugene. She also provided the FBI with copies of the club annuals from 1929 and 1930, requesting that they be returned to her after they were photographed. Edythe insisted that "during the period she resided with Gordon, she saw no actions on [his] part that would reflect sympathy for the Communist Party or the Soviet Union" and maintained that she knew of no Communist connections with either the Quill Club or the Theatrical Group at the Ford Forum, although she did recall that William Harrison was a member of the club. Around 1930, the couple separated, and Gordon "agreed to finance [Edythe's] education if, upon receiving a divorce, she would not sue for alimony."[76] Edythe received her M.A. in economics and history from Boston University in 1935. Meanwhile, Gordon had met a Russian textile worker organizer named Sonia (June) Croll. She and Gordon traveled to the Soviet Union together in the early 1930s and eventually married, had a son, and settled in New York.[77]

Dorothy West stayed in touch with Gordon throughout the 1930s and 1940s when she and her companion, Marian Minus, moved in leftist literary-political circles in New York. In a letter to Langston Hughes in 1934, she praises Gordon and Hughes as two black intellectuals who are "wide-awake" and capable of reaching the younger generation.[78] In interviews given in the 1970s and 1980s, however, perhaps because she did not wish to complicate her growing fame with connections to radical politics, she did not acknowledge Gordon's help or his influence on her work. Gordon, on the other hand, generously assisted West when she first came to New York by publicizing her work in Gwendolyn Bennett's column, stating that her stories in the *Boston Post* had "developed quite a following."[79] A reviewer for the *Washington Tribune* maintained that "had the Saturday Evening Quill Club done nothing but publish Dorothy West's story of 'An Unimportant Man,' its work would have been worth while."[80] The same may well be said about the Helene Johnson poems that Gordon was the first to publish. Certainly he must be credited with providing a substantive start for the cousins' writing careers.

On May 4, 1926, Charles S. Johnson, the editor of *Opportunity* magazine and organizer of the second literary contest, wrote to inform Dorothy and Helene about the results of the contest to which they had submitted their work. West had won half of the second short story prize for "The Typewriter." She shared the award and the fifty-dollar prize with Zora Neale Hurston for "Muttsy." With her story, described by Jean Toomer as "the best realized in the contest," West triumphed over her mentor, Eugene Gordon, who won fourth prize for his story "Rootbound" (the title of which Helene later used in an unpublished poem about a man who must decide between staying in America, despite its discrimination, or leaving his country).[81] Dorothy also surpassed Claude McKay, who won an honorable mention for "High-Ball." Helene won three honorable mentions for her poetry. Robert Frost, one of the poetry judges, admired "Magula," which he described as a "macabresque fantasy mingled with living emotion," and he thought "The Road" was the finest poem submitted.[82] Despite Rachel's attempts to lessen any disappointment should they not win by telling them that "everyone" got invitations to the dinner, the cousins had attended the awards ceremony on May 1, where they met writers who were to be lifelong friends: Countee Cullen, Langston Hughes, Zora Neale Hurston, Wallace Thurman, and Eric Walrond. The following December, Gwendolyn Bennett reported in her literary column "The Ebony Flute" that "Dorothy West and Helene Johnson are spending the winter in New York—I believe they are studying Journalism at Columbia University."[83] The cousins had arrived and New York was waiting for them.

CHAPTER 5

The Youngest Members of the
Harlem Renaissance, 1926–1931

ELATED BY THEIR SUCCESS at the second *Opportunity* awards dinner in May 1926, Dorothy and Helene joined the family on Martha's Vineyard, knowing they would soon return to New York. Although they were to establish friendships with the men of the Harlem Renaissance, particularly with men in New York's gay, biracial subculture, it was with women in the arts, across a broad spectrum of race, age, profession, and interest, that the cousins formed a network of literary, financial, and emotional support. Actresses Edna Thomas, Rose McClendon, Georgette Harvey, Fredi Washington, and Isabel Powell; singer Alberta Hunter; producer Cheryl Crawford; theatrical agent Elisabeth Marbury; short story writer and journalist Gwendolyn Bennett; professors Blanche Colton Williams (Hunter College) and Dorothy Scarborough (Columbia University); and writers Marian Minus and Zora Neale Hurston all moved in overlapping social and professional circles. Because of the matriarchal traditions in the Benson family history, and the women they knew in Boston's African American literary and cultural community, the cousins moved easily into this supportive milieu.

Zora Neale Hurston was one of the very first women they met at the awards dinner. According to West, "Zora loved me but she always had a little feeling about me because I was only seventeen and she was twenty-five" when the two divided the *Opportunity* award.[1] Of course, Zora was really thirty-five, but if she felt chagrin at sharing second prize for the short story with Dorothy, it did not bother her for long; soon she was referring to the cousins as her "little sisters" and inviting them to parties at her apartment on West Sixty-sixth Street. It was Zora who made their important introduction to Wallace Thurman and his avant-garde coterie at 267, the Stanford White mansion in Harlem converted to a rooming house, where aspiring artists met to drink bootleg gin and to plan their aesthetic assault on mainstream America. A few years later, West reciprocated by introducing Hurston to members of New York's haute bourgeoisie, all family friends from Martha's Vineyard, in hopes that they would promote her work. Hurston included Helene Johnson's poems in the short-lived journal *FIRE!!* which she co-edited, and when she went south on an anthropological research trip, she publicized Johnson's work, reading her poetry to students at the University of New Orleans. While Zora traveled the rural South, the cousins sent her newsy letters and current best-sellers, and she mailed them a box of fresh pecans for their first Thanksgiving in New York. Perhaps most important, Zora secretly sent the women her manuscripts for safekeeping while she was bound in intellectual indenture to her patron, the overbearing Mrs. Mason.[2] Of all her literary friends in New York, Zora felt that the cousins were the only ones she could really trust. Thus, on the night of the *Opportunity* awards dinner, a long, occasionally prickly, but mutually loyal and supportive friendship began among the three writers.

Along with Zora, the cousins met Blanche Colton Williams at the banquet. Williams, a contest judge, a former professor of English at Columbia University, and the chair of the English Department at Hunter College, was to become an important mentor to West; shortly after the awards banquet, she submitted Dorothy's prize-winning entry (along with those of the first prize winner, "Symphonesque" by Arthur Huff Fauset, and the fourth place winner, "Rootbound" by Eugene Gordon) to the O. Henry Memorial Award contest, and all three were published in *Prize Stories of 1926*. A few years later, Williams encouraged Angus Burrell to publish West's story "An Unimportant Man" in Columbia University's literary magazine.

In addition to meeting two women who were to be instrumental in their writing careers, the cousins would certainly have appreciated the positive critical response to their work from the literary establishment. Robert Frost, who judged the *Opportunity* contest, called Helene's first-prize winning poem "The Road" the "finest" poem submitted, and he praised her fourth-place entry "Magula" as a "macabresque fantasy mingled with living emotion."[3] Even before the cousins attended the awards dinner, *Opportunity* had published a number of Helene's poems, including "Trees at Night" and "My Race" (1925). Journalist Gwendolyn

Bennett promptly mentioned Helene in her column as "the youngest of the new group of negro poets." Jean Toomer, another contest judge, thought that Dorothy's entry "The Typewriter" was "the best-realized story . . . it is set down with swift economy."[4]

"The Typewriter" placed West among the two hundred writers whose work was selected for the O. Henry short story collection from over two thousand entries from magazines in 1925–26.[5] Thus, at the age of seventeen, she found herself in the company of her favorite writers: Edith Wharton, Dorothy Parker, F. Scott Fitzgerald, and Mary Roberts Rinehart. Works by Theodore Dreiser, Willa Cather, and Sherwood Anderson were also published in the volume. African American letters was well represented; in addition to Gordon's and West's stories, Fauset's "Symphonesque" placed among the top twenty and was mentioned on the book's cover.

"The Typewriter" is similar to "Hannah Byde," which would soon appear in the *Messenger* (June 1926), and to the three pieces West would publish in Gordon's *Saturday Evening Quill Club Annual:* "An Unimportant Man" (1928), "Prologue to a Life" (1929), and "Funeral" (1930). These stories combine the "proletarian aesthetic" of Eugene Gordon's fiction, which "documents the complex manner in which race, class, and gender often militate against individuals in a racist, sexist, and elitist environ-ment," with West's compassionate evocation of the vulnerable and dis-possessed.[6] Her fiction at this time, unusual for being written by a woman under twenty, depicts "unachieving, disappointed [men] who still have retained a measure of innocence" but who are unable to satisfy their frigid, bitter wives.[7] Margaret Perry notes the influence of Dostoyevsky on West's work (one of the few literary influences to which she would ever admit), not only in the claustrophobic, urban atmosphere of the characters' dingy apartments and the crowded streetcars in which they travel, but also in West's vision of the "incorruptible nature of children" (132). Spurned by their wives, the protagonists in these stories often iden-tify with the hopes and ambitions of their daughters. In protecting and supporting children against repressive mothers who try to force them into lives of bourgeois respectability, the men achieve a sort of redemption.

Like Dorothy's stories, Helene's poetry also met with immediate crit-ical success. Countee Cullen selected "Bottled," which would soon be published in *Vanity Fair,* for a poetry reading and wrote to congratulate her on the quality of her work.[8] In September 1926, "Fiat Lux," a stern indictment of cruelty and racism in a women's prison, appeared in the *Messenger*, while in the same month *Opportunity* published "Mother," a tribute to Ella Benson's sincere religious piety and her dedication to her daughter. In October the *Messenger* published "Love in Midsummer," a poem of sexual awakening that draws imagery from the unique natural environment of Martha's Vineyard. Countee Cullen and Wallace Thurman must have asked Helene for poems immediately after meeting her at the awards dinner, since her work quickly appeared in magazines they edited in the fall of 1926. Cullen published "Magula" in his guest-edited, all–African American issue of *Palms*. This prestigious journal of modernist poetry was owned and edited by Idella Purnell, an American teacher and librarian who lived in Guadalajara, Mexico.[9] In *Palms*, Cullen's aesthetic taste and editorial eye for theme and technique produced a remarkable selection by prominent African American writers. The October issue included, in addition to his own work and Johnson's "Magula," poems by Arna Bontemps, Georgia Douglas Johnson, Anne Spencer, Jessie Fauset, W.E.B. Du Bois, Richard Bruce Nugent, Gwendolyn Bennett, Walter White, Alain Locke, and Langston Hughes, as well as by Helene's fellow Bostonians William Stanley Braithwaite and Waring Cuney. The critical reputation of "Magula" has stood the test of time. According to Mitchell, it is "one of Johnson's more overtly political poems [that] succinctly illustrates the 'radical' nature of [her] verse." On one level the poem "caters to shallow consumers of Renaissance literary production, giving them . . . a flashy, exotic vision of Africa," although "by poem's end, Johnson has deftly destabilized those expectations" by communicating a vision of danger and vulnerability within the exotic jungle.[10] Johnson's compressed imagery suggests that dangers—sexual, racial, and cultural—emanate from systems of hegemonic power and domination.

Perhaps encouraged by Zora Neale Hurston's interest in the cousins, Wallace Thurman also championed Helene's poetry. In his 1928 essay "Negro Poets and Their Poetry," he maintained that "Helene Johnson alone of all the younger group seems to have the 'makings' of a poet."[11] Thurman and Hurston selected her tragic, eerie "A Southern Road," which depicts the aftermath of a violent lynching and prefigures the Billie Holiday song "Strange Fruit" (1939), for their journal *FIRE!!* (November 1926). The poem, frightening in its intensity and coldly suppressed rage, fits perfectly in the journal that was designed to so shock the bourgeoisie that it would be "banned in Boston." The poem draws on the tree imagery that Johnson uses to such effect in "Worship" and "Trees at Night" ("Slim Sentinels / Stretching lacy arms / About a slumberous moon"), although here the "blue-fruited black gum" tree bears a terrible burden.[12] With her appearance in *FIRE!!* Helene Johnson instantly joined the Harlem Renaissance avant-garde. The journal was intended not only to articulate Langston Hughes's aesthetic philosophy of cultural and racial autonomy, as set down in his essay "The Negro Artist and the Racial Mountain," but also to foment "rebellion against Victorian pretensions of respectability." The editors intended to interrogate "forbidden interracial and homosexual relationships [and] the color line" and to "expose the wild parties, and the prodigious consumption of alcohol which Prohibition had turned into a principled act of defiance."[13] Published in the issue with Johnson, which was illustrated by Aaron Douglas and Bruce Nugent, were Langston Hughes, Zora Neale Hurston, Countee Cullen, Arna Bontemps, Gwendolyn Bennett, and Waring Cuney. For shock value, Thurman included his own "Cordelia the Crude," a naturalistic story in the tradition of Zola, about a teenage prostitute in Harlem, while Nugent contributed a Firbank-esque celebration of homoeroticism which Wirth calls "a pioneering contribution to gay literature [and] the first by an African American writer."[14]

That Johnson's poetry found acceptance in such diverse journals as *Palms* and *FIRE!!* speaks to her level of technical proficiency and her sense of audience, and demonstrates the ways in which her work pushes and extends the boundaries of traditional, modernist, and postmodernist poetic structures. She was as comfortable employing the classical allusions, multiple languages, and intricate, intellectual arguments championed by Cullen as she was celebrating the quotidian experiences of ordinary Harlemites through vernacular speech and blues lyrics in a way that impressed Thurman, Hurston, and Langston Hughes. As Cheryl Wall astutely observes, in an exegesis of Johnson's "Sonnet to a Negro in Harlem," "the sonnet's representation of alienation in the inner city seems as current as hip-hop."[15] This sonnet may have been the one Johnson sent to Cullen for inclusion in his anthology of African American poetry *Caroling Dusk* (1927). He apparently asked for some other poems for the book, but she demurred, claiming "they were all pretty awful," hoping she was not delaying publication of the anthology, and promising to send "a couple of new ones" that she thought he would like because "one of them is a sonnet." In her letter to Cullen Helene notes, with characteristic New England modesty, that she has been "having more than my share of good luck, an overdose of it, and will probably need all the good wishes you can spare."[16]

As her correspondence with Cullen shows, Johnson knew the audience for her different poems. She was an informed reader who closely followed the debates on African American literature, art, music, and politics. Like West, Johnson published in the journals and anthologies where many of the aesthetic exchanges played out, and both women were well aware that the literature of the Harlem Renaissance existed on a continuum, with Cullen's classical work at one pole and Langston Hughes's vernacular writing at the opposite. The Cullen-Hughes debates, largely over stylistic and ideological choices, came to a head just as Johnson and West were publishing their work in 1926. Where Hughes incorporated the language of the masses and the musical rhythms of jazz and the blues in his poems, Cullen was a traditionalist. He adhered to Standard English, and he favored such formal structures as the ballad and the sonnet. Hughes, in contrast, avoided the elevated language, conventional rhyme scheme, and use of classical symbols that would define Cullen's poetry. In fact, Dorothy West regretted that of all the younger writers, only Cullen remained "remote in his lyricism."[17] In contrast, Cullen found Hughes's jazz poetry particularly difficult to stomach, as he makes clear in his 1926 article "Poet on Poet." In his view, Hughes "pursues his own way, scornful, in subject matter, in photography, and rhythmical treatment, of whatever obstructions time and tradition have placed before him." Citing a stanza of Hughes's "Negro Dancers,"

Me an' ma baby's
Got two mo' ways,
Two mo' ways to do de buck!

Cullen wonders, "in the light of reflection . . . if jazz poetry really belongs to that dignified company, that select and austere circle of high literary expression which we call poetry."[18] Four months later, in his now famous essay "The Negro Artist and the Racial Mountain," Hughes responds. He speculates that Cullen subconsciously "would like to be a white poet." He suggests that in choosing European models for his poetry, Cullen was in effect fleeing his own culture, and pointedly concludes, "And I doubted then that, with his desire to run away spiritually from his race, this boy would ever be a great poet."[19]

Although Helene Johnson was well aware of this intellectual sparring, she refused to take sides, and she avoided personalizing the debate. She was closer temperamentally to the younger, more avant-garde writers, yet her verse spans an impressive range and thus cannot be contained by any one philosophical camp. She avoided her era's heated political and aesthetic debates not because she was timid or disinterested, but because she realized that they offered false choices. She further realized that as the debates turned personal, they deflected attention from art. What was most important, she explained, was to bring "attention to the work and not the person."[20] To the end of her life, Johnson refused interviews because she feared people were interested in her as a female writer of the Harlem Renaissance rather than in her poetry. In this way, she was very different from Dorothy, who reveled in publicity throughout her life and enjoyed telling stories of the famous artists and writers she had known.

Meanwhile Wallace Thurman, who was vociferous in his support of Hughes's side of the controversy, felt that his own professional life was veering dangerously toward decadence and self-indulgence. Drawn to the cousins' New England dignity and integrity, as well as their talent, he became a close friend of both women and immediately put them into his satirical roman à clef about Harlem, *Infants of the Spring*. Although the book did not appear until 1932, his description must have been written shortly after he met them in the late spring of 1926. Their scene opens at his large loft at 267 West 136th Street. The landlady, businesswoman Iolanthe Sidney, owned extensive real estate in Harlem and offered free lodgings to artists like Thurman, Langston Hughes, and Bruce Nugent. In the novel, Thurman credits Zora Neale Hurston for introducing him to the cousins. "Sweetie Mae [Zora] was accompanied by two young girls, recently emigrated from Boston. They were the latest to be hailed incipient immortals. Their names were Doris Westmore [West] and Hazel Jamison [Johnson]. Doris wrote short stories. Hazel wrote poetry. . . . Raymond [Thurman] liked them more than he did most of the younger recruits to the movement. For one thing, they were characterized by a freshness and naïveté which he and his cronies had lost. And, surprisingly enough for Negro prodigies, they actually gave promise of possessing literary talent."[21]

The accuracy of Thurman's portrait of his literary circle is corroborated by West: "We called [Thurman] our leader . . . 'cause he had a marvelous personality and he had the big room, and you brought your little gin there, and you brought your little crackers there, and you sat around and ate and talked about the great books, the great American novels you were gonna write, and the great poetry."[22] In his own novel of the period, *Gentleman Jigger*, Bruce Nugent gives a vivid description of life at 267: "Two sixty-seven was a large brownstone-front house in Harlem . . . [a] great mansion built in a more generous day by the great Stanford White." Here, the coterie gathered to listen to "the irreverent and loquacious dialect witticisms" of Nola (Zora) and to draw inspiration from Rusty (Thurman). "Rusty had decided to be one of the most, if not *the* most, important Negroes in America. He was an opportunist. He was the leader . . . facile and shrewd . . . and he needed the ideas of these less aggressive imbeciles to use as proof of his own creative ability. Their opinions regarding him did mean a lot. Besides, he had created the 'salon.' "[23]

West and Johnson were indeed young, inexperienced, and painfully shy in the room full of jaded and witty iconoclasts. Asked if she ever discussed her own work at 267, West replied, "I guess so . . . [but] I was ignored. I was seventeen and a half. I was a woman."[24] Nevertheless, the cousins were prepared for their debut in New York: unlike some of the residents of 267, who did more talking and drinking than writing, they had been producing work for most of their lives. In fact, asked in 1987 when she had begun writing, eighty-year-old Johnson answered, "Ever since I can remember."[25] Similarly, by the time she arrived in New York, Dorothy's stories "had appeared for years among the 'tabloid' tales distributed by the Wheeler Syndicate to scores of daily and weekly papers throughout the country."[26] Despite all of the attention, the cousins preserved their New England breeding. Eugene Gordon reported to Gwendolyn Bennett that "they are so excessively modest that they do not speak of their work, even at Quill Club meetings where such things are supposed to be discussed."[27]

Back in Boston and Martha's Vineyard in the summer of 1926, the cousins wrote industriously. On the Vineyard, West began a novel about herself and her two cousins (which has not survived), and Helene worked on her poetry. Her poem "Metamorphism" paints a thrilling picture of the ocean surrounding the island. The poet begins with a caesura, asking, "Is this the sea?" What follows are a series of sensuously arresting, changing images. In one instance, lying in sharp relief against the alliterative quiet of "This lisping, lulling murmur of soft waters," is "This sudden birth of unrestrained splendor, / Tugging with turbulent force at Neptune's leash." The poet ends, again asking, "All these—the sea?" (27). The Vineyard was also to inspire a column on nature that Dorothy wrote for many years. Not surprisingly, Johnson and West have recently been embraced by ecocritics, who see them as early advocates for the environment; in verse and prose, the cousins highlight their lifelong opposition to environmental depredations on Martha's Vineyard.

Although the cousins continued to attend Eugene Gordon's Quill Club meetings in Boston, they knew that their destiny was in New York. Harry T. Burleigh, the composer, arranger, and organist, was a neighbor on Martha's Vineyard and had regaled them, since the women's childhood, with glamorous tales of the city. Now he urged Rachel and Ella to allow the young women to pursue their dreams and promised to supervise them. Thus reassured, the parents allowed their daughters to return to the city in December and to enroll in college extension courses. Gwendolyn Bennett promptly reported in her column that "Dorothy West and Helene Johnson are spending the winter in New York—I believe they are studying Journalism at Columbia University."[28]

The young women were eager to explore the city, but they were cautious at first because Rachel had warned them that "New York was not like Boston, [the people] were real prejudiced." One day, according to Dorothy, they felt thirsty and "went to get a soda. We called it tonic—because that's what they called it in Boston. We went to a drugstore and the people at the counter, they were drinking tonic. We said 'We'd like two tonics' and they said 'Go to the back of the store.' We knew then that everything my mother had said about New York was right!" When they got to the back of the drugstore, the pharmacist explained that in New York "tonic" refers to patent medicine, so the cousins returned to the counter for their soda after all. Soon, the cousins "fell, as everybody does, in love with New York." West recalls that "we went on the subway and got off in Harlem. And there were all these colored people all over the place, just on the street corners. We had never seen so many colored people."[29]

James Weldon Johnson describes the wide streets they would have seen, full of "gay crowds skipping from one place of amusement to another, lines of taxicabs and limousines standing under the sparkling lights of . . . famous night-clubs."[30] In 1928, Wallace Thurman depicted Seventh Avenue, "Black Broadway—Harlem's main street," where Dorothy and Helene boarded with Edna Thomas, as "one electric-lit line of brilliance and activity. . . . People are everywhere. Lines of people in front of the box office of the Lafayette Theater at 132nd Street, the Renaissance Motion Picture theaters at 138th Street and the Roosevelt Theater at 145th Street. . . . People going into the cabarets. . . . Adolescent boys and girls flaunting their youth. . . . Seventh Avenue is filled with deep rhythmic laughter. It is . . . Harlem's most representative street." Harlem's night life was "the *leit motif* of sophisticated conversation" in New York and London, and Thurman estimated there were about a dozen important clubs "to which white sophisticates, Greenwich Village artists, Broadway revelers and provincial commuters make eager pilgrimage," including Bamville, Connie's Inn, Small's Paradise, and the Cotton Club.[31]

Although the cousins had neither the means nor the inclination to attend these venues, they soon met the beautiful Fredi Washington, a friend of Edna Thomas. Fredi, who was to become a lifelong friend and supporter of Dorothy, was dancing in the chorus at the Club Alabam and at the Cotton Club. Fredi looked like Joan Crawford and had dramatic aspirations; soon she launched her career in theater and film. She had been born in Savannah, Georgia, the oldest of the nine children of a dancer and a postal worker. Fredi and her sister Isabel grew up in comfortable circumstances in a predominantly white neighborhood, but were sent to a convent school in Pennsylvania when their mother died and their father remarried. Upon graduation, Fredi joined her grandmother in New York and worked as a typist at Black Swan records.[32] In 1921 she toured in the chorus of Sissle and Blake's musical *Shuffle Along*. She eventually became a critically acclaimed actress who worked opposite Paul Robeson in the plays *Black Boy* and *The Emperor Jones*. Helene had a small part in the latter, perhaps through Fredi's influence. Dorothy followed Fredi's career with great interest and gently satirized her in the WPA sketch "Cocktail Party" (1939): "the actress surveyed the room with disdain. She was playing in a downtown hit. Her hair went up and her nose turned up and even her lips were slightly curled. She was light-skinned and lovely and remote as a queen among her subjects."[33] In the sketch, the actress ignores her fellow Harlemites, only to gush over the attentions of a Broadway producer. If Fredi objected to her portrait, it did not keep her from enthusiastically promoting Dorothy's writing career. She can be seen smiling proudly in every photo of a 1948 book signing for *The Living Is Easy* and probably helped organize the event. Fredi was known for her generosity toward other women; she took the young Lena Horne under her wing at the Cotton Club, although, according to the Washington family, Lena never acknowledged the help.

In the early 1930s, hopeful of a film career, Fredi went to Hollywood. Although she starred with Duke Ellington (with whom she had a long love affair) in the short film *Black and Tan* and later in Fannie Hurst's melodrama of passing, *Imitation of Life*, her racially ambiguous looks were against her; like Edna Thomas, Dorothy Dandridge, and to a certain extent Lena Horne, she was considered too fair-skinned for conventional African American roles but was never considered for a "white" role.

Helene and Dorothy also knew Fredi's sister, Isabel, who later married Adam Clayton Powell. Like Fredi, Isabel began work in New York as a typist for Black Swan records but soon began dancing at Connie's Inn and the Cotton Club. While some New York chorus girls may have led racy lives, the convent-bred Washington sisters were carefully protected. Their grandmother, Big Mama, monitored all of their social activities. Every night the Cotton Club sent a car for Isabel. "I was a 'soubrette,' " Isabel recalled, "that means I led the chorus and did specialty numbers." While Powell knew that the Cotton Club was segregated and that "only white people were allowed to go there," it did not bother her at the time. "I was too busy sleeping all day and performing at night. . . . I was glad to have a job . . . [and] Big Mama was very supportive; she was thrilled."[34] Isabel also had stage ambitions, and in 1929 Wallace Thurman selected her to play Cordelia Williams, "a typical chippy," in his play *Harlem*. She "stirred audiences with her vivid portrayal," giving the impression that she "has practically lived her part." Thurman's account of the challenges of casting an African American show highlights the professional uncertainties of black actors, and the importance of networking within the race, since "there are no casting agencies to visit. There is no Negro theatrical blue book to consult. There are no Negro dramatic houses, amateur or professional, to visit for scouting . . . [so] it is necessary to sit in speakeasies and cabarets, attend the vaudeville houses, and invade private . . . dances or parties."[35] Along with Isabel Washington, Thurman cast Rachel's friend, Inez Clough, who had just returned from the road tour of *In Abraham's Bosom*, and Helene Johnson, who understudied the dancers, and who traveled with the show to Detroit and Chicago. As it turned out, *Harlem* was the last performance for both Isabel and Helene. Isabel met Adam Clayton Powell during the run and gave up her career for marriage. Helene injured her leg in the summer of 1929 and retired to Martha's Vineyard to recuperate.[36] Since Adam Clayton Powell Sr. owned a home near the Benson-West cottage, and since the cousins knew her sister Fredi, Helene and the newly engaged Isabel probably saw each other that summer. In fact, Isabel adored Rachel West and took on her habit of baking cookies for and lending books to Vineyard children. In later years, Isabel fell out with Dorothy over the latter's penchant for feeding the local birds (the subject of many of Dorothy's nature columns for the *Vineyard Gazette*). Isabel claimed that they created a nuisance on her own porch, but Dorothy refused to give them up.

Later, Isabel and Fredi became civil rights activists, just as Helene and Dorothy began to examine issues of social justice in their work. In New York, Fredi wrote for Adam Clayton Powell's newspaper, the *People's Choice* and, along with Edna Thomas, worked to improve the conditions of black actors.[37] She, Thomas, Noble Sissle, and Leigh Whipper founded the Negro Actors Guild in 1937. Similarly, although Helene and Dorothy initially delighted in Harlem's glamour and excitement, they soon realized that the other face of the community involved overcrowded conditions, exorbitant rents, and poverty they had never witnessed in Boston. Eventually, Dorothy used her experiences as a social worker in some of her most poignant stories like "Pluto" and "Mammy," while Helene argued for social justice in "Regalia" and "Goin' No'th."

In January 1927, however, everything in New York seemed perfect. Helene was a lovely woman, with golden skin and long, wavy hair. She preferred solitude to company, however, and would often take a couple of doughnuts and go down to Battery Park, where she would sit for hours watching the sea and composing her poems. Dorothy, dark and petite with an irresistible smile and deep dimples, blossomed socially. Harry T. Burleigh considered her one of the most beautiful girls in New

York, an opinion corroborated by photographs and her own self-portrait in a novel, which depicts her "velvet skin, the dark hair like a cloud, the dark eyes like wells to drown in."[38] At first too shy to speak at Wallace Thurman's parties at 267, she gradually began to display her Benson gifts for observation and satire, honed in family conversations, where wit and mimicry were prized, as she entertained Thurman's crowd with devastating send-ups of the pretentious "blue-vein" families she sometimes visited because of Boston connections. By all accounts, Dorothy was vivacious and charming, and, like Helene, an excellent dancer. Countee Cullen, who was known for his ballroom dancing skills, sought her out as a partner at the newly opened Savoy Ballroom on Lenox Avenue.

The main focus for both women, however, at least in the early years, was to hone their craft and to support themselves as writers. Helene, perhaps with the help of John Erskine, her writing teacher at the Columbia University Extension, or Carl Van Vechten, sold her poem "Bottled" to *Vanity Fair.* Unfortunately, the thrill of seeing her work in one of the most prestigious of the "slicks" was marred when she was called to the office of Frank Crowninshield, the Boston Brahmin editor of the magazine. He told Helene he would give her a whole page in the magazine for her poetry; then he crudely propositioned her. "She came home in tears," West recalled, "we held hands and got down on our knees to pray. That was the end of her career at *Vanity Fair.*" Unlike Langston Hughes, who also benefited from Van Vechten's influence at the magazine and published a number of his poems there, and who apparently emerged unscathed from Crowninshield's office, Helene and Dorothy soon learned that Rachel's warnings about unscrupulous men in New York were not unfounded. "You don't know what we had to go through back then," West told interviewer Deborah McDowell, "and I'm so glad you don't. . . . In those days, women were just like excess baggage or fair game."[39] Van Vechten, the self-styled dean of African American artists, would not have objected to Crowninshield's behavior since he himself routinely harassed the young cousins. Parodied by Bruce Nugent as "Serge Von Vertner, the big white discoverer of High-Harlem [who] wrote perfect, neurotic, precious books spiced with the gayest sophistications [and] stared with undressing blue eyes from a red face deceivingly moronic," Van Vechten, despite his open homosexuality, could not keep his hands off young women like Dorothy and Helene.[40] Though many of his guests pandered to his self-indulgence in return for his literary connections, A'Lelia Walker stood up to him. West recalled her saying, "Carlo, let that child alone" and "Carl, stop goosing that child. Don't you do that to that child" as West walked past him.[41] Certainly, according to Bruce Nugent, who also rebuffed his advances, the cousins were not the only young African Americans, of either sex, who received Van Vechten's unwanted attentions.

The indignities suffered by West and Johnson in their pursuit of artistic recognition so scarred them that West still spoke about it fifty years later, and Helene virtually retreated from public life, yet such treatment was not unusual at the time. As women demanded recognition for their talents, some men, from positions of power and influence, harassed with impunity women whose interest in the arts seemed to call into question their moral integrity. For example, Anaïs Nin, a contemporary of West's and Johnson's and a fellow student in the writing classes at Columbia University Extension, came from a similar sheltered background and an artistic family. To support herself, Nin posed for commercial artists and modeled clothes, but she was repeatedly subjected to salacious remarks, hands thrust down her dress, and random groping.[42] Few women were as assertive as Zora Neale Hurston, who, after a man made a pass at her in an elevator, "coldcocked him with a roundhouse right that left him sprawled on the elevator floor."[43] A more common response was to seek protection in marriage, as did Nin and most of the cousins' friends. It must have become clear to them that if they were not to choose matrimony, in which they definitely had no interest, they needed to take steps to protect themselves from predatory males and to establish relationships with strong and influential women.

With friends like A'Lelia Walker and Edna Thomas, the cousins moved in Harlem's gay and bisexual subculture, and formed emotional bonds with a number of artistic, homosexual men. Although homosexuality was not discussed openly, it was expressed through elaborately coded references and rituals. Countee Cullen often took Dorothy to drag clubs, probably the Hamilton Club Lodge Ball that Langston Hughes describes in *The Big Sea*. Harlem at this time was "a homosexual mecca," and "the drag balls of the 1920s and 1930s were the safest and most visible spaces where queers could affirm [their] nonnormative nature" and where women would not be importuned by aggressive heterosexual men.[44] In

addition to Countee Cullen, Dorothy and Helene were close to Ed Perry,
Bruce Nugent, Eric Walrond, Harold Jackman, Richmond Barthé,
Alexander Gumby, and Alonzo (Al) Thayer. Thayer, a talented actor who
appeared in *Green Pastures*, was a longtime friend of Dorothy's. When
Dorothy was in Russia in 1932, Helene wrote to her that "your little
friend, Al Thayer, comes over here all the time to play poker."[45] A few
years later, Thayer gave a WPA interview in which he emphasized the
social importance of gay men during the Harlem Renaissance: "it was a
soft living for all young writers, artists, musicians and pseudo intellectuals
[who had] a passable wardrobe, a smooth line of chatter, and a flair for the
latest dances."[46] Ed Perry, who moved in theatrical circles, was a close
friend of Edna Thomas's and Countee Cullen's. Perry, like Dorothy, was a
supernumerary in *Porgy* and traveled to London with the company in
1929. There he lived with Cullen, who was in Europe on a Guggenheim
fellowship. Cullen and Perry went out of their way to entertain Dorothy,
inviting her to dinner at their apartment, escorting her to parties, taking
her to the theater, and showing her "a great deal of fun."[47] In her letters
to Rachel, West does not mention Cullen's recent failed marriage to
Yolande Du Bois, the daughter of W.E.B. Du Bois, or his "honeymoon"
in Europe with his friend Harold Jackman; nor does she allude to any sexual connection between Cullen and Perry.

Both Helene and Dorothy admired and respected gay men, although
they sometimes described them in the judgmental language of the
period. They were also naïve about the realities of homosexuality. In fact,
both women saw these men as possible, if not ideal, marriage partners,
having observed firsthand the successful relationships of couples like
Lloyd and Edna Thomas, and Carl and Fania Van Vechten. Of course,
many gay men in their circle, such as Countee Cullen and Wallace Thurman, fully expected to marry and to blend queer desire with social convention.[48] It is thus not surprising that although Helene seems to have
interacted with straight men, Dorothy actively pursued marriage with at
least three men of gay or ambiguous sexual orientation, including Countee Cullen, Langston Hughes, and Bruce Nugent. Helene encouraged
her cousin in these relationships, writing in 1931: "I think you ought to
marry whoever you want no matter what he is like, if you love him. . . .
The older we get, the less illusions we have, & as far as abnormality goes,
I don't think that's important at all."[49] At the time, Dorothy was living

with Edna and Lloyd Thomas, so she would certainly have seen the possibilities of such a union.

It is possible that the cousins were discussing Dorothy's feelings for Bruce Nugent. In 1928, the two were very close, and in December Nugent had written Dorothy a vaguely erotic letter while he toured with Thurman's musical *Harlem*. He sends her "much love and many kisses. . . . Golden leaves against a flame striped blue. And amethyst cliffs rearing from a night-drunk sea." He wishes "selfishly" that she were on the tour "to talk to" but realizes that he would "fall (too) easily into the role of a spiritual dependent . . . not too good for a young man who should form some sort of rock bottom character for himself." Most of the letter, however, reminds her that she is lucky not to be on the tour since the "sordid and Southern" cities would have "disillusioned" her, possibly a reference to segregated conditions that the company encountered on the road. Despite the passionate beginning, Nugent closes his latter with a safely platonic postscript: "Love to Helene and Aaron and Alta [Douglas]. Say hello to anyone who might expect it. Love, Bruce."[50] Two years later, West wrote wistfully to Countee Cullen, "[Helene] sends love to you. She thinks you and Bruce are the world's finest. I think I do, too, and I wish I had some influence over Bruce, or do you disapprove of people wanting to reform other people? Yet I loved Bruce and perhaps I still do. . . . I did want our lives to mean something together, and, of course, to me that meant a baby. That's all I've ever really wanted, and Bruce seemed so strong, and I liked his fine mind."[51]

Even as she confides in Cullen her unrequited love for Nugent, West floats the possibility of a relationship between she and Cullen. At a reading of Cullen's poetry by James Weldon Johnson, her eyes fill with tears and she immediately writes to Countee (although they are staying only a few blocks apart on Seventh Avenue): "I should like you to be here now, reading your poetry and telling me your dreams while I sat very still with my eyes shining. . . . I love to listen! I love the company of men. Myself quiet while some man's voice drones on."[52] Of course, West's use of "drones" seems at odds with her image of an adoring, uncompetitive helpmate to a creative man, while it may reveal her resentment at the professional success of Cullen and other male artists. Cullen must have parried her romantic enthusiasm, for she responds: "Got your note. Made me feel very young and sat down hard upon. It was such a cautious note! . . . My cheeks fairly blazed. I had the horrid thought that my effusive missive must have seemed to you a love letter."[53] Nevertheless, Cullen sends mixed signals, asking that she write to him again "in that vein." He may even have proposed marriage and a long engagement, for she writes: "Dear Baby, Of course I'll wait two years if you want me to . . . I don't mind a bit being poor. I sort of wanted us to climb holding on to each other. But, my darling, you are cautious, and that I can't change, and perhaps I don't want to." At the same time, Dorothy's own conflicts about marriage surface; observing the indifference of her friends Aaron Douglas and Rudolph Fisher to their wives, Alta and Jane, she wonders if "perhaps marriage is a dull business for women."[54] In April 1931, Cullen writes to her from Chicago, determined to set the record absolutely straight. Her letters are "poems," he is "tremendously flattered" that she likes his novel, and he has been "thinking of [her] in other connections. . . . You are a fascinating and loveable child . . . in spite of your terrible yearning toward grown up ship and sophistication. I like you too much to want to hurt you even ever so slightly in no matter how remote a future. You and I have never had a real heart-to-heart talk about those things which must figure very greatly in our lives if we are to have the supreme relationship to one another; and I am fearful lest you are more sanguine about your knowledge of certain things, and your ability to bear them than you are actually equipped to do so." He closes with an injunction that she "keep sweet and remember me with kindness" and encourages her to keep working on her novel.[55] By May, Dorothy seems to have accepted the situation, since Cullen writes with unintended irony: "what a gay time we had last night, although we weren't able to talk very seriously. . . . I'll call you first chance I get and will arrange to go dancing."[56] Just two years later, Dorothy was to echo her words to Cullen in letters to Langston Hughes while the two were in Russia, urging him to marry her and give her a baby, after which she would absolve him from sexual and emotional connection, and encourage him to pursue his literary career.

West alludes to homosexuality only obliquely in her story about herself and Hughes in Moscow, "Russian Correspondence." The cousins, however, often discussed the topic in letters, and Johnson explored same-sex love in her layered poem "A Boy Like Me." The poem is structured as an extended dialogue between two young boys who discuss their desire for a "delicious" little boy "to fit into our cradle." Initially it seems that they merely want a playmate, but the series of erotic metaphors accumulate. And by poem's end their plans for conception are made clear: "Please, God, the Father, / May I be a mother, too, / like you? made in your image?" (82). In invoking the duality of the Christian deity, Johnson brilliantly normalizes the notion of a male mother. Moreover, focusing on two males conceiving a child displaces same-sex desire from Johnson the female poet, while simultaneously allowing her to explore an important aspect of the self. Revealingly, the two little boys valorize bisexuality: they will raise their son to be "free and / strong / with double charm and alternate / propensities" (85).

A similar rejection of the heterosexual imperative is expressed in novels by the cousins' friends Wallace Thurman and Bruce Nugent. Both Thurman's 1929 novel *The Blacker the Berry* and Nugent's posthumously published *Gentleman Jigger* (2002) deliberately toy with gender and sexuality and challenge social roles. For example, in Nugent's text, the Thurman character (Rusty) and Stuartt, Nugent's autobiographical character, adopt masculine and feminine roles when entertaining guests. Rusty occupies the only chair, immaculately dressed in "razor-creased trousers" and a "mauve and white skullcap he affected [at home] to emphasize his smallness and blackness. He looked as though he felt like Anatole France" (27). Stuartt, dressed in loose-fitting clothes, sits on the floor "hugging his knees," "smiles up" at male guests, talks in "a calm and certain way, his gentle voice soothing and somnambulistic" and brags about "[his] high instep . . . he arched his foot for inspection" (29–30, 39). Even more significant than gay men in the lives of Johnson and West were their many close relationships with gay women or women of indeterminate sexuality who modeled for the cousins a life of professional or artistic fulfillment unhampered by the restrictions of conventional marriage.

The chic, beautiful, unmarried, Blanche Colton Williams, whom the cousins had met at the awards dinner, facilitated their matriculation at Columbia. Johnson took classes from the popular professor and novelist John Erskine, while West studied with Williams and with Dorothy Scarborough.[57] Williams (1879–1944), a graduate of Mississippi College for Women, came from a liberal, enlightened southern family. She had won a fellowship for graduate study at Columbia University, where subsequently she received a Ph.D. in 1910 and taught courses in the short story. Her classes at Columbia were enormously popular, and over time enrollment in them increased substantially, although soon after West studied with her she left Columbia permanently for Hunter College.

Williams strongly influenced West's personal and professional lives. She pioneered the teaching of college rhetoric and creative writing, and wrote detective novels (under a pseudonym) and several texts on the short story. In fact, she felt that "the short story is the literary medium that supersedes all others in America [and is] the most perfect literary form," an opinion with which West concurred.[58] Williams expressed strong opinions on the construction of the short story, which West seems to have taken to heart in her novels and later stories. She spurned literary elitism and championed accessible, popular, commercial fiction; she preferred writers like O. Henry who "mastered the art of surprise" and "emotionally moved their audience," although she disliked obscure language and "subtle shades of emotion."[59] Williams was interested in American dialects and particularly liked regional writing, believing that writers should write what they know. The stories she selected for the 1926 O. Henry prizes reflect her interest in regionalism, set as they are in Boston, Maine, New Orleans, San Francisco's Chinatown, and Texas (Arthur Huff Fauset's "Symphonesque"). A friend of many intellectuals of the Harlem Renaissance, Williams encouraged and promoted African American writers. A witty, elegant, and fashionably dressed woman, Williams never married, maintaining that it was impossible to combine an academic career with a husband and family. "When I decided to make my career the most important thing in my life, I aimed to be a better teacher than any other, if I could, and to look less like a teacher than any other scholar I knew," she once explained in an interview.[60] Certainly, Dorothy West, with her own interests in literature, art, and fashion, saw in this unique, attractive and single-minded professional woman a strong role model, and one of whom Rachel would definitely approve.

In addition to taking Williams's short story class at Columbia, Dorothy studied playwriting and the novel with Dorothy Scarborough (1878–1935). Scarborough was born in Smith County, near Tyler, Texas; her father was a Confederate veteran but her family, like that of Williams, was liberal, artistic, and progressive. Scarborough's father, a judge, moved the family to Waco so that his children could attend Baylor University. Her sister Martha held degrees from Vassar and Baylor, while her brother, George Moore Scarborough, was a successful Broadway playwright.

Rachel Benson West
as a young woman.
Schlesinger Library,
Radcliffe Institute,
Harvard University

Ella Benson
Johnson as a
young woman.
Courtesy of
Abigail McGrath

Ella Benson Johnson and her nephew, John Johnson,
at the World's Fair, New York City, 1939.
Courtesy of Abigail McGrath

Helene Johnson and her
aunt, Carrie "Dolly" Benson,
ca. 1924.
Courtesy of Barbara Franklin

Helene Johnson, 1931.
The inscription reads,
"to 'Darthy' with
Love & best wishes
Always Helene."
Schlesinger Library,
Radcliffe Institute,
Harvard University

Dorothy West
(with the
headwrap) and
Eugenia Rickson
(wearing the
cross), at
Gay Head,
Martha's
Vineyard,
Massachusetts,
August 21, 1938.
Schlesinger
Library,
Radcliffe
Institute,
Harvard
University

Helene Johnson's husband, William Warner Hubbell III, at Coney Ilsand in New York City, March 1948. Courtesy of Abigail McGrath

The *Porgy* cast, on the Boardwalk in Atlantic City, New Jersey, March 1929, just before leaving for London. First row center, left to right: Rose McClendon, Evelyn Ellis, with her hand on the donkey, and Georgette Harvey. Third row, underneath "Atlantic City," right to left: Richard Bruce Nugent, Philander Thomas, and Edward G. "Ed" Perry. Dorothy West is in the third row right, partially obscured. By permission of Thomas H. Wirth

Edna Lewis Thomas and
Lloyd Thomas, June 18,
1932, and December 8, 1938.
Yale Collection of American
Literature, Beinecke Rare
Book and Manuscript
Library. Photographs by
Carl Van Vechten.
By permission of the
Van Vechten Trust.

Rose McClendon,
ca. 1929.
The inscription
reads,
"To Brucie Wucie
Poo, from Rosie
Posie Pow. Rose."
By permission of
Thomas H. Wirth

Fredi Washington,
ca. 1935.

Zora Neale Hurston,
New York City, 1935.
Yale Collection of American
Literature, Beinecke Rare
Book and Manuscript Library

Elisabeth Marbury and
Elsie de Wolfe, ca. 1915.
From *My Crystal Ball* by
Elisabeth Marbury (1923)

Langston Hughes and
Dorothy West en route to
Russia, June 1932.
Yale Collection of American
Literature, Beinecke Rare
Book and Manuscript Library

Mildred Jones, Sylvia Garner, and Dorothy West, 1932. Yale Collection of American Literature, Beinecke Rare Book and Manuscript Library

Film group in Moscow, 1932. First row, left to right:
Dorothy West holding books, Sylvia Garner, Langston Hughes,
Louise Thompson, Juanita Lewis, and Mildred Jones.
Yale Collection of American Literature,
Beinecke Rare Book and Manuscript Library

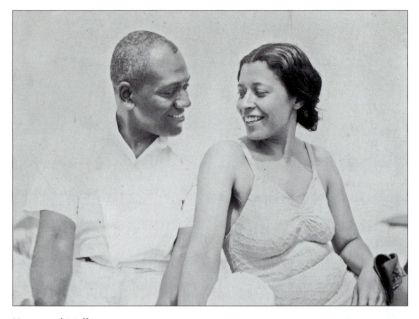

Henry and Mollie
Moon the year after
their marriage,
Long Island,
July 2, 1939.
Western Reserve
Historical Society,
Cleveland, Ohio

Dorothy West, Marian
Minus, and Snowball
at Oak Bluffs, late 1940s.
Courtesy of Barbara
Franklin

Dorothy West, Helene Johnson,
Eugenia Rickson, Abigail Hubbell,
and Sean, across the street from
the family cottage, Oak Bluffs,
Massachusetts, 1942.
Courtesy of Abigail McGrath

Dorothy West at a book signing for *The Living Is Easy*, New York City, May 13, 1948. Harold Jackman standing at left; Eugenia Rickson, across from West; Carl Van Vechten, at rear center; Mollie and Henry Moon at right. Countee Cullen/Harold Jackman Memorial Collection, Atlanta University Center, Robert W. Woodruff Library

Book signing for *The Living Is Easy*, New York City, May 13, 1948. Fredi Washington at left next to Dorothy West; Eugenia Rickson in middle, facing Washington; Grace Nail Johnson at far right. Schlesinger Library, Radcliffe Institute, Harvard University

Dorothy received bachelor's and master's degrees from Baylor, completed additional graduate work at the University of Chicago, and spent a year at Oxford, although women were not allowed to obtain degrees. She obtained her Ph.D. from Columbia University in 1917 and began teaching in the Extension Division. Scarborough, again like Williams, was interested in American regionalism, particularly the African American oral tradition, including folklore, the supernatural, hoodoo, and the blues. She was friendly with both the composer W. C. Handy and Charles Johnson, the editor of *Opportunity*. Johnson published her research on folk songs in the magazine; this material later formed part of her best-known book, *On the Trail of Negro Folk Songs* (1925). Like Blanche Colton Williams, Scarborough served as a judge for the *Opportunity* literary contests and was a strong supporter of Harlem Renaissance writers. In 1926, Scarborough wrote a letter to the editor of *Opportunity*, stating that "American literature and art will be much the richer when the vast potentialities of the Negro race are developed and given scope."[61] Her interest in the race did not, however, ring true for Dorothy. "Dr. S. pronounces Negro like a true Southerner. . . . She thinks Negro with a small 'n,' " Dorothy scribbled in her notebook for the class on playwriting.[62]

Scarborough became a minor celebrity when her controversial novel *The Wind* was made into a movie in 1926, starring Lillian Gish. The film, based on Scarborough's experiences in a bleak, arid part of Texas where the family had moved to help relieve the symptoms of her mother's tuberculosis, depicts a sensitive woman driven mad by the incessant wind and harsh environment of an isolated cattle ranch. Scarborough wrote critically on a number of social issues, including agricultural reform and child labor in the cotton fields, and may well have stimulated West's interest in the supernatural, in gender and class issues, and in the vulnerability of women and children, themes that she explored in many of her stories. West's work clearly shows Scarborough's influence, both in theme and in her use of regionalism in her novels.

Despite Dorothy's objection to Scarborough's southern pronunciation, she acknowledged years later that the professor had influenced her writing enormously. Scarborough clearly recognized West's talent and nurtured her first novel, even after West was forced to drop out of Columbia. It was probably Scarborough who taught West to write concisely, to minimize adjectives, to cut mercilessly, and to describe a novel in one sentence. Scarborough may also have worked with her on character development and taught her that the best character makes the greatest change, a principle West demonstrated with the evolution of the bigoted white grandmother in her novel *The Wedding*. It was in Scarborough's class that West first read Lajos Egri's *Art of Dramatic Writing*, which was "everybody's Bible at the time."[63] For reasons about which West was never clear, but probably had to do with Isaac's financial setbacks, the cousins left Columbia after about a year. Although Scarborough scolded her in February 1928 for "procrastination," she sympathized with her withdrawal and suggested that she complete the work out of class. Scarborough put West on a writing schedule, offered to review her work, and promised to help place the novel with an agent.[64] West worked on the book off and on until 1931, when she again contacted Scarborough, who replied, "I shall be glad to read it and to criticize it—if you can send it right away, and there will not be any charge. . . . I am glad to take an interest in an interesting story begun in my class."[65] West apparently sent Scarborough drafts of the book over the next year, and eventually, at Countee Cullen's suggestion, sent it to the literary agent John Trounstine. Trounstine was unable to place it, and in 1933 West announced to Cullen that she was returning to the short story, "my best and favorite form."[66] There is no record of further correspondence with Scarborough, who died suddenly of influenza in 1935. She had been a dedicated teacher and mentor to Dorothy.

Meanwhile, the cousins continued to submit their work for prizes and publication. In May 1927, Zora Neale Hurston wrote to the cousins, hoping they "ran away with" the third *Opportunity* contest, which had taken place two weeks earlier; in fact, the Boston contingent had acquitted itself quite well.[67] Eugene Gordon, Johnson, and West all won prizes. This time, Gordon divided the first and second prizes with another writer and also won a third prize, all for his short stories. West won a Special Buckner Award of ten dollars for her story "An Unimportant Man," which clearly shows Gordon's influence in style and theme, and which he would soon publish in the first issue of the Quill annual. Helene won second prize for her poem "Summer Matures," an erotic evocation of minutely observed nature imagery from Martha's Vineyard ("The pelican's thick pouch / Hangs heavily with perch and slugs. / The brilliant-bellied newt flashes / Its crimson crest in the white water") and classical allusions to Sapphic poetry (41).

Still working within formal poetic structure, she won fourth prize for "Sonnet to a Negro in Harlem." Like several other lyrics, including "Regalia," "Bottled," and "Rootbound," "Sonnet" offers an affirming portrait of African American men that, unlike those of many contemporary writers, reverberates with strength, dignity, and beauty. A frequent theme in Johnson's work is the talent, creativity, intelligence, and improvisational skill of black men, as illustrated by the young jazz musician in "Poem" (1927). Both a dramatic monologue and a performance piece, it foregrounds a smiling, process-wearing banjo player, singing and dancing onstage at Harlem's Lafayette Theater. In celebrating the artist, "Poem" responds to those in the larger culture who would object to the jazz-influenced song and dance, and especially to the straightened hair and flashing teeth. The speaker makes clear her position: "Gee, brown boy, I loves you all over" (38).

Gordon, representing the Quill Club, took a table for ten at the awards banquet and sat with his wife, Edythe Mae, two other Quill Club members, Alvira Hazzard and Florence Harmon, and the cousins. The other women at the table, all talented but essentially unknown Boston writers, must have underscored for Dorothy and Helene the importance of remaining in New York and of obtaining mainstream recognition. Edythe Mae Gordon published poems and short stories in the tabloid supplements of the African American press, and in 1928 her story "Subversion" was named a "distinguished short story" by the O. Henry Memorial Award Prize Committee. Alvira Hazzard was an active member of the Quill Club; she contributed a play and a poem to the first annual (1928), a play to the second (1929), and a poem to the third (1930). A teacher in the Boston public schools, she also wrote for the *Boston Post* and acted in plays produced by Maud Cuney-Hare at the Allied Arts Center. Florence Harmon, the treasurer of the Quill Club, worked with Gordon at the *Boston Post*. She wrote stylish, ironic, romantic stories which Gordon published in the first two issues. Her tone, plot, and characterization recall the work of fellow Bostonian Marita Bonner and are comparable to contemporary stories published in the "slicks" like the *Ladies' Home Journal*. It is unfortunate that her work should have been excluded from the mainstream press on racial grounds, just as the serialization of *The*

Living Is Easy was rejected by the *Ladies' Home Journal* because the editors feared that a book about Boston's black aristocracy might offend southern subscribers.[68]

For the July 1927 issue of *Opportunity* Gordon described the awards evening in an odd little piece called "The Opportunity Dinner: An Impression," in which he wrote: "I take up my [crusted brown roll] and write on its hard-shellacked surface 'Souvenir. Opportunity Awards Dinner, 1927, Quill Club.' . . . I take up my wife's silken-beaded bag and force the chunk of bread into it, wondering if I am observed and, if so, what my observer thinks."[69] One can't help wondering what Edythe thought, seeing a hard roll shoved into her dainty, beaded bag, but her response, like her presence at the table, is not reported in the article.

West, meanwhile, spent the winter of 1927 working on a novel in Dorothy Scarborough's class at Columbia. When she showed Cullen a draft, he claimed to recognize the inspiration for three characters, the actresses Edna Thomas and Georgette Harvey, and the theater director Cheryl Crawford, all of whom played important roles in Dorothy's life. Harvey and Crawford were associated with the Broadway play *Porgy*, whose cast West had joined as a supernumerary in early 1927. The show, which toured Atlantic City and Philadelphia before opening in London in 1929, reads like a Who's Who of African American theater: Rose McClendon, Georgette Harvey, Percy Verwayne, Wayland Rudd, Evelyn Ellis, and Leigh Whipper.

Edna Thomas, who joined the play for the London run, belonged to a closely knit circle of African American actresses who supported and encouraged each other in an uncertain and discriminatory professional climate. When Dorothy and Helene arrived in New York, Thomas extended her protection to them. Edna, who had no children of her own, became a surrogate mother to the young women. She introduced them to influential New Yorkers like Carl Van Vechten and to her circle of gay and bisexual men and women. Rachel constantly wrote to the cousins, impressing upon them the importance of Edna's kindness, and Dorothy doodled her name ("Aunt Edna") in her theater class at Columbia University.[70] When Dorothy was in Russia, Edna remembered her birthday with a gift of five dollars, and Helene wrote to her cousin: "She is very good to me . . . and she is your really and truly fine friend."[71] Edna 's circle included Inez Clough, a Bostonian actress and friend of Rachel's; Rose McClendon, the first lady of the African American stage; and the beautiful Washington sisters, Fredi and Isabel, all of whom contributed to the network of encouragement and support that sustained the cousins in their years in New York.

Edna was a stunningly beautiful and talented actress, dedicated to the development of African American theater, and to the improvement of working conditions for black actors and stagehands. Like Dorothy Dandridge several generations later, Edna "ran into difficulty in securing roles because she was too fair to be considered black, and yet she was not permitted to play 'white' roles."[72] As Dorothy was to depict in her novel *The Living Is Easy*, Edna's early life was fraught with trauma. Edna's mother, a twelve-year-old nursemaid in Lawrenceville, Virginia, had been raped and impregnated by a member of her employer's family as she slept beside her charge. Shortly after her birth from this union, Edna traveled with her mother and grandmother to Boston, where they settled among the genteel families of color in the West End.[73] At sixteen, having completed two years of high school, Edna moved into Boston's "blue-vein" society when she married a son of J. H. Lewis, the wealthy tailoring entrepreneur. The marriage was unhappy; Edna's husband was an alcoholic and a gambler, and eventually died of tuberculosis. Edna maintained a close relationship with her father-in-law since both were interested in racial uplift and philanthropic organizations. She studied singing, thinking that she might go on the stage, and she often performed in charity theatricals. She probably met Rachel West around this time at one of the musical and literary groups they both frequented. Dorothy West drew on Edna's history for the Duchess in her novel; like Edna, the Duchess, who can pass for white, redeems her mother's tragic past by marrying into Boston's brown Brahmin society. Another similarity between the two women was their talent for acting: just as the Duchess used her acting skills to traverse social barriers, so Edna played multiple social roles across a broad swath of New York's theatrical, literary, political, and philanthropic circles.

Eventually, Edna left Boston and worked as a social secretary for Madam C. J. Walker, the self-made millionaire and founder of a hair care empire. In addition to her secretarial duties, Edna tutored Madam Walker in reading and etiquette.[74] In 1916 Madam Walker moved to Harlem, where she opened a flagship hairdressing establishment next to her townhouse on 136th Street, and then commissioned the construction of an elegant mansion, the Villa Lewaro, in Irvington, New York. Edna became a close friend of Madam Walker's daughter, A'Lelia, and shared the Walkers' glamorous life of parties, philanthropy, and the arts. Enrico Caruso was a close family friend and suggested the name Villa Lewaro, a play on A'Lelia Walker's name. Madam Walker died in 1919, never having really enjoyed her new residence, but her daughter continued to put the Villa Lewaro and her considerable fortune at the service of the arts.

Through the Walkers, Edna met Lloyd Thomas, the manager of the beauty salon. Lloyd was handsome and cultured; he fancied himself an aesthete and was fond of quoting the Chinese poet Li Po.[75] His hobby was raising orchids and other exotic plants. Edna described him as "a dour, taciturn, indifferent man, of light complexion. . . . I had never met a man like this before and his indifference fascinated me."[76] Despite Lloyd's sexual orientation, the couple married and enjoyed an active social life. When A'Lelia Walker decided to open her supper club, the Dark Tower, Lloyd put his promotional and marketing skills at her disposal. Among the "many notables" present on the club's opening night, gushed Gwendolyn Bennett, were "Carl Van Vechten, Madame A'Lelia Walker, Dr. W.E.B. Du Bois, Eric Walrond, Jessie Fauset, and goodness knows who else."[77] Edna and Lloyd knew everyone in bohemian New York and, like Carl Van Vechten, traveled in its glamorous gay and bisexual subculture. Thanks to Van Vechten, the couple also frequented the salons of wealthy, influential patrons of the arts like the Askews. As theatrical director John Houseman recalled, "the Askews' Sunday 'at homes' were not parties: they were a continuing, well-organized operation with a clear and consistent objective: to exert . . . a dominant modernistic influence on the art fashions of [the] time."[78] Regulars included architect Philip Johnson (who used Edna's apartment for his trysts with nightclub owner Jimmie Daniels); composers Aaron Copland and Leonard Bernstein; photographer Lee Miller; choreographers Agnes de Mille and George Balanchine; and the Van Vechtens. "Other ladies distinguished for their elegance, their wifely position, or their creative talent were Edna Thomas . . . [and interior decorator] Muriel Draper" (98).

Despite her social connections, Edna was witty, unpretentious, and self-deprecating, with a penchant for drinking champagne and playing poker. Both Helene and Dorothy benefited from Edna's vast social network; in interviews, Dorothy frequently alluded to the "Park Avenue crowd" who entertained members of the Harlem Renaissance, and it was probably through Edna that she and Helene met such luminaries as George Bernard Shaw, Virgil Thomson, and Frederick Ashton. Lloyd, in contrast, was snobbish and aloof. He was a born teacher, however, and enjoyed being surrounded by "minions" who catered to him and in whom he could instill a thirst for knowledge. He struck the two cousins very differently: Lloyd was a strong influence on Helene, who appreciated his erudition and knowledge of poetry, although Dorothy found him "trifling" and disliked seeing him drift around the house all day in his bathrobe.[79]

Edna, like A'Lelia Walker and most of their friends, was bisexual (Walker married three times) but found relationships with women more emotionally fulfilling.[80] In the early 1930s she fell in love with the British aristocrat Olivia Wyndham; conveniently Olivia brought her fortune with her when she moved into the large Seventh Avenue apartment with Edna and Lloyd. They also rented rooms to theatrical friends, and over the years Helene and Dorothy often stayed there. Edna's official explanation for Olivia's presence, even to Van Vechten, who would scarcely have been shocked, was that Olivia was a houseguest who helped with expenses.[81] The two women lived together, in Manhattan and Brooklyn, and in a country house in Connecticut, with Lloyd intermittently present, for the rest of their lives.

Before settling into cozy domesticity with Edna, Olivia had been a member of Nancy Cunard's decadent circle of "Bright Young Things" in London after World War I. Part of the circle celebrated in the novels of Evelyn Waugh, Aldous Huxley, and Anthony Powell, Olivia consorted with Tallulah Bankhead, Noël Coward, Adele Astaire, and the Prince of Wales. "Wantonly promiscuous, Olivia was unstoppable. . . . At King's Road parties, when [she] was not disappearing with one person after another, male or female, she was playing pander, 'dragging people upstairs and putting them on top of each other.' "[82] Despite her flamboyant lifestyle, her family tree was impeccable: her mother and two aunts posed for John Singer Sargent's *The Three Graces*, and her cousin was Cynthia Asquith, daughter-in-law of Prime Minister Herbert Asquith. Olivia was not particularly attractive but had many endearing qualities: "she always showed extreme sensitivity to the sufferings of other creatures, animal as well as human [and] was deeply upset by any manifestation of exclusion, of selectivity, of judgment—anything even faintly implying discrimination" (67). Thus, like many artistic women of the period, Edna combined a discreet lesbian private life with a heterosexual public persona. Lloyd, once the nightclub folded, never worked again and never supported Edna financially, but he evidently cared for her and, according to Rachel, missed her when she was on tour. When Dorothy and Helene lived with the Thomases in their large apartment on Seventh Avenue at various times, they would have been exposed to this alternative lifestyle that gave Edna complete freedom to express herself emotionally and artistically without forfeiting her position in conservative African American society.

Before Olivia's arrival, and after the death of Edna's employer, Madam Walker, the Thomases were in a precarious financial position. Like many women in her circle, Edna often participated in amateur theatricals for charity. She was known for her ability to sing spirituals, and it was at a benefit performance for Rosamond Johnson's music school that Lester Walton of the Lafayette Players noticed her and immediately tried to sign her to the group.[83] Founded by Anita Bush in 1917, the Lafayette Players was a distinguished African American repertory company based in Los Angeles but active on both coasts; many of the actors also worked in the films of Oscar Michaux.[84] At first, Lloyd was unwilling to support Edna's desire to go on the stage, insisting that the commercial theater was vulgar and unrefined, and perhaps concerned about the racial indignities she might suffer on tour in other parts of the country. Eventually, however, Edna capitulated to Lester Walton's repeated offers and launched her career with the lead role in his production of *Confidence*, a one-act play by Frank Wilson. *Confidence* opened at the Putnam Theatre on Fulton Street in Brooklyn and later toured the East Coast. Edna was "an emphatic hit" in Philadelphia, Washington, D.C., and Norfolk, Virginia."[85] According to Leonard de Paur, she was "one of the three great ladies of the theatre we had at that time. . . . She, Rose McClendon, and Laura Bowman could have played any type of theatre that was ever staged." Thomas performed over one hundred roles with the Lafayette Players and also played on Broadway in Hall Johnson's *Run, Lil' Chillun* and *Lulu Belle*. Her youthful appearance enabled her to play ingénue roles until well into her fifties.[86] In 1936 she was a popular and critical success as Lady Macbeth in Orson Welles's Federal Theatre production. Welles was infatuated with her and deferred to her elaborately during rehearsals.

In 1926 Edna auditioned for the part of Bess in the Theatre Guild's production of *Porgy*, for which her friend Cheryl Crawford was an assistant director. Having been raised in Boston, Edna spoke like Katharine Hepburn and was unfamiliar with the Charleston dialect. Nevertheless, she practiced with poems of Paul Laurence Dunbar, won the part, and announced it to her friends. However, when the play's white authors, DuBose and Dorothy Heyward, saw Edna, they objected. She was "too refined . . . too white." The Heywards offered her the lesser part of Clara, but Edna was upset and left the production; instead, she understudied her friend Evelyn Preer in *Lulu Belle* and eventually took over the role.[87] In 1929, with the play poised for a London run, Cheryl Crawford persuaded her to reconsider and accept the role of Clara.

In March 1929, Dorothy wrote to Rachel excitedly: "Cheryl Crawford called me up this morning and told me I can go abroad. Isn't that wonderful! We are sailing the 26th. . . . This is so sudden because someone backed out . . . and Cheryl immediately thought of me." She assured Rachel that "Tommy [Edna] says earnestly that I must tell you that she will take really excellent care of me . . . [and] I may use her trunk. And Cheryl will be along too."[88]

Accompanying the production to London was Edna's friend Rose McClendon (1879–1936). Their careers were similar in that both women came to the legitimate stage relatively late, and both benefited from the fact that, as Broadway director John Houseman points out, "for years, show business had occupied a special place in [African American] city life as one of the few open roads to self-expression and fame" (177). McClendon was a striking woman, with aquiline features that reminded people of Eleanor Duse. She and Edna Thomas moved easily among the various factions of the Harlem theatrical milieu: the long-running Lafayette stock company, in which the two women had performed; the "small but powerful group of successful Negro performers and respected union members whose talent had won them full acceptance in the white world; . . . the intelligentsia—the teachers, social workers, advisors, and race relations experts," such as the members of the Urban League, who saw theater as a venue of racial uplift and were eager to influence its course; and the New York Communist Party, which had established a number of organizations in the arts. McClendon, according to Houseman, was one of several important African American actors who "had shown a willingness to collaborate [for artistic or other reasons] with United Front Organizations" (178). Bruce Nugent also alludes to her political affiliations, noting discreetly that she was a member of the "Group Theatre and other, even more radical aggregations."[89] Both Thomas and McClendon sought to improve conditions for African American actors and technicians, although it was not until the WPA Federal Theatre Project, directed by McClendon, John Houseman, and Hallie Flanagan, that African American stagehands, consistently refused admission to the union on grounds of color, were able to work as carpenters and electricians in their chosen professions.

McClendon was an important influence on Dorothy and Helene, and both were great fans; Dorothy knew her particularly well during the London run of *Porgy*, although they had met in 1927 in the New York production. At this time, Dorothy apparently organized or arranged something for McClendon, for she wrote to her: "Dear Dorothy, I want to thank you so much for Sunday afternoon. I was indeed honored and I shall never forget it—you are a darling little girl. Yours with much love, Rose McClendon."[90] In 1932 Helene, who was living with Edna and Lloyd in their apartment on Seventh Avenue, wrote to Dorothy: "I saw Rose McClendon on 7th Ave the other day alone and wanted to speak to her so bad. She looked beautiful. But she wouldn't remember me."[91] Helene's shyness probably prevented her from speaking, although McClendon would certainly have known who she was.

Born in Greenville, South Carolina, Rosalie Virginia Scott moved to New York with her parents, who were employed by a wealthy family as housekeeper and coachman. She was educated in the New York public schools and developed an early interest in acting. In 1904 she married Henry Pruden McClendon. Her husband, a trained chiropractor, could only find employment as a Pullman porter, but the couple established a gracious home in Harlem. Rose volunteered for social and philanthropic activities at Saint Mark's African Methodist Episcopal Church, the NAACP, the Urban League, and the Hope Day Nursery. She became very involved with children's theater in Harlem, where she wrote, directed, and costumed the plays. In 1916, wanting to learn more about stage craft, she won a scholarship to the Sargent School of Dramatic Art, later the American Academy of Dramatic Art (AADA).[92]

McClendon's first role was in *Justice* with the Bramhall Players, a company founded by Benjamin Butler Davenport and housed on his seventy-three-acre family estate in New Canaan, Connecticut, near Stamford. McClendon had gotten lost in rural Connecticut on her way to the audition and it was a hot day; before Davenport could greet her, "she angrily burst into a tirade against him for picking such an inconvenient place, for picking such a hot day for the interview, and for sending for her in the first place. She got the job."[93] McClendon was forty years old before she performed her first major role in *Roseanne* with Charles Gilpin in 1924. She was witty, feisty, and independent; when offered a part in the musical *Deep River* in 1926, "she refused to consider it, naming an amount which seemed to her exorbitant. Arguments that she was unknown fell on deaf ears . . . [so] she went back to her children's plays in Harlem. She got the part and the salary she had demanded" (215). She subsequently worked in *In Abraham's Bosom* (1926), *Porgy* (1927), and, shortly before her untimely death from pneumonia, in Langston Hughes's play *Mulatto* (1935). She had also begun rehearsing John Houseman's production of Euripides' *Medea*. Since no satisfactory text was available, Countee Cullen worked on the poetic translation from the Greek, and Virgil Thomson composed the music for an African American women's chorus. Unfortunately, McClendon's illness cut short the project.[94]

According to Nugent, "Rose remained the only glamorous Negro 'star' lady of the dramatic stage" (216). She was a close friend of John Houseman's and worked with important figures in twentieth-century theater such as the choreographers Martha Graham and Frederick Ashton, the composer Virgil Thomsen, and the producer Elisabeth Marbury. Throughout her career she continued to offer her services and assistance to groups and organizations, including the Group Theatre (the predecessor of the Negro Ensemble Company) and the Negro Experimental Theatre (formerly the Krigwa Players). She helped organize the Negro People's Theatre in 1935, and had been selected to direct the African American branch of the Federal Theatre, although the project passed to Hallie Flanagan when she became ill. Rose McClendon died in 1936 of pneumonia; the Rose McClendon Players were established in her honor by Dick Campbell and the African American soprano, Muriel Rahn, who succeeded McClendon in her last role as Cora in Hughes's *Mulatto*.

It was Cheryl Crawford who organized the London tour of *Porgy* and ensured that her close friends Edna Thomas, Georgette Harvey, and Rose McClendon, as well as the young Dorothy West, were included in the cast. Crawford, like Blanche Colton Williams, Dorothy Scarborough, and Elisabeth Marbury, was dedicated to promoting and supporting African Americans in the arts. She was particularly interested in helping women, although she was instrumental in building the careers of many young actors, including Diana Sands, Canada Lee, and Brock Peters. Crawford fell in love with the theater at about the same time that she realized her sexual orientation upon reading *Mademoiselle de Maupin*, the forbidden French novel by Théophile Gautier, which features a swash-buckling, cross-dressing, dueling, lesbian opera singer. As a young woman, Crawford loved to dance and, imitating Vernon and Irene Castle, taught herself "to follow and to lead" and then gave dancing lessons to neigh-borhood children, charging a quarter a lesson. At Smith College, she acted in a number of plays where she was usually given male roles. In the summer of 1924, dreading a return to Akron, she joined the Province-town Theatre on Cape Cod. Although she did not meet Eugene O'Neill, she did work with playwright Susan Glaspell and the radical feminist and journalist Mary Heaton Vorse. Upon graduation, and learning that the Theatre Guild was starting an acting school, she obtained an interview with Theresa Helburn, and, although she admitted that she wanted to direct, not to act, she was admitted to the course. Shortly thereafter, Helburn offered her a job as a casting secretary for the Guild, but Craw-ford held out for the position of third assistant stage manager. Helburn looked amazed at her temerity but then "slammed her hand on the desk. 'Okay! I'll give you a try, Go to it!'" Crawford later wondered "what persuaded her . . . but she had made her way as a woman in a man's pro-fession, and perhaps she wanted to give another woman a break."[95]

Since her theater salary was small, Crawford supplemented her income in other ways. Like Edna Thomas, she was a skilled poker player and was unusually successful because of what people called her "Indian face." She also possessed a platonic "sugar daddy," a "well-to-do stock-broker, a lonely bachelor who enjoyed bringing champagne and excel-lent bourbon in cobweb-decorated bottles to my apartment . . . where I always managed to have some indigent friends around to drink his liquor and be taken for a fine dinner at one of the nearby speakeasies" (39).

Finally, Crawford was a bootlegger, making "gin from good alcohol procured by the stockbroker. This I put in the bathtub with distilled water and juniper berries, bottling it in Gordon gin bottles, which could be bought for twenty-five cents each. I would load five or six cases of the stuff into a secondhand, four-gear Mercer touring car and drive to Amherst and Northampton where I could sell a bottle for two dollars and fifty cents" (39).

In 1927, a year after Crawford joined the Theatre Guild, the company produced *Porgy*, directed by Rouben Mamoulian. Years later, Dorothy West remembered with gratitude Crawford's willingness to hire her. In fact, Crawford went out of her way to employ nonprofessionals from Harlem: "some of the best bits in *Porgy* were played by people who had never been on stage before, and they added a great deal of authenticity to this folk drama" (39). Crawford made lifelong friends among the *Porgy* cast: "The company and I had a long love affair. Their uninhibited exuberance, their sense of fun and their ability to live 'for the day thereof' entranced me. Once a week a bunch of us went to Harlem, to Small's Paradise or the Lennox Club, or a rent party at one of their apartments, to sing and dance as if there was no tomorrow. Actually, we weren't sure there would be a tomorrow" (39).

In 1929 the company sailed for London. Crawford's "sugar daddy" had won fifteen hundred dollars for her on the stock market, and she planned to spend it all, buying clothes and enjoying a working vacation with her friends. "The eleven-day trip was a ball. The company would take over the second-class lounge by noon each day. There was a continuous dice game, a poker game and music" (42). West's letters to Rachel corroborate Crawford's account: "Yesterday [Edna] was quite high on champagne and won seven dollars at poker."[96] On another day she reports that "Each day [Edna] grows sweeter. She's stayed sober, too, though she and Cheryl and Rose and Maria and Georgette have a champagne club about every other night where they split four quarts. Last night was one of their club nights and I happened in and Cheryl recited some of the most marvelous poetry I've ever heard. Her voice is glorious. She loses her shyness when she's tight. She's quite grand."[97]

During the visit to England, in the company of Edna, Rose, Georgette, and Cheryl, Dorothy matured and became, in Wallace Thurman's words, "a cosmopolitan lady."[98] Reflecting on her stay in London she wrote to her mother: "I am quite at home now, and shall be sorry to leave. I have given much and learned much in the weeks I have been here. There is nothing so broadening as travel. Every day I realize that."[99] Although she was unable to accompany Edna on to Paris in the summer of 1929, she returned to Martha's Vineyard determined to find a way to live in Europe with Helene and to form a coterie of working artists, joining Countee Cullen, Eric Walrond, and Augusta Savage who were already there. Cullen and Walrond were both on Guggenheim fellowships, while Savage was sponsored by the Rosenwald and Carnegie foundations. In August Dorothy wrote to Wallace Thurman, suggesting that he join the group, but he demurred. Perhaps feeling gloomy about his disastrous, short-lived marriage to Louise Thompson, or possibly thinking of his own dissipated energies and lack of achievement at the salon at 267, he replied: "Such things generally turn out to be stupid unless colorful personality abounds, and then it grows tedious and unproductive." He kept his options open, however, adding "should I be able I too shall flee to Europe this fall."[100] In October, Countee Cullen wrote, urging her to come soon and reminding her of their plans for the "Utopian household we were to set up" in Paris, with themselves as the "guiding spirits of the venture."[101] West in turn wrote to Zora Neale Hurston, who was collecting conjure stories and Voodoo spells in New Orleans, telling her about the projected artists' colony and urging her to join them.[102]

Paris, however, was not to be. Cullen wrote to West the following August (1930) from his parents' home in Pleasantville, New Jersey, admitting he was "rather selfishly glad the grand gathering has been postponed until next year, for I am so improvident at the moment that I could not come," which may have been an oblique reference to his recent divorce from Yolande Du Bois.[103] Dorothy must also have needed money, for she returned to New York, while Helene remained in Boston with the family.

Hurston and West remained in touch, and since Hurston was still in New Orleans, she offered Dorothy the apartment on West Sixty-sixth Street for the fall. She may also have arranged for Dorothy to work for the best-selling author Fannie Hurst. Helene felt it was a wonderful opportunity for her cousin and was convinced "something splendid will come out of it."[104] Hurston undoubtedly had an ulterior motive, for she soon began sending West boxes of classified material from New Orleans. After assuring Dorothy that the cousins were "near my heart and always will be. I trust you and Helene more than anyone in the world. You are the fine gold in New York's show and shine," Hurston thanked her for putting her parcel away "so carefully" but then asked that Dorothy send her "all the typed sheets, secretly, and by registered mail," adding in capital letters "PLEASE DON'T LET ANYONE KNOW THAT YOU HAVE HEARD FROM ME OR SEE MY PAPERS BEFORE YOU MAIL THEM."[105] West's discretion was particularly important since Hurston was involved in a dispute with her patron, the egocentric and manipulative Charlotte Osgood Mason, who demanded exclusive access to Hurston's research and writing. Hurston, feeling isolated and paranoid, distrusted Langston Hughes, Alain Locke, and even her old friend Bruce Nugent. Though she knew none of the reasons for Hurston's strange behavior, West loyally supported her friend and respected her request for secrecy.

CHAPTER 6

Russian Interlude, Literary Salons, and *Challenge*

DOROTHY WEST met the theatrical agent Elisabeth (Bessy) Marbury (1856–1933) and her partner, the interior designer Elsie de Wolfe (1865–1950), shortly after her arrival in New York. The two women, who belonged to a circle of wealthy, socially conscious, unmarried women such as J. P. Morgan's daughter Anne, and Anne Vanderbilt, were to influence West in many ways, both personally and professionally. Either Zora Neale Hurston or Fannie Hurst, both clients of Marbury's literary agency, introduced West. Marbury, who had promoted the career of bandleader Lt. James Europe, was an early supporter of African Americans in the arts and, according to West, "one of the few whites who met with [the] wholehearted approval" of the prickly Wallace Thurman.[1] Since West's first interest was in playwriting, it was natural that she meet Marbury, considered by Dorothy Parker (whom West also met and liked) and the Algonquin group of writers to be one of the most influential agents in the world. As West told an interviewer, "Elisabeth Marbury and Elsie de Wolfe were Americans who went to Paris, and they were involved with literary matters, and they had a salon and the Hemingways and the Fitzgeralds and all would come."[2] That West perfectly understood the relationship between Marbury and de Wolfe, and hoped to model her own literary, sexually tolerant salon on theirs, is clear from a letter she wrote to Countee Cullen upon her return from Russia: "It has long been my dream to preside over a small salon. . . . There is so much I want for my friends. . . . I have in mind an experiment. . . . [Guests] will love my friends because they love me . . . and since there is no deception in my world, they will gradually learn and accept."[3]

During the late 1920s and early 1930s, West, Johnson, Hurston, Hurst, and Marbury formed a loosely affiliated circle of financial and emotional support. Hurst had offered Dorothy a job after Zora's departure for the South. Although Johnson felt optimistic for her cousin, sure that "something splendid [would] come out of it," the job turned out to be domestic in nature, and West quickly let Hurst know that she had crossed an invisible social line and that West, unlike Hurston, would not "put on an apron . . . that was Zora's background. It was not my background."[4] Meanwhile, Zora hired Helene to help with her research, though it was to remain secret. "No that mysterious woman, Zora's boss, does not know I'm working for Zora. Will let you know how it turns out," Helene wrote to Dorothy. Hurston knew West and Johnson's family and was invited to Martha's Vineyard and to Boston for Thanksgiving. According to Helene, Zora's younger brother Everett, a postal worker in Brooklyn, was madly in love with Dorothy and had broken off his engagement because of her.[5] In January 1931, Dorothy wrote to Zora from Boston with a "proposition" that she board with her at West Sixty-sixth Street. Hurston readily agreed, on the conditions that "#1. Please don't expect me to keep a very tidy kitchen. I aint that kind of a person. #2. That you just feel at home & dont expect to be company."[6]

Dorothy clearly knew Elisabeth Marbury well in 1929, for when she gave a reception for Rose McClendon shortly before *Porgy* left New York for London, Marbury sent roses for the party.[7] By midwinter, Dorothy was living with Edna and Lloyd Thomas, and she often visited Marbury on Sunday afternoons before attending Zora's weekly soiree. "Would you like to go to Zora's Sunday night?" she asks Countee Cullen, informing him that she would go to Zora's after seeing Marbury. "She'd so love to have you. And she has millions of marvelous anecdotes."[8] On one of her visits, Marbury told Dorothy that what she liked best about her was that she had never asked her for money. West was appalled that the thought should even have occurred to Marbury, since "I had an art."[9] In fact Marbury provided West with a far greater service than cash: she and Fannie Hurst persuaded the literary agent George Bye, who also represented Eleanor Roosevelt, to take West as a client. Bye in turn convinced the *Daily News* to give her a regular story column that sustained her through the 1940s.

In January 1931, Marbury got involved in the *Mule Bone* drama between Hurston and Langston Hughes. Hurston had shown Marbury the play she and Hughes had worked on, but she claimed it as her own

material and announced that it was to be performed in Cleveland by the
Gilpin Players. Realizing the play needed work, Marbury hired Wallace
Thurman to revise it. However, "once he got wind of the controversy,
Thurman returned the play to the Marbury agency untouched."[10] When
Zora's patron, Mrs. Osgood Mason, took Hughes's side and reprimanded
her, Zora wrote a note of apology, slyly adding: "Miss Elisabeth Marbury
sent for me last Saturday to call at her home. . . . She wanted to have me
try out for the radio. I was asked to sing one song to get my voice range,
& to see if my personality got over. She expressed satisfaction on both
points. I was told to prepare a 15 minute program & come back to
her."[11] The letter veers suddenly into a convoluted account of Zora's
sore throat and inability to keep the appointment with Marbury, but
clearly she was putting the jealous Mrs. Mason on notice that she had
another ally at least as powerful as her "godmother."

In the summer of 1931, Hurst and Hurston set off on a road trip to
visit Marbury at her estate in Kennebec County, Maine. Marbury and de
Wolfe had been briefly estranged in 1926, and during that time Marbury
had convinced Elizabeth Arden of cosmetics fame to purchase the adjoin-
ing land when the two began an affair. Arden had turned her property
into the famous Maine Chance Farm, one of the first luxury beauty spas.
En route to see Marbury, Hurst and Hurston stopped at Niagara Falls, and
Hurston sent Dorothy West "a pound or two of love from me to let you
know I remember."[12] It is tempting to conjecture what would have been
Zora's satirical take on Maine Chance Farm and its clientele, had she visited there with Marbury. According to Carla Kaplan, the editor of
Hurston's letters, Marbury was one of the people with whom Hurston
claimed to correspond, although those letters have not been found.

When Dorothy West met her, Marbury was seventy years old and
weighed over two hundred pounds. Despite being a heavy smoker, she
possessed clear, ageless skin; she dressed in masculine suits, spoke in a
deep, hoarse voice, and wore her hair in an old-fashioned pompadour.
Theatrical designer Cecil Beaton described her as "a huge old Buddha."[13]
Like Edith Wharton, Marbury came from an old New York society family, but she was inherently democratic, declaring in her 1923 autobiography that "the only real aristocracy in the world was the aristocracy of
brains" and insisting that "prejudice born of intolerance will go far
towards destroying a people and wrecking a nation."[14] Marbury was one

of the first people in the upper echelon of New York society to protest anti-Semitism, both personally and professionally, and she was a friend and admirer of the poet and Zionist Emma Lazarus. In the presidential election of 1928 she supported Al Smith because he wanted to abolish the Ku Klux Klan and repeal Prohibition.

Despite her liberal, iconoclastic opinions, Marbury's public persona was that of a tough-talking Broadway producer, and she was known for her "caustic, often ribald witticisms."[15] Many years later, West regaled Boston University students with stories of her visits to Sutton Place, the development Marbury had built, where she would receive guests as though she were "Queen Victoria on her throne."[16] According to West, "she had five servants, all English, and you had to go through them to get to her. They had the lovely English accents, and when you got to her she was booming in an American voice."[17] What Marbury possessed in social conscience, however, she sometimes lacked in social graces. Proclaiming "I revel in youth . . . I want to be surrounded by it," Marbury frequently asked Hurston and West to bring their writer friends to Sutton Place.[18] On one awkward occasion, she insisted that the group of African American artists and intellectuals sit and listen to the *Amos 'n' Andy Show* on the radio.[19] Of course, ever the entrepreneur, she may have been planning to produce her own African American program, hence her request that Hurston do a voice test, although nothing seems to have come of the idea. Wallace Thurman was of the party that evening, though he was not as offended by Marbury's faux pas as was Dorothy West. Sensing that Marbury liked him, he wrote the next day and requested five hundred dollars to complete his novel *Infants of the Spring*. Marbury not only sent the money but often found script-doctoring work for him in her various productions. Thurman found her more "genuine than anyone he had met . . . and her tongue was as sharp as his." When he completed the satirical *Infants of the Spring*, his tribute to Marbury is that "she is nowhere in its pages."[20]

A savvy businesswoman who initiated the royalty system, Marbury was also committed to theatrical reform and anticipated the mission of Actors Equity; like Rose McClendon and Edna Thomas, she was concerned about working conditions for stagehands and women in the chorus. She insisted that stagehands be fed and given overtime pay when rehearsals ran late, and she required that the chorus be paid a living wage and addressed with respect and courtesy.

In addition to giving her professional advice and assistance, Elisabeth Marbury and Elsie de Wolfe provided a model for West's personal life. When West met Marbury, she and interior designer Elsie de Wolfe had been a couple for thirty years, much like their friends Gertrude Stein and Alice B. Toklas. As with Stein and Toklas, the two women were very different physically. Marbury's appearance proclaimed her lifelong love of food; in fact, one of her first memories, as a child of six, was sneaking into the pantry and gorging herself on bananas, for which she had a passion. De Wolfe was reed-thin and maintained her figure through rigorous diet and exercise. Cecil Beaton found her "a vaguely plain woman with a marmoset face and only a pair of bright brown eyes to break the anonymity." De Wolfe had, however, impeccable, innovative taste; she was "a living factory of chic."[21] Her decorating philosophy was "plenty of optimism and white paint, comfortable chairs with lights beside them, open fires on the hearth, flowers wherever they belong, and mirrors and sunshine in all rooms."[22] Beaton held her personally "responsible for putting an end to Victorianism in the United States" and battling "the appallingly low level of bad taste throughout America" (204). Despite her own affluence, de Wolfe focused her design work on, above all, interior decoration that encouraged comfort and livability. West and Johnson had been brought up with a similar perspective by Rachel; despite the fact that the beauty and decoration of their home on Brookline Avenue was known in the community and frequently displayed to visitors, Rachel always insisted that the children were its raison d'être. West expresses de Wolfe's philosophy in "The Sun Parlor," a memoir in which she regrets that her obsession with painting and decorating a room precluded its enjoyment by a little cousin.[23] A point that would not have been lost on West, who was also very interested in fashion and interior design, was that de Wolfe did what she loved to do, and she made her passion a paying proposition. For a generous commission, she advised nouveau riche American millionaires on purchasing French antiques; she amassed a fortune that she and Marbury spent on travel and on decorating their various homes in New York, Maine, and France. Marbury seems to have been drawn to petite, vibrant, creative women, such as de Wolfe and Elizabeth Arden. She undoubtedly enjoyed Dorothy's knowledge of literature, fashion, art, literature, and interior decoration, and the two were friends until her death in 1933.

In her 1923 autobiography, which West surely read, Marbury spoke candidly of her relationship with de Wolfe. About a separation the two endured during World War I, when de Wolfe remained in France to nurse burn victims, Marbury wrote: "I rejoiced at her return for the interruption of such a companionship as ours had been a wrench. Such an experience can never be classed as painless dentistry for no anesthetic prevents the hurt." Indifferent to public opinion, Marbury made no secret of their intimacy: "We had suffered together. We had been happy together. We had shared our disappointments. We had revelled in our respective success. We had mutually known poverty and side by side had practised self-denial. We had earned, through years of hard work, the luxury which in later years we were to share."[24]

Underpinning the romantic attachment, however, is a dedication to their respective careers: Marbury acknowledges that without the independence of their professions, "we might easily have become victims of misrepresentation and of envy, had our anchorage been less secure" (302). Ironically, shortly after the book was published, de Wolfe announced her marriage to an elderly British peer. It was clearly a marriage of convenience as the two rarely lived together, and it does not appear to have fazed Marbury, who insisted in her book that "every woman should marry if this is humanly possible for her," although, like many of the couples West and Johnson knew in New York, her definition of marriage seems elastic. Marbury concludes her book, which she dedicated to de Wolfe in a romantic poem, by asserting "I think that I can truthfully state that the great secret of our happiness has lain in the fact that neither of us ever attempted to dominate the individuality of the other" (302). With the exception of a diamond bracelet that she left to Elizabeth Arden, Marbury willed her entire fortune to de Wolfe.

During this period, West, Johnson, and Hurston were closely connected. The trio formed "an intimate literary community [that provided] warmly affirmative support for each other's writings . . . and worked out ideas" among themselves.[25] Hurston's interest in folk culture and the material she sent to the cousins for safekeeping undoubtedly sensitized West and Johnson to the richness of a culture they had experienced little of in Massachusetts. West and Johnson certainly read Hurston's "classified" information, which included children's games, work songs, intercepted love letters, accounts of conjure ceremonies, and revivalist sermons. A few years later, West's WPA essays drew on her own family's oral history of rural customs such as quilting and berrying, as well as ghost tales and children's games they recalled from South Carolina.[26] Perhaps inspired by Hurston's interest in rural preachers, West wrote about urban messiahs such as Daddy Grace and Father Divine and revivalists like Billy Sunday. West's fiction also shows Hurston's influence. Episodes in *The Living Is Easy*, particularly the accounts of the wild, tomboyish Cleo (Rachel), recall Hurston's autobiographical self in *Dust Tracks on a Road*, as well as Janie in *Their Eyes Were Watching God*. Even West's last novel, *The Wedding*, includes tall tales that suggest stories Hurston collected in *Mules and Men*. Helene Johnson, too, used more vernacular in her poetry after moving to Harlem and meeting Hurston.

After their initial closeness, the three women drifted apart. Hurston was a powerful personality, accustomed to dominating rooms and commanding friends to "come a running" when she wanted to see them.[27] She was also, according to West, a "snoop" who listened at friends' doors and intimidated them with Voodoo spells.[28] Even in the early 1930s Dorothy had begun to distance herself a bit, leading Johnson to urge her to "write to Zora sometimes."[29] Other events came between them. Hurston could be two-faced in her relationships, frequently playing people off against each other as she did with Langston Hughes and Alain Locke, Langston Hughes and Mrs. Mason, and Langston Hughes and Carl Van Vechten. She could also be savagely witty at her friends' expense, as when she observed that of the twenty-two African Americans heading to Russia to make a race movie, "only two in the crowd look anything like Negroes."[30] Other complications affected the relationship. When West returned from Russia, she placed some papers and her new fur coat in Zora's storage unit; the area was burgled, however, and the coat and papers disappeared. West always claimed that "Zora needed money . . . and staged the robbery, and took my little fur coat."[31] West was more upset by the loss of her papers, but she complained to Claude McKay that she could have gone to Paris if "that wretch hadn't walked off with my coat."[32] Similarly, in 1937 Zora asked Carl Van Vechten if he knew of Helene's whereabouts since she "put a box of papers in storage for me"; these may have been materials that Johnson had worked on secretly, unbeknownst to Hurston's patron, Mrs. Mason, or may have been some of the papers Zora sent to West and Johnson when she was collecting folklore in Florida.[33] In the same letter, Hurston gossips unsympathetically about Helene, claiming she has broken up her home and left her husband. After 1937, in fact, no letters between the three women seem to have been written, nor do West's letters in the 1940s contain any reference to Hurston.

In the spring and summer of 1932, however, West and Johnson were both living in Zora's apartment on West Sixty-sixth Street. Their initial burst of literary success had diminished and neither was very productive. West's family novel, *Five Sheaves*, about which Dorothy Scarborough, her teacher at Columbia, was optimistic, was finally revised but she still had found no publisher.[34] Perhaps unconsciously reflecting on her situation, she wrote to Cullen: "From my back window I see a brick wall."[35] Rachel came to stay with the cousins for an extended visit, which apparently precluded their socializing or going out with their friends, as Cullen wrote several times to Dorothy asking how long her mother would remain. Johnson published only two poems that year, both in *Opportunity*. "Monotone" seems to sum up the general mood of 1932: "My life is but a single attitude / An endless preface / An old day-by-day."[36]

Helene was keeping herself occupied by volunteering with a peace organization, and one day they called and asked for her assistance. Helene was out, but Dorothy agreed to lend a hand at the Fellowship of Reconciliation. When she arrived she found that her friends Henry Moon, a journalist at the *Amsterdam News*, and actress Rose McClendon were there as part of a committee tasked with recruiting African American actors to make a film in Russia on black and white relations in the United States. Louise Thompson, Wallace Thurman's ex-wife and a member of the Harlem Chapter of Friends of the Soviet Union, headed the committee. Since few professional actors were willing to accept the terms, such as purchasing their own tickets and receiving salary in worthless Russian currency, the committee was asked to invite any suitable African Americans who wished to go. The group eventually included the actors Wayland Rudd (whom West knew from *Porgy*) and Sylvia Garner; Taylor Gordon, a writer, singer, and protégé of Carl Van Vechten's; Loren Miller, who would become a prominent civil rights lawyer in Los Angeles; newspapermen Ted Poston and Henry Moon; two attractive divorcees, Mildred Jones, a graphic artist and recent graduate of Hampton Institute, and Mollie Lewis, a pharmacy graduate of

Meharry Medical College; singer Juanita Lewis; Louise Patterson, a labor researcher; and writers Langston Hughes, who had driven across the country from California to make the sailing, and Dorothy West. Helene was apparently unable to raise the money for the trip. West, who had been trying to get back to Europe, decided to go despite her indifference to politics or communism; her father was willing to pay her way (although she later claimed that Moon, who was in love with her, gave her some money for her passage), and she was, after all, interested in Dostoyevsky and the theater. She arrived in the USSR with only twenty dollars to her name.

In the 1930s travel to the USSR by African Americans was not unusual. Despite the strong anticommunist bias and religious orientation of the black community, young African Americans unable to find employment in Depression-era America found that their technical skills were welcome in Moscow. A few years after Dorothy's visit her mentor, Eugene Gordon, by then an editor of the women's pages for the *Boston Post*, traveled around the country, writing articles for the Russian press on nutritious meal-planning. Homer Smith, a young journalism major at the University of Minnesota, was hired by the Moscow post office and became a correspondent for the black press in America. Smith was on the platform to welcome the group of would-be actors as they steamed into the station. As he recalls, "the morning after their arrival the Negroes were brought together at the Meschrabpon Film Studio to meet the director, Karl Younghans. . . . There were raised eyebrows and puzzled expressions. . . . These were the toiling masses of American Negroes?" The filmmakers were distressed to see that "there most certainly were no callous-handed sharecroppers, stevedores or truck drivers . . . furthermore, most of them had never even experienced the ruder and cruder forms of Jim Crow, having lived North of the Mason-Dixon line."[37] Even worse was the fact that none of the group, except Sylvia Garner and Juanita Lewis, could sing. Whole scenes involving the singing of spirituals had to be eliminated, adding to Langston Hughes's burden of reworking the script.

The group was shown to their accommodations in the prestigious Grand Hotel, "a block from the Kremlin, in the heart of the capital. It had enormous rooms with huge, pre-tzarist beds, heavy drapes at the windows and deep rugs on the floors."[38] Dorothy wrote to her aunt Dolly, "I can see the gold domes within the Kremlin walls."[39] Since it was summer, the view from Dorothy's window did not include the hungry, barefoot street urchins huddled around makeshift campfires that she observed in the winter and described in her essay "Room in Red Square." She did note the discrepancy in social classes, such as the "amazing Lincolns . . . outside the bourgeois hotels, maintained by the most reckless chauffeurs in the world," and next to them, "the picturesque peasant in his smock and straw shoes."[40] She reported to her mother that "the food is good, though it costs a lot. . . . I pay two roubles for a small portion of cake. The straw-berries are delicious. We buy them from street vendors and they sell them in a cone twisted out of newspapers. . . . But there is no such thing as toilet paper."[41] The food in the Grand Hotel, however, left much to be desired: "the dining room had no menu; guests . . . were served whatever was available. Day after day this consisted of weak Russian borsch, some Irish potatoes, cabbage and black bread."[42] Kasha was omnipresent, but citrus and fresh fruit were impossible to obtain. Caviar, though rationed, was plentiful, and since Langston Hughes liked red caviar and Dorothy liked black, they would often meet on the street and exchange their caviar rations.[43] Some members of the group found the food hard to digest, though West reported to her mother that she hadn't been sick, which she attributed to the fact that "I don't eat much of this Russian food." Instead, accompanied by her friends Mollie Moon and Mildred Jones, she went "daily to one of the four or five really magnificent hotels here, and there I order recklessly and have a grand meal. These restaurants are left over from the old regime of the Czar, and are therefore gorgeous with fine French cooking and excellent service and a soft orchestra." Although she expressed guilt at eating well while the Russian peasants queued for hours for hard bread, West and her friends reveled in the absence of racial dis-crimination. "It's grand to go into a place and know you are welcome. The head waiters know us now and greet us with such heartwarming bows."[44] Needless to say, West did not express her pleasure in the waiters' bows to the more radical members of the group, such as Louise Patter-son, and she always insisted that nothing she saw in Russia could have persuaded her to become a Communist.

Dorothy's closest friends in Russia were artist Mildred Jones, with whom she shared a large room in the Grand Hotel, and Mollie Moon, whom Dorothy and Helene had known in New York. Dorothy and

Mildred quickly became close: "I like her so much," Dorothy wrote to her mother. "She is intelligent and very fine."[45] A few weeks later she describes Mildred to Rachel as "a lovely kid . . . serious-minded, intelligent, very fine. I want you to meet and like her." By this time West had decided that Mildred was "a more suitable companion than Mollie." Fortunately, Mollie also enjoyed Mildred's company and so "hasn't minded the threesomes."[46] Mollie was popular both with Russian men and the men in the group, such as Leonard Hill and Henry Moon, so, according to West, she did not feel excluded by Dorothy and Mildred's friendship. Although West never mentions going out with Russians, Mollie, along with "most of the girls from the cast were dated for days in advance."[47]

Mollie Lewis, a lifelong friend of Dorothy's and Helene's, hailed from Hattiesburg, Mississippi. Like Zora, she routinely lied about her age, but was probably born between 1907 and 1912. Chester Himes, her cousin by marriage, described her as "a strikingly attractive woman whose features in repose reminded one of the colored lithographs of East Indian Maharanees. Her complexion was of a color termed 'yellow' by other Negroes and 'tan' by white people. She had raven black hair, slightly curled, which she often wore parted in the center and gathered in a bun at the back in what was considered a Spanish style. And she had huge dark slumberous eyes colored a muddy maroon and curtained by fringes of black lashes incredibly thick and long: the kind of eyes generally described as 'bedroom eyes.' "[48] Mollie was intelligent as well as beautiful; in 1928 she graduated from the Meharry Medical College School of Pharmacy. After she and her husband divorced, Mollie moved to New York at Zora Neale Hurston's invitation, where she began taking classes at Columbia and the New School for Social Research, and where she eventually became a social worker. No sooner did she arrive in New York, however, than her hostess decamped on one of her research trips. A stranger to the city, Mollie was sitting alone in Zora's apartment one day when Dorothy stopped by. Dorothy promptly invited her for Easter dinner at the home of Edna and Lloyd Thomas; they attended a party given by some of the Thomases' cosmopolitan, interracial friends, "and Mollie was thrilled. She had not known such people existed. So she liked it, and then gradually she met many people."[49]

Helene, Dorothy, and their cousin Eugenia all enjoyed Mollie's company, although she was, according to Boston standards, "kind of a wild one."[50] Later, Dorothy and Mollie shared an apartment in Zora's building, where Mollie began to build a diverse social life. West's WPA essay "Cocktail Party" describes one of Mollie's parties after her marriage: "Our smiling hostess stood in her open door. Behind her was a surge of varicolored faces, the warm white of fair Negroes, the pale white of whites, through yellows and browns to rusty black." The hostess "was on the city payroll, had graduated from a first-class Negro college, belonged to a good sorority, had married respectably, and was now entrenching herself in Negro society. There had been one or two flamboyant indiscretions in her past, and so every once in a while, to assure herself . . . she had lived them down, she entertained at a lavish party."[51] Zora, however, was skeptical of Mollie's social aspirations, or perhaps a little jealous of someone who seemed to enjoy even more success flattering influential whites than she did. Zora "didn't quite trust Mollie [and] she used to snoop . . . [and] she practiced voodoo. Mollie believed in all that myth, so she swore Zora was practicing voodoo on her."[52] Upon Mollie's departure to Russia, she bequeathed her job as a theater usher to Helene, although Helene complained to Dorothy that Mollie sent postcards from Russia to the white employees at the theater but did not send one to her, thus reinforcing the idea white people have that "our kind like them a little better than their own."[53]

This gesture seems a precursor of Mollie's lifelong determination to acquire prominent white friends; eventually, as the wife of Henry Moon and the founder of the Urban League Guild, she socialized with the Winthrop Rockefellers, Eleanor Roosevelt, Henry Luce of *Time* magazine, Tallulah Bankhead, the Alfred Lunts, the heads of the AFL and the CLO, and Elisabeth Marbury's friend Anne Morgan.[54] Although Chester Himes satirized her as Mamie Mason, "who only ever wanted to be the 'Hostess with the Mostess' and to serve the Negro problem up to white people and be loved by white people for this service," Mollie justified her social ambitions as necessary for the support of the race: "At an early age I became aware of my obligation to participate in organized efforts to level the onerous barriers which locked me and my people in a ghastly cultural, political and economic ghetto. Neither I nor my family had sufficient income to make significant financial contribution to this cause. We did, however, have commitment, energy and time to contribute. Over the years I have made this kind of voluntary contribution

to various organizations and causes—the Harlem Art Center, the
Wilwych School and others. But my principal effort has been my vol-
unteer work on behalf to the National Urban League through the
National Urban League Guild. I was a founder of the Guild and have
been its Chairperson for more than 30 years."[55] In 1947, *Opportunity*
praised "Mrs. Mollie Moon, New York social worker" who "holds the
helm of this inspired interracial voluntary group." The Urban League had
begun in 1911 with $275 in its treasury, but thanks to Mollie's social
contacts and strenuous fund-raising in the auxiliary Guild, in 1947 the
organization confidently launched a $450,000 campaign chaired by
Henry R. Luce.[56] Mollie was best known for the elaborate Beaux Arts
Ball, an annual fund-raiser attended by New York's most prominent
artists, socialites, and philanthropists. In 1942, Hazel Scott, the wife of
Adam Clayton Powell, and actor Canada Lee entertained Tallulah
Bankhead, Langston Hughes, Countee Cullen, and the Alfred Lunts. The
event, held in Harlem's Savoy Ballroom, raised $2,500 in the middle of
wartime.[57]

Mollie was never intimidated by her powerful friends. In 1948 she
broke the color bar at the Rainbow Room when she invited Winthrop
Rockefeller to co-host the ball. In an interview in which she discussed
her friend, Dorothy chuckled when remembering the time Mollie sued
Rockefeller's wife, the famously litigious Bobo. The suit never went to
trial, and Mollie received a large settlement.[58] Dorothy always loved and
respected Mollie and never begrudged her her society friends. In fact,
Mollie is one of the few people, living or dead, on whom Dorothy
bestowed unreserved praise in her 1978 interview with Genii Guinier.
Henry Moon, who had unsuccessfully pursued Dorothy, married Mollie
Lewis a few years after the Russian trip; together they became a power
couple in New York's philanthropic and cultural circles.

Moon had asked Dorothy to go on the trip to Russia, thinking she
was too involved in the hectic, Harlem life of parties, dancing, and bootleg liquor, and hoping to have her to himself in Moscow. It was Langston
Hughes to whom Dorothy was immediately attracted, however. On the
voyage over, they updated each other on their activities in the five years
since their meeting at the *Opportunity* dinner in 1927, and Hughes certainly flirted with Dorothy. Photographs show the two affectionately
entwined on deck chairs. One evening, after a champagne party, they

"went out and looked at the stars. The moon was big and friendly. The sea was calm."[59] In Helsinki Hughes took her for a carriage ride into the country, and they stopped for tea at an old inn.

Hughes's literary reputation, charming personality, and handsome face clearly appealed to West; physically and intellectually, he fit the same mold as Countee Cullen and Bruce Nugent, with whom Dorothy had been involved a few years earlier, and toward the end of the trip she repeated her pattern and proposed marriage. Like Cullen and Nugent, he was simply asked to provide a baby, after which he could maintain an independent artistic life, free of domestic entanglement. As in the case of his predecessors, it should have been, but wasn't, obvious to Dorothy that her feelings were not reciprocated. West seems to have been singularly naïve with regard to men's intentions toward her in real life, though she portrays them more accurately in fiction. In "Russian Correspondence" she describes Tack (that is, "Lang"), a boyish, free-spirited painter. The narrator, a hysterical American woman with whom he is having an affair in Moscow, first urges Tack, who is en route to Baku, to pursue his art and "be a wild boy," but then becomes frantic as she realizes that he has abandoned her for his Russian interpreter.[60] As the ironic title implies, the narrator's feelings are completely one-sided, and this is exactly what happened in real life. When West followed Hughes to Baku, she found he had already departed for Uzbekistan. She was met at the Baku station by Mildred Jones.

The situation, in fact, was complicated because, in addition to pursuing Hughes, Dorothy had fallen in love, perhaps for the first time in her life, with Mildred. The contrasting styles of the two women are revealed in a shipboard photograph: Jones reclines languidly in a deck chair, displaying a sophisticated haircut and a sultry pout, while West sits perky and cross-legged on the deck, like a little girl. Langston Hughes was also attracted to Mildred, who often typed up poems he had translated from the Russian and Chinese. In a letter to Carl Van Vechten he describes Mildred, "a bobbed girl whom I don't believe you've ever met," as "the beauty-sensation of the season. She goes to parties with the local Who's Whos. And knows everybody of importance. She's a nice kid who hasn't learned a word of Russian yet."[61] One of Mildred's conquests was chief of the Press Division of the Foreign Affairs Commissariat, Constantine Oumansky, who "was on the verge of becoming mentally unbalanced in his ardor for the smiles and favors of chic, bob-haired, peach-colored Mildred Jones."[62]

Despite all the male attention, it was apparently Jones who initiated the relationship with West. In a photograph of Jones and West on the ship's deck, separated by the matronly figure of Sylvia Garner, Mildred directs a brooding, sidelong glance toward West, who smiles cheerfully into the camera. Jones apparently sensed a rival in Hughes from the beginning, since she too invited West for a carriage ride in Helsinki as soon as West had returned from the outing with Hughes. Mildred's ardor apparently unnerved Dorothy, who suddenly decided she wanted to marry Langston and start a family. In a long, emotional letter to Hughes, West proposes; she admits the relationship with Mildred, which she seems to believe has upset him, but trusts that he will forgive her. She is, however, still conflicted and is unwilling to break completely or to hurt Mildred because "her *feeling* for me is deep and sincere. I cannot wound her in any way. . . . It is simply that this is the first time I have had the stamina to admit to myself that I do not, and I do not now remember when I did, want her as she wants me."[63] Essentially, West not only wanted Hughes to rescue her from her first lesbian relationship but also to salvage Mildred's pride. Presumably, no woman, no matter how much she might desire a lesbian relationship, could be expected to turn down a man as eligible as Langston Hughes. After all, Mildred herself had married the charismatic newspaper editor W. A. Scott in 1929. Scott, the founder of the *Atlanta World*, had left his wife and two children for Mildred, but the marriage lasted only two months.[64]

Sensing, correctly, that Hughes might ignore her letter (although he kept it), West tells him she will leave Russia and travel to Paris with Mollie Lewis, because otherwise Mildred will want to continue their intimacy "and I could not torture her or myself by my nearness."[65] Still hoping that he will hustle her away from temptation and restore Mildred's peace of mind, West suggests that she and Hughes go to Latvia to obtain their exit visas, but he manages to elude her. Hughes, needless to say, did not get involved. Under his sociable demeanor he was ambitious, and pathologically private, and surely would have avoided any sort of homoerotic triangle. Nor did he have any intention of limiting his options by acquiring a wife and family. In Russia he amused himself with Sylvia Chen, a Chinese-Jamaican "modernistic" dancer whom he described to Carl Van Vechten as "my girl friend at the moment."[66] Interestingly, he took Dorothy to meet Sylvia; Dorothy was impressed with Sylvia's English accent and reported to Rachel that the woman was "very interesting, though she shows off a little." West was actually more interested in the interracial marriage between Sylvia's sister and a Russian, observing that they were very affectionate and that "prejudice is quite unknown here."[67]

Meanwhile, Dorothy's father died unexpectedly (although he was over seventy), and Rachel asked her to return to Boston. Realizing there was no future with Hughes, Dorothy reconsidered the relationship with Mildred and, instead of traveling with Mollie, who had decided to go on to Berlin, she left Moscow with Mildred. On the train, Dorothy suddenly burst into tears. To Mildred's questions, she could only say "I am saying good-bye to my youth."[68] Perhaps Dorothy was acknowledging the loss of her long-maintained sexual innocence. In 1929, Wallace Thurman had commented that her "stories lacked passion and that [her] virginal state might be in some way responsible," and he urged her and Helene to "get rid of the puritan notion that to have casual sexual intercourse is a sin," adding, "don't repress . . . your sex urge, just because you are Puritan enough to believe that hell fire awaits he who takes a bite of the apple, unless you are profoundly inoculated with the illusion of love."[69] Now West knew that while she had certainly succumbed to the sex urge, she was unsure whether she was really in love. Nevertheless, when they stopped in London, they were "so happy." West was eager to show Mildred the little bed-sitter she had shared with Edna Thomas two years earlier, when she probably first understood the possibility of lesbian love in the company of Edna, Georgette Harvey, and Cheryl Crawford. To her disappointment, however, the building had been converted into a gentlemen's club. Despite their passionate Russian affair, West mentioned Mildred only obliquely as "a woman whom I loved very much."[70] Although West never spoke or wrote about homosexuality, the many unhappy couples in her fiction, who have chosen each other for superficial, socially acceptable characteristics, may well function as coded references to the hegemony of heteronormative relationships.

West was not the only cousin involved in a passionate affair. While Dorothy was away in Russia, Helene had also fallen in love. In October 1932 she wrote to West, confiding, "I've been in love again and you

know what that means to me. I'm normal again now, tho, darling."
Helene was likely discussing William Warner "Bobo" Hubbell III, a
third-generation New Yorker whom she and Dorothy had met at the
Thirty-fourth Street Macy's, where he worked as an elevator man.
Hubbell endeared himself to the cousins at the nearby Metropolitan
Opera House, where he held a second job as an usher. Since the cousins
could only afford standing room tickets, he would routinely usher them
to vacant seats. The romance apparently intensified, because two months
after the October letter Helene wrote, "Bobo wants me to marry him.
He wanted to get the license last week, but I'd rather go to Germany and
anyway . . . he'd never get along with the Bensons tho he is a nice loyal
kid."[71] The trip to Germany did not materialize, and Helene and Bobo
soon wed. They moved to an apartment on Saint Nicholas Avenue in
mid-Harlem, overlooking City College, and Helene eventually became
the only literary sister (with the exception of Isabel Washington Powell)
to give birth.

Once back in the United States, Mildred Jones applied for jobs in
New York state government, while Dorothy returned to Rachel's new
home at 23 Worthington Street in Boston, where she remained for the
next few years as she created and edited a literary magazine. Interestingly,
West was able to maintain cordial relations with both Hughes and Jones
after the Russian interlude and to press them into assisting her with her
magazine. Jones designed the covers and layout for the first issues, while
Hughes's stories were a major coup for the young and unknown editor.
Even Henry Moon, reconciled to his lack of success with West, contributed several pieces, while Hurston enthusiastically praised her
courage in the new venture.

In Boston, West resumed her correspondence with Countee Cullen.
Passing through New York in the summer of 1933, after the deprivations
of Russia, she was struck by the "well-dressed women . . . how they burst
upon my vision! Clothes, clothes, clothes, after all those months of not
letting them matter . . . the chic hats, the charming socks, and above all,
the shoes."[72] Despite the temptations of the city she has decided, she
writes, to "lead a retiring life" in Boston far from the distractions that had
dissipated her creative energies in New York.[73] She also expresses concern
about Cullen's career and regret that he is dissipating his energies in
attending his elderly, widowed father (who was, nevertheless, paying his

bills). She is unsure of exactly what she wants to do but knows it involves providing "a space for young dark throats to sing heard songs."[74] West had probably suggested they co-host a salon at 23 Worthington Street that would bring recognition to their own writing and that of their friends. But Cullen, ever adept at avoiding any commitment, personal or professional, sidestepped the plan, protesting that he would be "an impediment, a sort of literary ox (not even a lion!)" in her "pretty parlor."[75]

Perhaps realizing that Cullen's response was typical of what she could expect from her male colleagues, West next decided to use the three hundred dollars given to her by the Soviet government upon her departure to fund a literary journal. She probably drew on Eugene Gordon's experience with the *Saturday Evening Quill*, although he was now in Russia and unable to assist her, but surely another inspiration was that of Pauline Hopkins's *Colored American Magazine*. In the previous generation, Hopkins's journal had done exactly what West wanted to do, namely, "publish the work of young poets and fiction writers, most of whom had no other outlets for their efforts." In fact Hopkins, who lost her editorial position—just as West was destined to do—because of political wrangling by male colleagues at the journal, "produced more and better fiction and poetry [during her tenure] than at any other time in its history."[76]

West was only twenty-five, but the letters she wrote soliciting support and material, and negotiating with printers, show a mature and self-possessed woman. She received little help from Langston Hughes, Countee Cullen, Bruce Nugent, or any of the men in the Harlem Renaissance movement. Nevertheless, by calling on her extensive network of friends, she obtained work from Hughes, Nugent, and Cullen, as well as from Sterling Brown, Margaret Walker, Richard Wright, Alain Locke, Ralph Ellison, Arna Bontemps, Alfred Mendes, Frank Yerby, and Pauli Murray. Needless to say, the poetry of Helene Johnson—of whom Hughes wrote enthusiastically, "somebody ought to bring out a book of hers"—was also featured."[77] In the second issue, West announced that, just as her mentor Blanche Colton Williams had judged the *Opportunity* contests and published the best stories, so she would be judging a contest at West Virginia State College and publishing the winning entries. Almost immediately, the journal was criticized for its apolitical stance, but West refused to sacrifice aesthetics to polemic. By the third issue, she had begun to articulate the philosophy of the journal; she wanted to combine a modernist style with an interest in proletarian literature; "with Jessie Fauset and W.E.B. Du Bois, she became the third African American writer to cross the great chasm between romanticism (such as that of Alice Dunbar-Nelson and Angelina Grimke) and modernism."[78]

As West explained in later years, editing a magazine was a male prerogative, and "it was very hard for one little woman back then."[79] When Richard Wright sought to wrest control from her and intimidated her with letters from his lawyers, demanding the copyright of his essay "Blueprint for Negro Writing," she acquiesced immediately. She feared that Wright's colleagues from the University of Chicago were Communists, and she did not want to get involved with the political element. Nevertheless, West "expanded the African American tradition to include women in the role of responsible and influential promoters of culture. . . . As the literary community is placing more emphasis on revising the African American tradition and, specifically, the role of women in that tradition, it is West's publishing successes, not her failures" that resonate.[80]

West probably met Marian Minus (1913–1972), with whom she was to live and write for over a decade, in the early 1930s. Dorothy had moved back to New York in the spring of 1934 to supervise the publication of *Challenge*. Through Mollie Lewis she obtained a job as a Home Relief investigator, and she and Mollie shared an apartment in Harlem between July 1934 and the summer of 1935. Marian Minus was a college student at the time; during vacations she stayed with her mother on West 117th Street, and West and Minus probably met through mutual friends. Marian Minus was an exceptionally accomplished and intelligent woman from an academic family. A magna cum laude graduate of Fisk University, she had majored in sociology, played basketball and tennis, and pledged Delta Sigma Theta sorority.

Marian's grandmother, Laura Lyles, was the model for the character of Gram in West's novel *The Wedding*. The child of poor white millworkers in Newbury, South Carolina, Laura Lyles raised her social status through marriage to an African American teacher. In her story "The Fine Line," Minus offers a poignant account of her grandmother's early life and the motivation for her marriage. Cadie Culkey's mill job is the sole support of her family, which consists of a slatternly mother, raggedy siblings, and a bigoted, tubercular father who clings to white privilege and invokes the Bible to justify his racism. One night, unable to eat the family's greasy, unappetizing dinner, Cadie leaves the house and hears a young man improvise a blues about the red southern moon; she intuits an erotic message. She steals into the forbidden garden of black neighbors and picks some figs, "firm and full inside their rich, dark skins." Plucking the fruit, she feels "the fig lying heavy in her hand, and in the moonlight she could see the thick white fluid where it smeared her fingertips."[81] Although the owner of the garden is angry at Cadie's trespass, and apprehensive about its racial ramifications, his wife invites the girl into the house for a glass of cool milk; there Cadie sees an order and harmony missing in her own home. Marian's mother, Laura Whitener Minus, "a small, plump fair woman," attended high school and normal school and also married an educator.[82] Laura Lyles Whitener, who stayed with her daughter, son-in-law, and granddaughter, grew increasingly bitter about having to "live colored." She took her frustration out on little brown-skinned Marian, although, on her death bed, she begged the child's forgiveness.[83] When Marian was about five, her parents left South Carolina for Ohio, where her father, Claude Wellington Minus, taught at Wilberforce University. When West met Marian and her mother, the latter (possibly widowed) was working as a seamstress. Later, Laura Minus worked for the WPA, and she may have helped West obtain her position as WPA interviewer. West interviewed Laura Minus in 1938 about her experiences with "ghosts" in several New York apartments. At some point in the early 1930s, perhaps during one of Marian's vacations from Fisk, she and Dorothy had spent a quiet evening together listening to Andre Kostelanetz and to operatic arias on the radio. It was, Minus recalled, "the calmest and friendliest night I've ever spent in New York."[84] In June 1935, upon graduation from Fisk University, Marian won a Rosenwald fellowship to pursue a Ph.D. in social anthropology at the University of Chicago.

In August 1936, Minus wrote to West, who had just published the fifth issue of *Challenge* and was vacationing on Martha's Vineyard. She tells "Dot" that she is "like someone with a precious touch who knows the value of its light and shields its flame from the shifting and shiftless winds." She urges Dorothy to "find time to write" at the beach and regrets that Helene, who had married in 1933, and whose last poem, "Let Me Sing My Song," had been published in *Challenge* in May 1935, is not writing. She apparently knew Mildred Jones and tells Dorothy: "I tried to write Mildred because I wanted to and yet I ended only with a miserable note. Perhaps it is because I know she is a plutocrat and I don't want her to be." Minus alludes to the evening she and West had spent together, saying "you will never know the depth and extent of my gratitude or the reason for it." She concludes with a cryptic appeal that West "remember that 'there is neither good nor evil in the world, but only being and doing.' And that in being and doing we are sure only of some ultimate pain which in the end is the only beauty we know." She closes with "Affectionately, Marian."[85] West apparently read between the lines and reciprocated Marian's feelings. In October she visited Marian in Chicago, where they probably became lovers. After West left, Minus wrote wistfully that "when five o'clock comes and if it is still raining, I shall turn my feet from the path they will think leads to the Partridge Inn and you."[86]

Marian Minus, according to West, was "an intellectual" who "was always willing to help others." She was interested in social justice and in the leftist politics that she would share with Richard Wright, Margaret Walker, Bob Davis, Frank Marshall Davis, and other members of the South Side Writers' Group in Chicago. In fact, she edited Richard Wright's work and "did quite a bit for him."[87] Minus and Wright were both involved with the Communist Party and supported Earl Browder, the party's presidential candidate in 1936. Marian, however, was growing disenchanted, and she advised Wright that the party was forcing him to subordinate his talent to propaganda. Apparently unaware of Minus's relationship with West, Wright pursued her avidly, warmed by her "Negro smile full of Negro sunshine."[88] His friends thought he was in love with her, and West herself claimed he wanted to marry Marian.[89] When he learned that Marian was gay, he professed to be shocked, although she made no attempt to deny her sexual orientation. In fact, Margaret Walker remembers that although homosexuality was never discussed in their circle, Marian "dressed mannishly and looked lesbian in a male fashion."[90]

Minus spent two years at the University of Chicago and completed all of her course work, but she did not write her dissertation or receive a Ph.D. She wrote papers on the culture and mythology of Malaysia, in which she cites Ruth Benedict, the same anthropologist with whom Zora Neale Hurston worked at Columbia, as well as a detailed account of weaving techniques in Peru.[91] Her interest in textiles, fabrics, and

fashion, which may have stemmed from her mother's work as a seamstress, was also an avocation that she and Dorothy shared. She often
shopped for fabric for Dorothy and herself, which Laura Minus made
into fashionable outfits for the two women. Minus herself was a good
seamstress who could shorten Dorothy's coat and do "a beautiful job."[92]
Minus's work in cultural anthropology led her to study consumer trends,
particularly among African American shoppers, and eventually to a job
at Consumers Union, where she still worked in 1969.[93]

By 1937 the two women were living with Marian's mother on West
117th Street. Minus persuaded West that *Challenge* magazine needed a
more relevant, political focus and suggested that Richard Wright guest-
edit an issue devoted to the South Side Writers' Group. Wright had been
working for the WPA in Chicago but had followed Minus to New York,
where he hoped to transfer his WPA position. Envisioning *Challenge* as an
African American journal of the proletariat, he accepted Minus's offer and
even secured financial backing from the *Daily Worker*. Ralph Ellison,
whom West always suspected of being an FBI informer, helped Wright
canvas for subscriptions. While Wright may have hoped to pursue the
relationship with Minus, he was anxious to distance himself from West,
and the bourgeois, decadent aura of the journal's previous six issues. His
first move was to change the name of the journal to *New Challenge* and
to place his name on the masthead as editor. He listed West and Minus as
associate editors and Sterling Brown, Robert Hayden, Loren Miller,
Langston Hughes, and Margaret Walker as contributing editors. He
secured original work from Frank Marshall Davis, Ralph Ellison, and
Margaret Walker. Henry Lee Moon, Alain Locke, and Marian Minus contributed book reviews. Minus offered a positive, perceptive discussion of
Hurston's *Their Eyes Were Watching God*, in direct contradiction of
Wright's recent, scathing review of the book in the *New Masses*. Neither
Dorothy West nor Helene Johnson published anything in this number.
Perhaps the most dramatic piece was Wright's "Blueprint for Negro Writing," which he intended as the journal's manifesto. In his essay Wright
ridicules the writers of the Harlem Renaissance—some of whom, like
Alain Locke and Henry Moon, are represented in the issue—as "French
poodles" that showed off their parlor tricks for white patrons.[94] Feeling
angry and betrayed, West reversed the editorial positions, listing herself
and Minus as editors and demoting Wright to associate. Wright realized

too late not only that West and Minus were lovers but also that the journal was not solvent, as Minus had led him to believe. Immediately, his lawyer contacted West, demanding that she release the copyright of his work. Fearing that the Communist Party was behind him, West complied and closed the journal. The debacle does not seem to have soured relations between West and Wright since, in 1938, Countee Cullen wrote to West, in his capacity as editor of the *Journal of African Affairs* (Claude McKay was co-editor), requesting that she review Wright's book *Uncle Tom's Children* and assuring her that "it would please him to have you review his book."[95]

The *New Challenge* situation seems not to have affected the relationship between West and Minus either. Both continued to write short stories and to work on their own novels as well as on a collaborative novel, loosely based on Isaac West, called *Jude*. In November 1937, Minus filed for unemployment but obtained a position at Consumers Union a month later. Her close friend from Fisk University, Dorothy Steele, worked at Consumers Union and was later responsible for hiring Helene Johnson and Gwendolyn Bennett. Minus's article "The Negro as a Consumer" in *Opportunity* (September 1938) drew on her experiences in Chicago, Harlem, and the South, where lack of consumer education in the black community led to shoddy goods, disenfranchised workers, child labor, and high mortality rates as a result of patent medicines. Meanwhile, West continued to work for Home Relief and drew on many of the situations she witnessed for her own writing. She had, she wrote to Langston Hughes, "seen so much and learned so much. I have first hand knowledge of hunger and sickness and despair. I have a head full of tragic stories."[96] Although the work took an enormous psychological toll, she witnessed events that were later transmuted into some of her best work, like "Mammy" (1940), a tale of racial passing and infanticide, and "Pluto" (1938), an account of Harlem children living below the poverty line.

In April 1938, however, the Home Relief Bureau referred her for a position with the Works Progress Administration (WPA) in the Writers' Project. Elmer Carter, an editor of *Opportunity*, wrote an "unqualified recommendation" for West, describing her as "one of the most promising Negro writers in America."[97] Under the auspices of the WPA, over 6,500 published writers in twenty-six states were asked to record oral histories of thousands of Americans in different ethnic groups, with the idea of publishing them in a huge anthology and writing travel guides to the United States. In addition to West, the Writers' Project employed Zora Neale Hurston in Florida, Richard Wright in Chicago, and Ralph Ellison, Langston Hughes, Claude McKay, Chester Himes, and Ted Poston in New York. In October 1938, West was promoted to senior newspaperman. Her crisp, ironic sketches of Harlem life such as "Cocktail Party," "Amateur Night at the Apollo," and "Daddy Grace" show her eye for detail and her ability to swiftly sketch character and atmosphere.

Even though both women continued to publish stories through the 1940s, West in the *New York Daily News* and Minus in *Woman's Day* magazine, their financial situation became precarious after the dismantling of the WPA and the coming of World War II. West was essentially supporting Rachel in Boston, as well as herself in New York, since money that had been left to them by Isaac West was tied up and unavailable. In 1941, she applied for a Guggenheim but was turned down. In August 1942, Minus wrote to West, who was waiting for her to arrive for their vacation with Rachel on Martha's Vineyard, that they were in danger of being evicted and that the landlord had threatened to put their furniture on the street and garnish West's wages from the *Daily News*. Minus complained that she was completely penniless and asked if Aunt Scotter might find her a job.

The following year, despite their plans to collaborate on a novel, and the insistence of their agent, George Bye, that they had great potential, West moved back to Martha's Vineyard, ostensibly to help Rachel care for her ailing sister Carrie. After Carrie recovered from her stroke, Dorothy stayed on with Rachel and never again returned to New York. West continued to write and in 1945 applied for a Rosenwald but was rejected. Minus may have been living with West in 1945 when the latter wrote to Countee Cullen, congratulating him on the fact that Lena Horne was to star in his musical *St. Louis Woman*, and adding "both Marian and I wish you all the success in the world."[98] In any case, Marian was a constant visitor through the 1940s, and Dorothy's much younger cousin, Barbara Franklin, remembered West and Minus caring for her affectionately. Marian was also an accomplished carpenter and mechanic. Helene Johnson's daughter, Abigail McGrath, recalls that a common neighborhood sight was Marian under the hood of a car, with Dorothy

standing by, handing her wrenches. The eight short stories Minus published in *Woman's Day* between 1945 and 1951 invariably feature a male
protagonist who works in construction, trucking, roofing, or commercial
fishing. While the accurate details certainly indicate that Minus was adept
at these trades, the stories reveal almost nothing about her personality or
her private life with West.

One exception is "Twice in His Lifetime," published in 1949. The
story opens as Stan prepares for a reunion with his wife, Janie, from
whom he has been separated for six months. "The separation had been
her idea, but he had shouted that she wanted a coterie, not a husband,
and she had shouted back that he might be right."[99] Stan is distressed by
"her compulsion to be surrounded by admirers, her voracious need for
devotion that he could not fulfill because he was only one person"—and
one who could not articulate his own feelings (78). Although he has
always "given her everything she had ever asked for," he finds it almost
impossible to grant her request "for the chance to decide if she wanted
their marriage to continue" (40). The six months have passed, however,
and he is preparing to meet her. "Stan dressed carefully . . . for being
well-groomed was one of the few things he was certain she really liked
about him. He wore the underwear, fine linen from Finchley's, that had
been her extravagant gift on his birthday, and he covered it with the suit
he'd had made especially for this day" (72). Although Janie's first words
to him are "That's a very handsome suit, Stan," it is obvious that she is
more interested in flirting with the friend he has brought along for
moral support, and in telephoning another man with whom she has a
later date, than in reuniting with her husband (74). Stan has been dogged
throughout the day by an adolescent memory of a gold watch he had
proudly won in a literary contest. Much as he loved the watch, he could
not wear it because he is one of those individuals whose magnetic field
makes a watch lose time. Eventually, he pawns it to buy a new tennis
racquet, realizing that "it had lost none of its value, but it was useless to
him. . . . On another wrist it would keep a careful record of time, but on
his it would always fail. What mattered was that he had won it. Whoever
had the watch after him could never have that" (72). Needless to say, in
the end Stan and Janie go their separate ways.

West and Minus remained close until around 1950, which would
tally with the story Minus wrote in 1949, and the story may well reflect

a coded description of the end of their relationship. Although West went on to write two novels, *The Living Is Easy* (1948) and *The Wedding* (1995), Minus never published again after 1951. In 1958 she was appointed personnel director at Consumers Union, where she remained until her retirement. She eventually established a household with Edna Pemberton, where West occasionally visited, and Minus and Pemberton moved in a literary and artistic circle with ties to the Harlem Renaissance that included Countee Cullen's widow Ida Cullen, Harold Jackman, Gwendolyn Bennett, the Bruce Nugents, and the Carl Van Vechtens. West, an extremely private person, never discussed the relationship with Minus. Her interests, until her death, revolved around her friends and family, her pets, and above all, her writing.

For Helene Johnson, the decade and a half in New York, before the birth of her daughter in 1940, was her most productive as an artist. During this period her careful attention to nature continued, but her oeuvre expanded to encompass meditations on race and gender, love and romance, spirituality, war, nonconformity, old age, same-sex relationships, and poverty. Though she had been aware of privation and racial and sexual bias while living in Boston, it was in New York that she saw poverty up close and experienced the glass ceiling firsthand. As a result, notes her daughter, "her personality became more radical, politically, socially, and economically."[100]

Where West engaged the public and advanced her work, Johnson maintained a strict screen of privacy. Unlike Dorothy, she refused to give interviews or public readings, and even her daughter wrote that her mother "had a lot of hermit in her" and that she was "extremely eccentric."[101] Johnson was no doubt aware of these perceptions. We imagine she would say that she merely marched to the beat of her own drummer. She expresses this very sentiment in "The Street to the Establishment," one of several poems she wrote late in life.

> You're the old. I'm the new
> I'm the multi. You're the few
> You're the gained, the attained,
> the begun, the become,
> the prize that's been won
> the picked from the which.

You're part of the mural on the wall,
the spire that cannot fall.
I'm the aborted
I'm the itch.

Perhaps because Johnson took such a fiercely independent path, she never received the prizes, honors, and other public recognition that came to West later in life. Still, the poem's upbeat rhythm and wonderful slant rhyme reveal a steely resoluteness; others may seek to shove her to the margins, to deem her unworthy of inclusion, but she knows that she can't be excluded.

Certainly the years that Johnson and West spent in New York were enhanced by the network of support and friendship that they enjoyed. Helene rarely initiated relationships, as West did, but she was passionately loyal and dedicated to the women in her family and to her daughter, Abigail. In the end, although she wrote something every day of her life, she chose to be a mother. In interviews during the last years of her life, Dorothy West also expressed her appreciation of those who helped her: the women in her family, Edna Thomas, Fredi Washington, Mollie Moon, Rose McClendon, Elisabeth Marbury, Jacqueline Onassis, and many others. Dorothy and Helene lived and created literature during extremely difficult times and with minimal financial support. Through it all they certainly shared Zora Neale Hurston's reflection on friendship: "Who can know the outer ranges of friendship? [It seems to me] that trying to go through life without friends, is like milking a bear to get cream for your morning coffee. It is a whole lot of trouble, and then not worth much after you get it."[102]

Epilogue

AFTER PUBLISHING *The Living Is Easy* to wide acclaim in 1948, Dorothy West lived, in her words, a "retiring" life on Martha's Vineyard. Of the three cousins, only Helene Johnson remained in New York, where she raised her daughter and worked with Marian Minus, Gwendolyn Bennett, and Dorothy Steele at Consumers Union. Eugenia Rickson and her husband, military veteran Marion Ray Jordan, moved to Onset, Massachusetts, a resort town next to Cape Cod. Though the cousins were no longer in the public eye, writing remained of utmost importance and an essential aspect of their identity. Helene Johnson's daughter, Abigail McGrath, recalls that her mother ceased writing poetry professionally, but "she continued to live life with the soul of a poet until she died. Moreover, she wrote a little something every day of her life, even if it was an ad for a car ('Cadillac is Badillac') or a review of a film."[1]

West also continued to write, despite the demands of her widowed mother and the obligation to care for a number of elderly relatives. After the deaths of her mother in 1954 and her Aunt Carrie in 1958, Dorothy lived alone in the Vineyard house. For over twenty years she wrote columns, "The Highlands Water Boy" and "The Cottagers' Corner," for the *Vineyard Gazette*, reporting on the African American community of Oak Bluffs and recording her bird watching and the subtle interplay of people and nature on the island. She also worked on *The Wedding*, a novel about the elite African American summer colony on Martha's Vineyard. Feeling out of tune with the times, she decided against publishing the book for fear it would be deprecated by the 1960s militants, who had no interest in the black aristocracy. It was also during this time that West renewed her friendship with Elizabeth Pope White, a childhood friend from the Vineyard.

Much like Dorothy West and Helene Johnson, Liz, as West called her, had moved to New York in the 1930s, where she worked for the Federal Theatre Project and became immersed in literary and artistic Harlem.

Liz was, according to West, a talented actress, a dancer, a costume designer, and an avid Shakespearean. In 1960, after returning to the Vineyard, she decided to produce a film of *Othello* with an all-black cast and an Afro-Caribbean jazz score, a project that consumed her energy and resources for the next twenty years. West joined the project as location manager, although she modestly described her job as "gofer," saying, "We were both healthy as horses with unlimited energy—it was fun for me— my station wagon standing ready to be packed with props, coolers, and whatever paraphernalia Liz was seeking." The film premiered in 1980, starring Yaphet Kotto as Othello, and won several awards.[2]

Meanwhile *The Living Is Easy*, like all of the novels by Harlem Renaissance women writers, had gone out of print. In 1982 the Feminist Press, spurred by Adelaide Cromwell, who provided an afterword, reissued the novel. Cromwell was a professor at Boston University and had met West thirty-five years earlier "picking blueberries on Martha's Vineyard." Their friendship grew, and in the early 1970s she invited West to address her African American Studies class. The effect was, she reports, "electrifying." Both West and the students relished her memories of the Harlem Renaissance, and the lectures became "an awakening for her, a prologue to her rediscovery."[3] The publication of *The Wedding*, at Jacqueline Onassis's urging, and *The Richer, the Poorer* in 1995, brought additional fanfare. West continued to receive invitations to speak at colleges and universities, and she was interviewed by publications across the country. Well into her eighties, she found herself feted by celebrities and pursued by admirers. The awards and acclaim showered on her in her final years capped an exhilarating journey and proved a fitting tribute. In the end, only West remained of all the literary sisters who had traveled with her on the road to artistic expression and to a life free of racial and gender proscriptions.

Notes

Prologue

1. Wallace Thurman, "Negro Poets and Their Poetry," in *The Collected Writings of Wallace Thurman*, ed. Amritjit Singh and Daniel M. Scott III (New Brunswick: Rutgers University Press, 2003), 210. Komunyakaa and Frost are quoted in Verner D. Mitchell, introduction to *This Waiting for Love: Helene Johnson, Poet of the Harlem Renaissance, ed.* V. Mitchell (Amherst: University of Massachusetts Press, 2000), 9–10.
2. Helene Johnson, "The Road," in *This Waiting for Love*, 25.
3. Cheryl A. Wall, *Worrying the Line: Black Women Writers, Lineage, and Literary Tradition* (Chapel Hill: University of North Carolina Press, 2005), 6.
4. Spillers is quoted in Wall, *Worrying the Line*, 7.
5. *Give Us Each Day: The Diary of Alice Dunbar Nelson*, ed. Gloria Hull (New York: Norton, 1986), 21.
6. As quoted in *Dorothy West: Where the Wild Grape Grows, Selected Writings 1930–1950*, ed. Verner D. Mitchell and Cynthia Davis (Amherst: University of Massachusetts Press, 2005), 27.
7. Claude McKay to Dorothy West, January 21, 1936, in *West: Where the Wild Grape Grows*, 208.
8. The manuscript is located in the Dorothy West Papers, Schlesinger Library, Radcliffe Institute for Advanced Study, Harvard University. A chapter, "At the Swan Boats," is included in *West: Where the Wild Grape Grows*, 57–62.
9. John K. Hutchens, "People Who Read and Write." *New York Times*, May 17, 1946, BR13.

Chapter 1   "Nothing So Broadening as Travel": *Porgy*, 1929

1. Adele Newson, "An Interview with Dorothy West," *Zora Neale Hurston Forum* 2 (1987): 22.
2. Cheryl Crawford, *One Naked Individual: My Fifty Years in the Theatre* (New York: Bobbs-Merrill, 1977), 15.
3. Eleonora Duse (1858–1924), an internationally acclaimed classical actress from Italy, had been entertained at the White House by President Grover Cleveland. She was noted for her affairs with both women and men, including the playwright Pirandello and the poet D'Annunzio.
4. Richard Bruce Nugent, "On Georgette," in *Gay Rebel of the Harlem Renaissance: Selections from the Work of Richard Bruce Nugent*, ed. Thomas H. Wirth (Durham, NC: Duke University Press, 2002), 211–213.
5. In Chester Himes, *Pinktoes* (Jackson, MS: Banner Books, 1996), Henry and Mollie Moon are satirized as Joe and Mamie Mason. Also see Himes's

autobiography, *The Quality of Hurt: The Early Years* (New York: Paragon House, 1990), 71.

6. Dorothy West to Countee Cullen, May 14, 1945, Countee Cullen Papers, Amistad Research Center, Tulane University (hereafter CCP).

7. Genii Guinier, "Interview with Dorothy West, May 6, 1978," in *The Black Women Oral History Project*, ed. Ruth Edmonds Hill (Westport, CT: Meckler, 1991), 169.

8. Himes, *Quality of Hurt*, 116.

9. Nellie McKay, "Foreword," in *Shadowed Dreams: Women's Poetry of the Harlem Renaissance*, ed. Maureen Honey (New Brunswick: Rutgers University Press, 2006), xxvii.

10. Cheryl A. Wall, *Worrying the Line: Black Women Writers, Lineage, and Literary Tradition* (Chapel Hill: University of North Carolina Press, 2005), 6.

11. For in-depth discussion of early actresses and stage performers, see Jayna Brown, *Babylon Girls: Black Women Performers and the Shaping of the Modern* (Durham, NC: Duke University Press, 2008), and Nadine George-Graves, *The Royalty of Negro Vaudeville: The Whitman Sisters and the Negotiation of Race, Gender, and Class in African American Theater, 1900–1940* (New York: St. Martin's Press, 2000).

12. Carole Ione, *Pride of Family: Four Generations of American Women of Color* (New York: Harlem Moon, 2004), 174. Carole Ione was the granddaughter of the famous actor Leigh Whipper; her grandmother also performed in vaudeville on the TOBA circuit.

13. Richard Bruce Nugent to Dorothy West, December 5, 1928, on stationery of the Grand Central Hotel, St. Louis, Missouri, in Dorothy West Papers, Schlesinger Library, Radcliffe Institute for Advanced Study, Harvard University.

14. Robert Frost is quoted in *Opportunity: A Journal of Negro Life,* June 1926, 174.

15. See Zora Neale Hurston to Dorothy West and Helene Johnson, May 22, 1926, inviting the women to take her apartment while she traveled through the South collecting folklore, in *Dorothy West: Where the Wild Grape Grows, Selected Writings 1930–1950*, ed. Verner D. Mitchell and Cynthia Davis (Amherst: University of Massachusetts Press, 2005), 182–183.

16. Brown, *Babylon Girls*, 171.

17. Richard Bruce Nugent, *Gentleman Jigger* (Philadelphia: Da Capo, 2008), 106.

18. Desiree French, "Dorothy West: A Child of the Harlem Renaissance Remembers Those Exciting Times," *Boston Globe,* August 12, 1989, 20.

19. Dorothy West to Rachel West, March 12, 1929, in *West: Where the Wild Grape Grows*, 183–184. Thurman's *Harlem: A Melodrama of Negro Life in Harlem* opened on Broadway on February 20, 1929, at the Apollo Theater. After ninety-three performances, mostly to sold-out houses, Thurman took the play on the road to Detroit, Chicago, Toronto, and Los Angeles. For more on the play, see *The Collected Writings of Wallace Thurman*, ed. Amritjit Singh and Daniel M. Scott III (New Brunswick: Rutgers University Press, 2003), 306.

20. Conversation with Abigail McGrath, Helene Johnson's daughter, on June 22, 2008, about the family's interest in and dedication to show business; she recalls the family insisting, even in the 1960s, that the only chances for an attractive woman like herself were marrying a rich man or going into show business.

21. For a conversation about Irene Bordoni, see Johnson's letter to West, December 3, 1929, in *This Waiting for Love: Helene Johnson, Poet of the Harlem Renaissance*, ed. Verner D. Mitchell (Amherst: University of Massachusetts Press,

2000), 108–109. Playbills and correspondence with Irene Bordoni are also in the Dorothy West Papers, Schlesinger Library, Radcliffe Institute for Advanced Study, Harvard University (hereafter DWP).

22. Dorothy West to Rachel West, April 6, 1929, DWP.

23. The account of Ethel Waters and the cigarette is from Abigail McGrath's unpublished novel, "Three Little Women: A Memoir Based on a Couple of Facts." In the 1978 interview with Genii Guinier, Dorothy West attributes the fire to Bertha Baumann and Bessie Trotter: "they were smoking—and a curtain caught fire, and the house burned down" (185). For information on theatrical guests at the Shearer guesthouse, see Jill Nelson, *Finding Martha's Vineyard: African Americans at Home on an Island* (New York: Doubleday, 2005), and Karen E. Hayden and Robert C. Hayden, *African-Americans on Martha's Vineyard and Nantucket: A History of People, Places, and Events* (Boston: Select Publications, 1999).

24. For a discussion of women artists who rejected the "heterosexual imperative" (a term coined by Weiss), see Andrea Weiss, *Paris Was a Woman: Portraits from the Left Bank* (San Francisco: Harper, 1995); Shari Benstock, *Women of the Left Bank* (Austin: University of Texas Press, 1986); Lois Gordon, *Nancy Cunard: Heiress, Muse, Political Idealist* (New York: Columbia University Press, 2007); and Cherene Sherrard Johnson, "'This plague of their own locusts': Space, Property, and Identity in Dorothy West's *The Living Is Easy*," *African American Review* 38, no. 4 (2004): 609–624.

25. All quotations in this paragraph are from Adele Logan Alexander, *Homelands and Waterways: The American Journey of the Bond Family, 1846–1926* (New York: Vintage, 2000), 492. Rachel may have met Carrie Bond Day (1889–1948) since Carrie, a graduate of Radcliffe, had many Boston connections and her cousins were close friends of Rachel's friends Bessie and Maud Trotter. Carrie Bond Day's story "The Pink Hat" won third prize in the 1926 *Opportunity* contest. See Alexander's family memoir, *Homelands and Waterways*, for more on Carrie Bond Day and her circle of artistic and professional women who chose not to marry.

26. See Guinier, "Interview with Dorothy West," 194, for the Eleanora Sears story, and Cleveland Amory, *The Proper Bostonians* (New York: E. P. Dutton, 1947), for a discussion of the prominent Sears family. See "Eleanora Sears Wins," *New York Times,* September 28, 1910, 8, for an account of her September 1910 mixed doubles win.

27. Dorothy West to Rachel West, May 19, 1929, in *This Waiting for Love*, 101.

28. Katrine Dalsgård, "Alive and Well and Living on the Island of Martha's Vineyard: An Interview with Dorothy West, October 29, 1988," *Langston Hughes Review* 12, no. 2 (Fall 1993): 36.

29. The description of BBC broadcasts, activities in London, and John Payne are from *West: Where the Wild Grape Grows*, 30; and *This Waiting for Love*, 101–102. For more on Robeson's visit to England, see Martin Duberman, *Paul Robeson: A Biography* (New York: Ballantine, 1989). For more on John Payne, see Frank Taylor, *Alberta Hunter: A Celebration of the Blues* (New York: McGraw-Hill, 1987).

30. Helene Johnson to Countee Cullen, spring 1929, CCP.

31. Ibid.

32. Countee Cullen to Dorothy West, July 3, 1931, DWP.

33. Gordon, *Nancy Cunard*, 92. Famous lesbians in Paris included the American heiress Natalie Barney and her partners Romaine Brooks (the painter) and

Oscar Wilde's niece, Dolly Wilde; the novelist Djuna Barnes and Thelma Wood (whose previous lover was Edna Millay); and the writer Colette and the Baroness X. Edna, through her close friends the Carl Van Vechtens, probably knew of Gertrude Stein and Alice B. Toklas; actresses Greta Garbo and Mercedes de Acosta; Tallulah Bankhead and Patsy Kelly; and the journalists Janet Flanner and Solita Solano, who was from Boston.

34. Adelaide Cromwell, *The Other Brahmins: Boston's Black Upper Class, 1750–1950* (Fayetteville: University of Arkansas Press, 1994), 139.

35. Verner D. Mitchell, introduction to *This Waiting for Love*, 11. For additional analysis of Johnson's poetry, see Nina Miller, *Making Love Modern: The Intimate Public Worlds of New York's Literary Women* (New York: Oxford University Press, 1998).

36. Wallace Thurman to Dorothy West, in *This Waiting for Love*, 104–105. West's "London" novel is lost and may have vanished in the 1930s during the "robbery" of Zora Neale Hurston's storage unit in which Dorothy's Russian fur coat also disappeared.

CHAPTER 2   THE BENSON FAMILY COMES TO BOSTON

1. Eugenia was born on February 28, 1907; she married Marion Ray Jordan, a military veteran, and died in Onset, Massachusetts, on July 16, 1999, as Eugenia Rickson Jordan (Social Security Death Index, http://ssdi.rootsweb.ancestry.com/).

2. John Johnson, telephone interview with the authors, November 10, 2009; he quotes his mother, Scotter Benson Johnson, and her description of her father. The Dorothy West quotations are from her 1948 novel *The Living Is Easy* (New York: Feminist Press, 1982), 90–91.

3. These manuscripts are in the Dorothy West Papers, Schlesinger Library, Radcliffe Institute for Advanced Study, Harvard University (hereafter DWP).

4. Dorothy West, "Anecdotes Interview with Mrs. Ella Johnson," October 26, 1938, WPA Federal Writers' Project, 1936–1940, Manuscript Division, Library of Congress.

5. Ibid. Also see Ben Benson household, 1880 U.S. census, De Kalb, Kershaw, S.C., roll T9–1232, p. 58.3000, enumeration district 71.

6. See Zora Neale Hurston's autobiography, *Dust Tracks on a Road* (New York: Harper Perennial, 2006); although Ella and Rachel's father was much kinder to them than Hurston's father was to her, their mothers were similar in their passionate dedication to education and social mobility.

7. Dorothy West, "The Purse," in *The Richer, the Poorer: Stories, Sketches, and Reminiscences* (New York: Anchor, 1995), 189–190.

8. Alice Walker, *In Search of Our Mothers' Gardens* (New York: Harcourt Brace, 1983), 230. For a published version of West's WPA interviews with her aunts, see *Dorothy West: Where the Wild Grape Grows, Selected Writings 1930–1950*, ed. Verner D. Mitchell and Cynthia Davis (Amherst: University of Massachusetts Press, 2005).

9. The account of Ella's nursing activities and the Gypsy camp are from Abigail McGrath's unpublished novel "Three Little Women: A Memoir Based on a Couple of Facts." Until 1908, black nurses were trained only at the New England Hospital for Women and Children. The first black registered nurse, Mary Eliza Mahoney, graduated in 1879. In 1908, Dr. Cornelius Garland opened the Plymouth Nurses' Training School and Hospital on E. Spring-

field Street. See John Daniels, *In Freedom's Birthplace* (Boston: Houghton Mifflin, 1914), 187, on Boston's educational opportunities.

10. Abigail McGrath said her mother did not know until she was five that Dorothy and Eugenia were not her sisters. In Genii Guinier, "Interview with Dorothy West, May 6, 1978," in *The Black Women Oral History Project*, ed. Ruth Edmonds Hill (Westport, CT: Meckler, 1991), 169, Dorothy refers to Helen as her sister.
11. Dorothy West, "Fond Memories," in *The Richer, the Poorer*, 172.
12. West, "Anecdotes Interview"; and Dorothy West, "Mrs. Ella Johnson," October 20, 1938, WPA Federal Writers' Project, 1936–1940, Manuscript Division, Library of Congress.
13. Dorothy West, "The Richer, the Poorer," in *The Richer, the Poorer*, 53–57; West, *Where the Wild Grape Grows*, in *West: Where the Wild Grape Grows*, 122–159.
14. McGrath, "Three Little Women."
15. John Johnson, telephone interview with the authors, November 16, 2009.
16. Abigail McGrath, "Afterword: A Daughter Reminisces," in *This Waiting for Love: Helene Johnson, Poet of the Harlem Renaissance*, ed. Verner D. Mitchell (Amherst: University of Massachusetts Press, 2000), 124.
17. McGrath, "Three Little Women."
18. Johnson, telephone interview; also see Karen E. Hayden and Robert C. Hayden, *African-Americans on Martha's Vineyard and Nantucket: A History of People, Places and Events* (Boston: Select Publications, 1999), 183.
19. Dorothy West, "The Purse," in *The Richer, the Poorer*, 183, 190.
20. Rachel's transcriptions of the juke tunes and sketches of herself and her friend Josie Kennedy dancing to them, as well as West's letter to a publisher describing her mother's childhood and soliciting interest in a book about her, are in DWP, folders 37–38.
21. Nadine George-Graves, *The Royalty of Negro Vaudeville: The Whitman Sisters and the Negotiation of Race, Gender and Class in African American Theater, 1900–1940* (New York: St. Martin's Press, 2000), 15.
22. Jayna Brown, *Babylon Girls: Black Women Performers and the Shaping of the Modern* (Durham, NC: Duke University Press, 2008), 105.
23. West, *Living Is Easy*, 29.
24. Katrine Dalsgård, "Alive and Well and Living on the Island of Martha's Vineyard: An Interview with Dorothy West, October 29, 1988," *Langston Hughes Review* 12, no. 2 (Fall 1993): 41.
25. West, *Living Is Easy*, 13.
26. Hurston, *Dust Tracks on a Road*, 13.
27. In her October 20, 1938, WPA interview with Dorothy West, Ella lists one of her residences as Springfield, Mass., a popular destination for southern migrants.
28. Sam B. Warner, *Streetcar Suburbs: The Process of Growth in Boston, 1870–1900* (New York: Atheneum, 1972), 113.
29. Daniels, *In Freedom's Birthplace*, 187.
30. Mary Antin, *The Promised Land* (New York: Penguin, 1997), 210.
31. Daniels, *In Freedom's Birthplace*, 195.
32. At some point Benjamin Benson lived with his daughters because West quotes him as saying that the family needed a home as big as the Boston Museum to accommodate their large brood. In "My Baby," reprinted in *West: Where the Wild Grape Grows*, West pictures her Grampa "in the grandfather chair, chewing tobacco, spitting into a tin can when it was summer and into the stove when it was winter" (89–90).

33. Rachel lived with forty-four-year-old Margaret Gately, a widow, and her twelve-year-old daughter Marguerite. U.S. Bureau of the Census, 1900, Boston, ward 21, Suffolk, MA, roll T623–686, p. 3A.
34. McGrath, "Three Little Women."
35. Johnson, telephone interview, November 10, 2009.
36. Marcel Proust, *Remembrance of Things Past*, trans. Terence Kilmartin and C. K. Scott Moncrief (New York: Random House, 1981), 846.
37. Brown, *Babylon Girls*, 118.
38. Walter J. Stevens, *Chip on My Shoulder* (Boston: Meador, 1946), 35.
39. Dorothy West, "Prologue to a Life" and Hannah Byde," in *West: Where the Wild Grape Grows*, 70–78 and 79–85, respectively; West, "An Unimportant Man," in *The Richer, the Poorer*, 137–160.
40. Dorothy West, "At the Swan Boats," in *West: Where the Wild Grape Grows*, 58–59.
41. West, *Living Is Easy*, 64.
42. The account of the wreck is from "Steamer Dewey Wrecked," *New York Times*, February 16, 1899, 2. See also *Boston City Directory* for the years 1891–1900, Freedman Bank Records, and U.S. Bureau of the Census, 1880, Richmond, Henrico County.
43. *Boston City Directory*, 1900.
44. See Daniels, *In Freedom's Birthplace*, for more information on African American neighborhoods in Boston.
45. West, *Living Is Easy*, 86–87.
46. U.S. Bureau of the Census, 1910, Boston, ward 21, Suffolk, MA, roll T624–623, p. 11B.
47. Rickson's World War I draft registration card, dated September 12, 1918, and filed at the Roxbury (Massachusetts) Court House, lists him as Eugene Franklin Rickson of 131 Warwick Street, Boston. He was born May 25, 1875, is listed as Negro, and was employed as a chauffeur with J. W. Schooner. For nearest relative, he names Minnie C. Rickson of 478 Brookline Avenue.

CHAPTER 3　　PAULINE HOPKINS AND AFRICAN AMERICAN
　　　　　　　　LITERATURE IN NEW ENGLAND

1. For West's comments on Wright and other writers, see Deborah E. McDowell, "Conversations with Dorothy West," in *Harlem Renaissance Re-examined: A Revised and Expanded Edition*, ed. Victor Kramer and Robert Russ (Troy, NY: Whitston, 1997), 72. For comments about Helene Johnson, see Genii Guinier, "Interview with Dorothy West, May 6, 1978," in *The Black Women Oral History Project*, ed. Ruth Edmonds Hill (Westport, CT: Meckler, 1991), 205.
2. Pauline Hopkins, "Address at the Citizens' William Lloyd Garrison Centenary," in *Daughter of the Revolution: The Major Nonfiction Works of Pauline E. Hopkins*, ed. Ira Dworkin (New Brunswick: Rutgers University Press, 2007), 355.
3. West describes the family's church attendance in *The Living Is Easy* (New York: Feminist Press, 1982), 308–309; "Penny" is Eugenia.
4. Dorothy West, "Pluto," in *The Richer, the Poorer: Stories, Sketches, and Reminiscences* (New York: Anchor, 1995), 104.
5. Blythe Coleman is quoted in Yvonne Guzman, "Family and Friends Honor Dottie West in Memorial Service," *Vineyard Gazette,* August 25, 1998, 11. "My eyes can fill with tears when I know that children are hungry," commented West in her 1978 interview with Genii Guinier (198–199). Indica-

tive of her lifelong concern for children, West established and bequeathed her estate to a foundation dedicated to supporting children and needy families, the Dorothy West Charitable Foundation.

6. Lorraine Roses, "Interviews with Black Women Writers: Dorothy West at Oak Bluffs, Massachusetts, July 1984," *SAGE* 2, no. 1 (Spring 1985): 49.

7. Pauline Hopkins, *Contending Forces: A Romance Illustrative of Negro Life North and South* (New York: Oxford University Press, 1988), 82.

8. Pauline Hopkins, "Some Literary Workers," in *Daughter of the Revolution*, 143, 147. Harriet Wilson's 1859 novel, *Our Nig; or, Sketches from the Life of a Free Black*, is now recognized as the first by an African American woman.

9. Pauline Hopkins, *Winona: A Tale of Negro Life in the South and Southwest,"* in *The Magazine Novels of Pauline Hopkins*, ed. Henry Louis Gates (New York: Oxford University Press, 1988), 388.

10. For discussions of Hopkins and fire imagery, see Kate McCullough, "Slavery, Sexuality, and Genre: Pauline Hopkins and the Representation of Female Desire," in *The Unruly Voice: Rediscovering Pauline Elizabeth Hopkins*, ed. John Cullen Gruesser (Urbana: University of Illinois Press, 1996), 21–49; Siobhan Somerville, *Queering the Color Line: Race and the Invention of Homosexuality in American Culture* (Durham, NC: Duke University Press, 2000); and Lori Stone, "Spirit of Resistance: A Study of the Effects of Compulsory Heterosexuality in Selected Novels by African-American Women" (M.A. thesis, University of Illinois, 1994).

11. Pauline Hopkins, "The Mystery within Us," *Colored American Magazine* 1, no. 1 (May 1900): 15.

12. Pauline Hopkins, "Elijah William Smith: A Colored Poet of Early Days," in *Daughter of the Revolution*, 278; Lois Brown, *Pauline Elizabeth Hopkins: Black Daughter of the Revolution* (Chapel Hill: University of North Carolina Press, 2008), 26.

13. Pauline Hopkins, "Phenomenal Vocalists," in *Daughter of the Revolution*, 118.

14. James Whitfield is quoted in Joan Sherman, "James Monroe Whitfield, Poet and Emigrationist: A Voice of Protest and Despair," *Journal of Negro History* 57, no. 2 (April 1972): 173–174; the Frederick Douglass quote is from Victor Ullman, *Martin R. Delaney: The Beginnings of Black Nationalism* (Boston: Bedford, 1971), 145.

15. James Monroe Whitfield, *"America" and Other Poems* (Buffalo, NY: James S. Leavitt, 1853), 9.

16. Pauline Hopkins, "Mark Réné De Mortie," in *Daughter of the Revolution*, 363, 365–366.

17. Brown, *Pauline Elizabeth Hopkins*, 34.

18. Ibid., 61–64. Hopkins writes in *Contending Forces*: "Near the head of G. [Grove] and P. [Phillips] Streets stands the well-known Twelfth Baptist Church . . . world renowned under its beloved pastor and founder, Leonard Grimes" (277).

19. Brown, *Pauline Elizabeth Hopkins*, 46. Records of the marriage are available at the Boston Public Library's microfiche room. We thank Tess Vismale for locating this document for us.

20. Pauline Hopkins, "Autobiographical Sketch," *Colored American Magazine* 2, no. 3 (January 1901): 218.

21. Donald M. Jacobs, ed., *Courage and Conscience: Black and White Abolitionists in Boston* (Bloomington: Indiana University Press, 1993), 228; and *Boston City Directory,* 1865.

22. See, for example, Hopkins, *Contending Forces*, chap. 16. Stewart's address is listed in the 1822 *Boston City Directory* and also in Jacobs, *Courage and Conscience*, 226.
23. Pauline Hopkins, "Rev. Leonard Andrew Grimes," in *Daughter of the Revolution*, 371. For more on Twelfth Baptist Church and the Reverend Thomas Paul, see George Williams, *History of the Twelfth Baptist Church, Boston Mass., From 1840–1874* (Boston: James H. Earle, 1874); and Roy E. Fikenbine, "Boston's Black Churches: Institutional Centers of the Antislavery Movement," in Jacobs, *Courage and Conscience*, 69–89.
24. Fikenbine, "Boston's Black Churches," 180–181. Rock was the first black lawyer certified to try cases before the U.S. Supreme Court.
25. Hopkins, "Autobiographical Sketch," 218.
26. *Annual Report of the School Committee of the City of Boston, 1865* (Boston: J. E. Farwell), 34.
27. Ibid., 103, 188. Also see *Boston Latin and High Schools Tercentenary Report, 1635–1935* (City of Boston Printing Department, 1935), 19, 21.
28. Hopkins's high school records, including the Girls' High School ledger for 1872–1879, are available at Boston's Dearborn Middle School. Although most scholars cite 1859 as Hopkins's birth year, her high school records consistently show that she was born in August 1856. The 1856 birth year is corroborated by the 1865 Massachusetts State Census and the 1870 U.S. Census. Hopkins graduated from Girls' High in 1875 and returned for additional studies in September 1878, when her age was twenty-two years and one month.
29. Brown, *Pauline Elizabeth Hopkins*, 90.
30. Hannah Wallinger, *Pauline E. Hopkins: A Literary Biography* (Athens: University of Georgia Press, 2005), 37.
31. Hopkins, "Autobiographical Sketch," 218.
32. Brown, *Pauline Elizabeth Hopkins*, 107–109.
33. Pauline Hopkins, "One Scene from the Drama of Early Days, in *Daughter of the Revolution*, 7–8.
34. The Hopkins Colored Troubadours program that contains these quotes is reproduced in Wallinger, *Hopkins: A Literary Biography*, 37.
35. Brown, *Pauline Elizabeth Hopkins*, 109, 111–112.
36. Hopkins, "Phenomenal Vocalists," 119–120.
37. Zora Neale Hurston, "Stories of Conflict," *Saturday Review of Literature* 17 (April 2, 1938): 32.
38. Helene Johnson, "Goin' No'th," in *This Waiting for Love: Helene Johnson, Poet of the Harlem Renaissance*, ed. Verner D. Mitchell (Amherst: University of Massachusetts Press, 2000), 63, 66.
39. For example, William Hopkins helped organize a program to celebrate the passage of the Fifteenth Amendment, ratified on February 3, 1870, to grant the franchise to African American men. Military units, civic organizations, and veterans groups convened in the Boston Common on April 14, 1870, and walked the half mile to Faneuil Hall for the 3:00 P.M. program. Participants included Rev. Leonard Grimes, the Hopkins family minister; U.S. senator Charles Sumner; abolitionists Wendell Phillips and William Lloyd Garrison; attorneys Robert Morris and Edwin Garrison Walker; Stephen S. Foster; and novelist William Wells Brown. Pauline and her mother may have attended the ceremony, since William Hopkins served on the Committee of Arrangements, and they may also have met William Wells Brown. The flyer "Boston Celebration of the 15th Amendment, Thursday, April 14th, 1870" is owned by the authors.

40. James Oliver Horton and Lois E. Horton, *Hard Road to Freedom: The Story of African America* (New Brunswick: Rutgers University Press, 2001), 205–206.

41. Paul Laurence Dunbar, "Douglass," in *The Life and Works of Paul Laurence Dunbar*, ed. Lida Keck Wiggins (New York: Dodd, Mead, 1907), 287.

42. Ida B. Wells, "Southern Horrors: Lynch Law in All Its Phases," in *Southern Horrors and Other Writings; The Anti-Lynching Campaign of Ida B. Wells, 1892–1900*, ed. Jacqueline Jones Royster (New York: Bedford, 1996), 64–65.

43. Hopkins, "Some Literary Workers," 144.

44. Dorothy Sterling, *Black Foremothers: Three Lives*, 2nd ed. (New York: Feminist Press, 1988), 93, 96.

45. Pauline Hopkins, "Club Life among Colored Women," in *Daughter of the Revolution*, 179.

46. Wallinger, *Hopkins: A Literary Biography*, 98; Pauline Hopkins, "Women's Department," *Colored American Magazine* 1, no. 2 (June 1900): 121.

47. William Dupree is quoted in Pauline Hopkins, "How a New York Newspaper Man Entertained a Number of Colored Ladies and Gentlemen at Dinner," in *Daughter of the Revolution*, 226–227.

48. Pauline Hopkins, *Of One Blood: Or, the Hidden Self*, in *Magazine Novels of Pauline Hopkins*,, 444.

49. Hopkins, "Higher Education of Colored Women," in *Daughter of the Revolution*, 196.

50. Ibid., and U.S. Federal Census for 1900, Oakland ward 3, Alameda, California, roll T623–82, p. 13A.

51. Adelaide Cromwell, *The Other Brahmins: Boston's Black Upper Class, 1750–1950* (Fayetteville: University of Arkansas Press, 1994), 82.

52. Brown, *Pauline Elizabeth Hopkins*, 410.

53. According to Ira Dworkin (*Daughter of the Revolution*, 357), Hopkins's December 11, 1905, speech at Boston's William Lloyd Garrison Centenary appeared in the *Boston Guardian*, December 16, 1905, 4, under the title "Colored Woman Makes Chief Address." Trotter included another of her speeches in his *The Two Days of Observance of the One Hundredth Anniversary of the Birth of Charles Sumner* (Boston: Boston Sumner Centenary Committee, 1911), 48–49.

54. Pauline Hopkins to Monroe Trotter, April 16, 1905, in *Daughter of the Revolution*, 241.

55. Guinier, "Interview with Dorothy West," 174.

56. Pauline Hopkins, "Whittier, The Friend of the Negro," in *Daughter of the Revolution*, 251–252.

57. Hopkins, "Club Life among Colored Women," 179.

58. Wallinger, *Hopkins: A Literary Biography*, 105–106.

59. Brown, *Pauline Elizabeth Hopkins*, 532.

60. Revealingly, each time she used the pseudonym Shirley Shadrach, she also published an article under Pauline E. Hopkins and/or Sarah A. Allen, which hints that the pseudonyms served to mask the fact that so much of the *Colored American Magazine* on occasion was penned by Hopkins. Dorothy West used a similar tactic while editor of *Challenge* from 1934 to 1937. West explains, "I didn't want to write under my own name, 'cause I edited the book. You can never tell how people will react, 'There she is, writing her own things.'" Katrine Dalsgård, "Alive and Well and Living on the Island of Martha's Vineyard: An Interview with Dorothy West, October 29, 1988," *Langston Hughes Review* 12, no. 2 (Fall 1993): 42.

61. Hopkins, "Autobiographical Sketch," 237.

CHAPTER 4   BOSTON GIRLHOODS, 1910–1925

1. Abigail McGrath, "Afterword: A Daughter Reminisces," in *This Waiting for Love: Helene Johnson, Poet of the Harlem Renaissance*, ed. Verner D. Mitchell (Amherst: University of Massachusetts Press, 2000), 124.

2. Henry Lee Moon, "Black Proper Bostonians," review of *The Living Is Easy*, by Dorothy West, *Crisis* 55, no. 10 (October 1948): 308.

3. Dorothy West, *The Richer, the Poorer: Stories, Sketches, and Reminiscences* (New York: Anchor, 1995), 2; Genii Guinier, "Interview with Dorothy West, May 6, 1978," in *The Black Women Oral History Project*, ed. Ruth Edmonds Hill (Westport, CT: Meckler, 1991), 159.

4. Deborah E. McDowell, "Conversations with Dorothy West," in *Harlem Renaissance Re-examined: A Revised and Expanded Edition*, ed. Victor Kramer and Robert Russ (Troy, NY: Whitston, 1997), 288.

5. Helene Johnson, "Regalia," in *This Waiting for Love*, 47. All future references to Johnson's poems are from this volume.

6. Adelaide Cromwell, *The Other Brahmins: Boston's Black Upper Class, 1750–1950* (Fayetteville: University of Arkansas Press, 1994), 52.

7. Guinier, "Interview with Dorothy West," 197; McDowell, "Conversations with Dorothy West," 300.

8. Guinier, "Interview with Dorothy West," 194; *Boston City Directory*, for the years 1898–1924.

9. Rachel West to Dorothy West, February 10, 1933, Dorothy West Papers, Schlesinger Library, Radcliffe Institute for Advanced Study, Harvard University (hereafter DWP). For more detail on Isaac West's childhood in Richmond, Virginia, and on African American emigration to Massachusetts, see *Dorothy West: Where the Wild Grape Grows, Selected Writings 1930–1950*, ed. Verner D. Mitchell and Cynthia Davis (Amherst: University of Massachusetts Press, 2005).

10. U.S. Bureau of the Census, 1910, Boston, Suffolk County, MA, roll T624–623, p. 11B; *Boston City Directory*, 1910. For a photograph of the Cedar Street house, see *West: Where the Wild Grape Grows*. Eugene and Minnie both worked for a family on Commonwealth Avenue. Rickson was the chauffeur, and Minnie would not have been listed since she lived in with the family.

11. Dorothy West, *The Living Is Easy* (New York: Feminist Press, 1982), 37.

12. Tony Hill, "Where Do We Go from Here: The Politics of Black Education, 1780–1980," *Boston Review*, October 1981, 1. Louise Day Hicks, a politician and lawyer from predominantly Irish South Boston (not to be confused with the African American South End), became known for her staunch opposition to court-ordered busing in the 1960s and 1970s.

13. McGrath, "Afterword," 124.

14. Ibid., 123.

15. Sarah Deutsch, "Boston as a Women's City," *Organization of American Historians Newsletter* 32, no. 1 (February 2004): A8.

16. Cromwell, *Other Brahmins*, 146. Wilson's husband, Butler Wilson, was a prominent lawyer and a longtime president of the NAACP.

17. Maud Cuney Hare to Dorothy West, 1929, Dorothy West Collection, Howard Gotlieb Archival Research Center at Boston University.

18. Helene Johnson, mail interview with Cheryl A. Wall, June 1987.

19. Guinier, "Interview with Dorothy West," 208.

20. McDowell, "Conversations with Dorothy West," 286; and Guinier, "Interview with Dorothy West," 205.

21. McDowell, "Conversations with Dorothy West," 286.
22. Guinier, "Interview with Dorothy West," 189.
23. Dorothy West, "Funeral," in *The Richer, the Poorer*, 63.
24. Guinier, "Interview with Dorothy West," 193, 196.
25. West, *Living Is Easy*, 220.
26. Dorothy West to Carrie Benson, DWP, box 1, folder 1, n.d.
27. Dorothy West, "An Unimportant Man," in *The Richer, the Poorer*, 140.
28. West, *Living Is Easy*, 298.
29. John Johnson, telephone interview with the authors, November 16, 2009.
30. Dorothy West, "The Black Dress," in *West: Where the Wild Grape Grows*, 86–87. Margaret's appearance is identical to F. Scott Fitzgerald's description of Nicole Diver in the beginning of his novel *Tender Is the Night*, which had been published in installments in *Scribner's* magazine, beginning in January 1934. West stated often that Fitzgerald was a model for herself, Wallace Thurman, and other writers of the Harlem Renaissance.
31. West, *Living Is Easy*, 299–300.
32. T. J. Bryan, "Helene Johnson," in *Notable Black American Women*, ed. Jessie Carney Smith, 588–589 (Detroit: Gale, 1992).
33. Dorothy West, "My Baby," in *West: Where the Wild Grape Grows*, 89; the "family genius" quote is from Guinier, "Interview with Dorothy West," 205.
34. McGrath, "Afterword," 125.
35. West, *Living Is Easy*, 299.
36. Cleveland Armory, *The Proper Bostonians* (New York: E. P. Dutton, 1947), 39.
37. Walter J. Stevens, *Chip on My Shoulder* (Boston: Meador, 1946), 85.
38. Guinier, "Interview with Dorothy West," 187.
39. Cromwell, *Other Brahmins*, 158.
40. Guinier, "Interview with Dorothy West," 205. The "bows and curtsies" quote is from West, *Living Is Easy*, 169–170.
41. *Boston Latin and High Schools Tercentenary Report, 1635–1935* (City of Boston Printing Department, 1935), 14.
42. A series of sketches is in the DWP, box 2, folder 37.
43. Dorothy West, "The Gift," in *The Richer, the Poorer*, 177.
44. Guinier, "Interview with Dorothy West," 189.
45. Dr. R. H. Bailey, Registrar, Boston Latin Academy (formerly Girls' Latin School), to the authors, August 19, 1998.
46. Brighton High essay, DWP, box 2, folder 41.
47. Dorothy West, "Fond Memories," in *The Richer, the Poorer*, 172–173.
48. A small, undated notebook in DWP, box 2, folder 23, appears to contain notes for *The Living Is Easy* West writes that Grampa Benson, who taught himself to read, worked for the Kennedy family in South Carolina and was paid one dollar a day. He may have come to Martha's Vineyard with the Kennedys.
49. Dorothy West to Isaac West, August 19, 1912, DWP; in *West: Where the Wild Grape Grows*, 3.
50. West, "Fond Memories," 176.
51. Fern Gillespie, "The Life and Legacy of Lois Mailou Jones," *Howard Magazine* 8, no. 2 (Winter 1999): 10; Barbara Townes is quoted in Jill Nelson, *Finding Martha's Vineyard: African Americans at Home on an Island* (New York: Doubleday, 2005), 61–63.
52. Guinier, "Interview with Dorothy West," 177; the information on Burleigh is from David Levering Lewis, *When Harlem Was in Vogue* (New York: Penguin, 1997), 28–29.

53. Irene Bordoni to Dorothy West, DWP, box 1, folder 5, n.d.

54. Brighton High essay, DWP, box 2, folder 41; in *West: Where the Wild Grape Grows*, 15.

55. *West: Where the Wild Grape Grows*, 16.

56. Eugene Gordon, editorial note on the inside front cover of the *Saturday Evening Quill,* June 1928. West discusses Gordon's invitation in Katrine Dalsgård, "Alive and Well and Living on the Island of Martha's Vineyard: An Interview with Dorothy West," *Langston Hughes Review* 12, no. 2 (Fall 1993): 39–40.

57. Edythe Mae Chapman Gordon Kelley, interviews with the FBI, March 16 and May 19, 1954, , BS 100–14710; information obtained under the Freedom of Information Act.

58. Gordon's World War I draft registration card, dated June 5, 1917, lists his address as 2505 Mozart Place NW, Washington, D.C., and his occupation as Janitor's Assistant for Terrill and Little. Ancestry.com WWI Draft registration cards, 1917–1918; Washington County, District of Columbia; roll 1556844, draft board 9.

59. Lorraine Elena Roses, ed., *Selected Works of Edythe Mae Gordon* (New York: G. K. Hall, 1996), xxi; and Edythe Mae Gordon Kelley, FBI interview, March 16, 1954.

60. Eugene Gordon, FBI files, NY 100–14692.

61. In 1917, Gordon joined the U.S. Army's first officer candidate class for African American men. He was commissioned an officer with Company C, 367th Infantry Regiment, and posted to France. The 367th remained at the front until the Armistice, under almost constant fire in the battles of the Argonne and Metz. Military Personnel Records information obtained under the Freedom of Information Act; National Personnel Records, 9700 Page Avenue, St. Louis, MO 63152.

62. A copy of the article is in the FBI files, NY 100–14692.

63. Eugene Gordon, "The Contest Spotlight," *Opportunity: A Journal of Negro Life,* July 1927, 204.

64. As quoted in Fern Gillespie, "The Life and Legacy of Lois Mailou Jones," *Howard Magazine* 8, no. 2 (Winter 1999): 8.

65. In 1869, Ruffin had become Harvard Law School's first African American graduate. The following year he became the fourth African American to serve in the Massachusetts legislature, succeeding Charles L. Mitchell, John J. Smith, and David Walker's son, Edwin Garrison Walker.

66. Eugene Gordon, "Massachusetts: Land of the Free and Home of the Brave Colored Man," *Messenger* 7, no. 6 (June 1925): 243.

67. Florida Ruffin Ridley, "Other Bostonians," *Saturday Evening Quill,* June 1928, 54–56.

68. After moving to Pittsburgh, Schalk married John W. Johnson, an advertising agent. In 1946, she founded the Pittsburgh chapter of the Jack and Jill Club, an organization dedicated to the development of African American children.

69. Langston Hughes, *The Big Sea* (New York: Hill and Wang, 1998), 219.

70. Waring Cuney, "No Images," in *Caroling Dusk: An Anthology of Verse by Black Poets,* ed. Countee Cullen (New York: Carol Publishing, 1993), 212.

71. Errol Hill and James Vernon Hatch, *A History of African American Theatre* (New York: Cambridge University Press, 2006), 332.

72. The FBI file on Eugene Gordon, 100–14710, states that "the November 3, 1946 issue of the *Boston Chronicle*, a weekly newspaper published in Boston

and devoted to negro affairs, stated its editor, William Edward Harrison, was elected Chairman of the Communist Party Organization in Ward 12, Boston, Massachusetts."

73. The Du Bois and Dunbar Nelson comments are from the April 1929 *Saturday Evening Quill*, in a section titled "Excerpts from Comments on the First Number of *The Saturday Evening Quill.*"

74. FBI files on Eugene Gordon, 100–14692 and 100–14710. A report in file 100–14710 states: "Boston informant T-1, of unknown reliability, an individual in a position to know of the Communist Party's efforts to infiltrate various organizations in Boston, Massachusetts in the 1920's and early 1930's, advised that during the late 1920's, the Theatrical Group of the Ford Hall Forum, as well as the Saturday Evening Quill Club, were Communist infiltrated."

75. FBI file 100–14710 on Eugene Gordon.

76. Edythe Mae Gordon Kelley, FBI interviews.

77. June was born Sonia Croll in Odessa in 1901. She entered the United States illegally and married Carl Reeve, executive chairman of the Communist Party of Pennsylvania and Delaware. After marrying Eugene Gordon, June assumed the alias Mrs. Langston Hughes to evade the Immigration and Naturalization Service. She eventually became the executive director of the Emma Lazarus Federation of Jewish Women's Clubs. See Cynthia Davis and Verner Mitchell, "Eugene Gordon, Dorothy West, and the Saturday Evening Quill Club," *CLA Journal* 52, no. 4 (June 2009): 393–408.

78. Dorothy West to Langston Hughes, February 2, 1934, in *West: Where the Wild Grape Grows*, 200.

79. Gwendolyn Bennett, "The Ebony Flute," *Opportunity: A Journal of Negro Life,* October 1926, 322.

80. In the April 1929 *Saturday Evening Quill*, in a section titled "Excerpts from Comments on the First Number of *The Saturday Evening Quill.*"

81. Charles S. Johnson to Dorothy West, May 4, 1926, in *West: Where the Wild Grape Grows*, 180–182.

82. As quoted in Gwendolyn Bennett, "The Ebony Flute," *Opportunity: A Journal of Negro Life,* September 1926, 292.

83. Gwendolyn Bennett, "The Ebony Flute," *Opportunity: A Journal of Negro Life,* December 1926, 391.

CHAPTER 5   THE YOUNGEST MEMBERS OF THE
             HARLEM RENAISSANCE, 1926–1931

1. Genii Guinier, "Interview with Dorothy West, May 6, 1978," in *The Black Women Oral History Project*, ed. Ruth Edmonds Hill (Westport, CT: Meckler, 1991), 165.

2. Valerie Boyd, *Wrapped in Rainbows: The Life of Zora Neale Hurston* (New York: Scribner, 2002), 184; also see letters from Hurston to Helene Johnson and Dorothy West, November 22 and December 5, 1928, in *This Waiting for Love: Helene Johnson, Poet of the Harlem Renaissance*, ed. Verner D. Mitchell (Amherst: University of Massachusetts Press, 2000), 99–100. All Helene Johnson poems quoted in the text are from this volume.

3. Frost is quoted in *Opportunity: A Journal of Negro Life,* September 1926, 292, and June 1926, 174.

4. Gwendolyn Bennett, "The Ebony Flute," *Opportunity: A Journal of Negro Life,* July 1926, 232; Charles S. Johnson quotes Toomer in a letter to Dorothy

West, June 28, 1926, Dorothy West Papers, Schlesinger Library, Radcliffe Institute for Advanced Study, Harvard University (hereafter DWP).

5. Blanche Colton Williams, introduction to *O. Henry Memorial Award Prize Stories of 1926* (New York: Doubleday, 1928), vii.

6. Sharon Jones, *Rereading the Harlem Renaissance: Race, Class, and Gender in the Fiction of Jessie Fauset, Zora Neale Hurston, and Dorothy West* (New York: Praeger, 2002), 156.

7. Margaret Perry, *Silence to the Drums: A Survey of the Literature of the Harlem Renaissance* (Westport, CT: Greenwood, 1976), 133.

8. Helene Johnson to Countee Cullen, December 17, 1926, Countee Cullen Papers, Amistad Research Center, Tulane University (hereafter CCP).

9. Purnell eventually left Mexico and moved to Los Angeles, where she worked in the aircraft industry during the war and later became a leader in the Church of Scientology in L.A.

10. Verner D. Mitchell, introduction to *This Waiting for Love*, 12–13.

11. Wallace Thurman, "Negro Poets and Their Poetry," in *The Collected Writings of Wallace Thurman*, ed. Amritjit Singh and Daniel M. Scott III (New Brunswick: Rutgers University Press, 2003), 210.

12. Helene Johnson, "Trees at Night" and "A Southern Road," in *This Waiting for Love*, 23, 35. All Helene Johnson poems cited in the text are from this volume.

13. Thomas H. Wirth, introduction to *Gentleman Jigger*, by Richard Bruce Nugent (Philadelphia: Da Capo 2008), xi.

14. Ibid., xii. The British writer Ronald Firbank (1886–1926) penned witty, conversational novels designed to épater le bourgeois; they usually involved interracial and homoerotic romance and campy scenes of clerics chasing naked choirboys around ancient cathedrals.

15. Cheryl A. Wall, foreword to *This Waiting for Love*, x.

16. Helene Johnson to Countee Cullen, December 17, 1926, CCP.

17. Dorothy West, "Elephant's Dance," in *The Richer, the Poorer: Stories, Sketches, and Reminiscences* (New York: Anchor, 1995), 217.

18. Countee Cullen, "Poet on Poet," *Opportunity: A Journal of Negro Life,* February 1926, 73.

19. Langston Hughes, "The Negro Artist and the Racial Mountain," *Nation* 122 (June 23, 1926): 692.

20. Abigail McGrath, "Afterword: A Daughter Reminisces," in *This Waiting for Love*, 123.

21. Wallace Thurman, *Infants of the Spring* (Boston: Northeastern University Press, 1992), 230–231.

22. Genii Guinier, "Interview with Dorothy West, May 6, 1978," in *The Black Women Oral History Project*, ed. Ruth Edmonds Hill (Westport, CT: Meckler, 1991), 183.

23. Nugent, *Gentleman Jigger*, 72, 74.

24. Guinier, "Interview with Dorothy West," 183.

25. Helene Johnson, mail interview by Cheryl A. Wall, June 1987.

26. Eugene Gordon, "Negro Fictionists in America," *Saturday Evening Quill,* April 1929, 20. John "Jack" Wheeler was a newspaperman who formed the Wheeler Syndicate to distribute sports, comic strips, and other features. He published work by Ring Lardner, Joseph Alsop, and F. Scott Fitzgerald and sent Hemingway to Spain to cover the Civil War. Gordon refers here to the stories West wrote for his column in the *Boston Post* that were distributed through the syndicate.

27. Gwendolyn Bennett, "The Ebony Flute," *Opportunity: A Journal of Negro Life,* October 1926, 322.

28. Gwendolyn Bennett, "The Ebony Flute," *Opportunity: A Journal of Negro Life,* December 1926, 391.

29. Danica Kirka, "Dorothy West—A Voice of Harlem Renaissance Talks of Past," *Los Angeles Times,* January 1, 1995.

30. James Weldon Johnson, *Black Manhattan* (New York: Da Capo, 1991), 160–161.

31. Wallace Thurman, "Negro Life in New York's Harlem," in *Collected Writings of Wallace Thurman,* 40–41, 46–47.

32. All information on Washington is from Donald Bogle, *Bright Boulevards, Bold Dreams: The Story of Black Hollywood* (New York: Ballantine, 2005), and Isabel Washington Powell, telephone interview with the authors, January 22, 2003.

33. Dorothy West, "Cocktail Party," in *A Renaissance in Harlem,* ed. Lionel C. Bascom (New York: Amistad, 2001), 275.

34. Powell, telephone interview.

35. The description is from a review found in the Wallace Thurman Papers, James Weldon Johnson Memorial Collection, MSS 12, box 3, folder 44, Beinecke Library, Yale University.

36. Wallace Thurman to Dorothy West and Helene Johnson, August 30, 1929, in *Dorothy West: Where the Wild Grape Grows, Selected Writings 1930–1950,* ed. Verner D. Mitchell and Cynthia Davis (Amherst: University of Massachusetts Press, 2005), 185.

37. Bogle, *Bright Boulevards, Bold Dreams,* 151.

38. Dorothy West, *The Wedding* (New York: Anchor, 1995), 97.

39. Deborah E. McDowell, "Conversations with Dorothy West," in *Harlem Renaissance Re-examined: A Revised and Expanded Edition,* ed. Victor Kramer and Robert Russ (Troy, NY: Whitston, 1997), 293.

40. Nugent, *Gentleman Jigger,* 20.

41. McDowell, "Conversations with Dorothy West," 293; Katrine Dalsgård, "Alive and Well and Living on the Island of Martha's Vineyard: An Interview with Dorothy West," *Langston Hughes Review* 12, no. 2 (Fall 1993): 33.

42. Noel Riley Fitch, *Anaïs: The Erotic Life of Anaïs Nin* (New York: Little Brown, 1993), 45–47.

43. Boyd, *Wrapped in Rainbows,* 130.

44. Sam See, " 'Spectacles in Color': The Primitive Drag of Langston Hughes," *PMLA* 124, no. 3 (May 2009): 799.

45. Helene Johnson to Dorothy West, December 8, 1932, in *This Waiting for Love,* 115.

46. Frank Byrd, "Harlem Parties: Interview of Alonzo Thayer," WPA Federal Writers' Project Collection, Manuscript Division, Library of Congress.

47. Dorothy West to Rachel West, May 19, 1929, in *This Waiting for Love,* 101.

48. See Arnold Rampersad, *The Life of Langston Hughes* (New York: Oxford University Press, 1986), 1:66–72, for a discussion of the sexuality of Cullen, Hughes, and Alain Locke, and of Cullen's interest in marriage.

49. Helene Johnson to Dorothy West, February 24, 1931, in *This Waiting for Love,* 111.

50. Richard Bruce Nugent to Dorothy West, December 5, 1928, DWP.

51. Dorothy West to Countee Cullen, March 18, 1931, CCP.

52. Dorothy West to Countee Cullen, March 13, 1931, CCP.

53. West to Cullen, March 18, 1931, CCP. In the same letter, West writes, "You are sweet to say you want me to write to you again in that vein."

54. Dorothy West to Countee Cullen, Sunday, 1931[?], CCP.

55. Countee Cullen to Dorothy West, April 16, 1931, Dorothy West Collection, Howard Gotlieb Archival Research Center at Boston University.

56. Countee Cullen to Dorothy West, May 7, 1931, Dorothy West Collection, Howard Gotlieb Archival Research Center at Boston University.

57. McDowell, "Conversations with Dorothy West," 270; see also the *Vineyard Gazette*, March 12, 1948.

58. Blanche Colton Williams, *Our Short Story Writers* (Freeport, NY: Books for Libraries Press, 1969), ii. For West's comments on Williams, see McDowell, "Conversations with Dorothy West," 281.

59. Williams, *Our Short Story Writers*, 202.

60. "History of the Colton Family in the United States," http://freepages. genealogy.rootsweb.ancestry.com/~coltoninfo/blanchcoltonwilliams.htm.

61. Dorothy Scarborough, letter to the editor, *Opportunity: A Journal of Negro Life*, June 1926, 194. For more on Scarborough, see Michael P. Dougan, "Dorothy Scarborough," in *American National Biography*, ed. John Garraty and Mark Carnes, 19:345–346 (New York: Oxford University Press, 1999).

62. West's class notebook, DWP, box 1, folder 12.

63. Guinier, "Interview with Dorothy West," 159.

64. Dorothy Scarborough to Dorothy West, February 1928, DWP, box 1, folder 12.

65. Dorothy Scarborough to Dorothy West, 1931, DWP, box 1, folder 11.

66. Dorothy West to Countee Cullen, September 6, 1933, in *West: Where the Wild Grape Grows*, 198.

67. Zora Neale Hurston to Dorothy West and Helene Johnson, May 22, 1927, in *This Waiting for Love*, 97.

68. For stories by Edythe Mae Gordon, Hazzard, and Harmon, see Lorraine Elena Roses and Ruth E. Randolph, eds., *Harlem's Glory: Black Women Writing, 1900–1950* (Cambridge: Harvard University Press, 1996).

69. Eugene Gordon, "The Opportunity Dinner: An Impression," *Opportunity: A Journal of Negro Life*, July 1927, 208.

70. West's class notebook, DWP, box 1, folder 12.

71. Helene Johnson to Dorothy West, April 24, 1933, in *This Waiting for Love*, 120.

72. Glenda E. Gill, *A Study of the Federal Theatre, 1935–1939* (New York: Peter Lang, 1989), 67.

73. George W. Henry, *Sex Variants: A Study of Homosexual Patterns* (New York: Paul Hoebber, 1948), 563.

74. Abigail McGrath, interview with the authors, September 15, 2008.

75. Abigail McGrath, interview with the authors, October 8, 2008.

76. Henry, *Sex Variants*, 566.

77. Gwendolyn Bennett, "The Ebony Flute," *Opportunity: A Journal of Negro Life*, November 1927, 340.

78. John Houseman, *Run-Through: A Memoir* (New York: Simon and Schuster, 1972), 97.

79. Abigail McGrath, telephone interview with the authors, August 18, 2008; and West to Cullen, March 13, 1931, CCP.

80. McGrath, telephone interview.

81. Gill, *Study of the Federal Theatre*, 72, 74.

82. Julie Kavanagh, *Secret Muses: The Life of Frederick Ashton* (New York: Pantheon, 1997), 81–82.
83. *New York Age*, May 20, 1939, in Edna Thomas vertical file, Moorland-Spingarn Research Center, Howard University; Gil, *Study of the Federal Theatre*, 69.
84. Gill, *Study of the Federal Theatre*, 6, 67.
85. *New York Age*, November 6, 1920, 6, in Edna Thomas vertical file, Moorland-Spingarn Research Center.
86. Gill, *Study of the Federal Theatre*, 75 (quotation), 70.
87. *Washington Afro-American*, February 11, 1939, in Edna Thomas vertical file, Moorland-Spingarn Research Center.
88. Dorothy West to Rachel West, March 12, 1929, in *West: Where the Wild Grape Grows*, 183–84.
89. Richard Bruce Nugent, "On Rose McClendon," in *Gay Rebel of the Harlem Renaissance: Selections from the Work of Richard Bruce Nugent*, ed. Thomas H. Wirth (Durham, NC: Duke University Press, 2002), 216.
90. Rose McClendon to Dorothy West, DWP, box 1, folder 12.
91. Helene Johnson to Dorothy West, December 8, 1932, in *This Waiting for Love*, 116.
92. AADA was founded in 1884 by Franklin Haven Sargent, a speech professor at Harvard, after the university refused to open a drama school. When McClendon attended, the school was housed in Carnegie Hall.
93. Nugent, "On Rose McClendon," 215.
94. Houseman, *Run-Through*, 129.
95. The Helbrun and Crawford quotes are from Cheryl Crawford, *One Naked Individual: My Fifty Years in the Theatre* (New York: Bobbs-Merrill, 1977), 33.
96. Dorothy West to Rachel West, April 2, 1929, DWP.
97. Dorothy West to Rachel West, April 12[?], 1929, DWP.
98. Wallace Thurman to Dorothy West, August 30, 1929, in *This Waiting for Love*, 103.
99. Dorothy West to Rachel West, May 19, 1929, in *This Waiting for Love*, 101.
100. Thurman to West, August 30, 1929.
101. Countee Cullen to Dorothy West, October 10, 1929, DWP, in *West: Where the Wild Grape Grows*, 31.
102. Zora Neale Hurston to Langston Hughes, winter 1929, in *Zora Neale Hurston: A Life in Letters*, ed. Carla Kaplan (New York: Doubleday, 2002), 158.
103. Countee Cullen to Dorothy West, August 25, 1930, DWP.
104. Helene Johnson to Dorothy West, December 3, 1929, in *This Waiting for Love*, 108.
105. Zora Neale Hurston to Dorothy West, November 5, 1928, in *Hurston: A Life in Letters*, 129–130.

CHAPTER 6   RUSSIAN INTERLUDE, LITERARY SALONS, AND CHALLENGE

1. Dorothy West, "Elephant's Dance," in *The Richer, the Poorer: Stories, Sketches, and Reminiscences* (New York: Anchor, 1995), 224.
2. Genii Guinier, "Interview with Dorothy West, May 6, 1978," in *The Black Women Oral History Project*, ed. Ruth Edmonds Hill (Westport, CT: Meckler, 1991), 169.
3. Dorothy West to Countee Cullen, July 4, 1933, Countee Cullen Papers, Amistad Research Center, Tulane University (hereafter CCP).

4. Helene Johnson to Dorothy West, December 3, 1929, in *This Waiting for Love: Helene Johnson, Poet of the Harlem Renaissance*, ed. Verner D. Mitchell (Amherst: University of Massachusetts Press, 2000), 108; Guinier, "Interview with Dorothy West," 172.

5. Helene Johnson to Dorothy West, October 23, 1930, in *This Waiting for Love*, 110.

6. Zora Neale Hurston to Dorothy West, January 1931, in *Zora Neale Hurston: A Life in Letters*, ed. Carla Kaplan (New York: Doubleday, 2002), 199–200.

7. Thank-you note from McClendon with a notation that Marbury had sent roses, in the Dorothy West Papers, Schlesinger Library, Radcliffe Institute for Advanced Study, Harvard University (hereafter DWP).

8. Dorothy West to Countee Cullen, March 13, 1931, CCP.

9. Guinier, "Interview with Dorothy West," 169.

10. Valerie Boyd, *Wrapped in Rainbows: The Life of Zora Neale Hurston* (New York: Scribner, 2002), 216.

11. Zora Neale Hurston to Charlotte Mason, January 12, 1931, in *Hurston: A Life in Letters*, 200.

12. Zora Neale Hurston to Dorothy West, June 11, 1931, in *Hurston: A Life in Letters*, 221.

13. As quoted in Alfred Lewis, *Ladies and Not-So-Gentle Women* (New York: Penguin, 2000), 415.

14. Elisabeth Marbury, *My Crystal Ball* (New York: Boni and Liveright, 1923), 45, 193.

15. Lewis, *Ladies and Not-So-Gentle Women*, 392.

16. West, "Elephant's Dance," 224.

17. Guinier, "Interview with Dorothy West," 169.

18. Lewis, *Ladies and Not-So-Gentle Women*, 391.

19. Guinier, "Interview with Dorothy West," 169.

20. West, "Elephant's Dance," 224.

21. Cecil Beaton, *The Glass of Fashion* (London: Weidenfeld and Nicolson, 1954), 207, 204.

22. Ruth Franklin, "A Life in Good Taste," *New Yorker,* September 27, 2004, 142.

23. "The Sun Parlor" is reprinted in West, *The Richer, the Poorer*, 195–199.

24. Marbury, *My Crystal Ball*, 302.

25. *This Waiting for Love*, 90.

26. See *Dorothy West: Where the Wild Grape Grows, Selected Writings 1930–1950*, ed. Verner D. Mitchell and Cynthia Davis (Amherst: University of Massachusetts Press, 2005), for four of the WPA essays.

27. Zora Neale Hurston to Dorothy West, March 22, 1937, in *This Waiting for Love*, 121.

28. Guinier, "Interview with Dorothy West," 220.

29. Helene Johnson to Dorothy West, October 23, 1930, in *This Waiting for Love*, 110.

30. Zora Neale Hurston to Charlotte Mason, July 6, 1932, in *Hurston: A Life in Letters*, 263.

31. Guinier, "Interview with Dorothy West," 173.

32. Dorothy West to Claude McKay, September 13, 1935, in *West: Where the Wild Grape Grows*, 204–205.

33. Zora Neale Hurston to Carl Van Vechten, October 23, 1937, in *Hurston: A Life in Letters*, 408.

34. Countee Cullen to Dorothy West, May 10, 1932, DWP.

35. Dorothy West to Countee Cullen, June 3, 1932, CCP.
36. Helene Johnson, "Monotone," in *This Waiting for Love*, 58. All quotations of Helene Johnson's poems are from this volume.
37. Homer Smith, *Black Man in Red Russia* (Chicago: Johnson Publishing, 1964), 25.
38. Langston Hughes, *I Wonder as I Wander* (New York: Hill and Wang, 1956), 73.
39. Dorothy West to Carrie Benson, summer 1932, DWP.
40. Dorothy West [Mary Christopher], "Room in Red Square," *Challenge* 1, no. 1 (March 1934): 10.
41. Dorothy West to Rachel West, June 29, 1932, in *West: Where the Wild Grape Grows*, 186–187.
42. Smith, *Black Man in Red Russia*, 26.
43. Guinier, "Interview with Dorothy West," 164.
44. Dorothy West to Rachel West, July 1932, in *West: Where the Wild Grape Grows*, 187.
45. Dorothy West to Rachel West, June 29, 1932, in *West: Where the Wild Grape Grows*, 186.
46. Dorothy West to Rachel West, July 1932, in *West: Where the Wild Grape Grows*, 188.
47. Smith, *Black Man in Red Russia*, 29.
48. Chester Himes, *Pinktoes* (Jackson, MS: Banner Books, 1996), 26. Census records show that Mollie Lewis was born on July 31, 1907.
49. Guinier, "Interview with Dorothy West," 220.
50. Ibid.
51. Dorothy West, "Cocktail Party," in *A Renaissance in Harlem*, ed. Lionel C. Bascom (New York: Amistad, 2001), 271.
52. Guinier, "Interview with Dorothy West," 220.
53. Helene Johnson to Dorothy West, December 8, 1932, in *This Waiting for Love*, 118.
54. "The Urban League Guild," *Opportunity: A Journal of Negro Life,* October–December 1947, 205.
55. Himes, *Pinktoes*, 26; Mollie Moon, "Personal Statement," August 29, 1977, in response to a questionnaire authored by Jessie Carney Smith, Special Collections, Franklin Library, Fisk University.
56. "Urban League Campaign Gets Underway," *Opportunity: A Journal of Negro Life,* July–September 1947, 152.
57. "Urban League Guild," 205.
58. Guinier, "Interview with Dorothy West," 219.
59. Dorothy West to Rachel West, June 18, 1932, DWP, in *West: Where the Wild Grape Grows*, 33.
60. Dorothy West [Mary Christopher], "Russian Correspondence," *Challenge* 1, no. 2 (September 1934): 14–15.
61. Langston Hughes to Carl Van Vechten, March 1, 1933, in *Remember Me to Harlem: The Letters of Langston Hughes and Carl Van Vechten, ed. Emily Bernard* (New York: Knopf, 2001), 102.
62. Smith, *Black Man in Red Russia*, 29.
63. Dorothy West to Langston Hughes, October 27, 1932, in *West: Where the Wild Grape Grows*, 190.
64. For more on the W. A. Scott–Mildred Jones marriage, see Leonard Ray Teel, "W. A. Scott and the Atlanta *World*," *American Journalism* 6, no. 3 (1989): 158–178.

65. West to Hughes, October 27, 1932.
66. Hughes to Van Vechten, March 1, 1933.
67. Dorothy West to Rachel West, March 6, 1933, in *West: Where the Wild Grape Grows*, 192.
68. Deborah E. McDowell, "Conversations with Dorothy West," in *Harlem Renaissance Re-examined: A Revised and Expanded Edition*, ed. Victor Kramer and Robert Russ (Troy, NY: Whitston, 1997), 293.
69. Wallace Thurman to Dorothy West, in *This Waiting for Love*, 104–105.
70. Katrine Dalsgård, "Alive and Well and Living on the Island of Martha's Vineyard: An Interview with Dorothy West," *Langston Hughes Review* 12, no. 2 (Fall 1993): 36.
71. The letters are in *This Waiting for Love*, 114, 117.
72. Dorothy West to Countee Cullen, June 4, 1933, CCP.
73. Dorothy West to Countee Cullen, December 1933, CCP.
74. Dorothy West to James Weldon Johnson, October 23, 1933, in *West: Where the Wild Grape Grows*, 198.
75. Countee Cullen to Dorothy West, July 16, 1933, DWP.
76. Joyce Durham, "Dorothy West and the Importance of Black 'Little' Magazines of the 1930s: *Challenge* and *New Challenge*," *Langston Hughes Review* 16, nos. 1 and 2 (Fall/Spring 1999–2001): 21.
77. Langston Hughes to Dorothy West, February 22, 1924, in *West: Where the Wild Grape Grows*, 201.
78. Durham, "Dorothy West and the Importance of Black 'Little' Magazines," 26.
79. McDowell, "Conversations with Dorothy West," 291.
80. Durham, "Dorothy West and the Importance of Black 'Little' Magazines," 29, 31.
81. Marian Minus, "The Fine Line," *Opportunity: A Journal of Negro Life,* November 1939, 336.
82. Dorothy West, "Ghost Story: Interview of Laura Minus," November 18, 1938, WPA Federal Writers' Project, 1936–1940, Manuscript Division, Library of Congress.
83. Guinier, "Interview with Dorothy West," 154–55.
84. Marian Minus to Dorothy West, n.d., DWP.
85. Marian Minus to Dorothy West, August 1936, DWP.
86. Marian Minus to Dorothy West, October 21, 1936, in *West: Where the Wild Grape Grows*, 209.
87. Dalsgård, "Alive and Well," 39.
88. Hazel Rowley, *Richard Wright: The Life and Times* (New York: Henry Holt, 2001), 122.
89. Dalsgård, "Alive and Well," 39.
90. Margaret Walker, *Richard Wright: Daemonic Genius* (New York: Amistad, 1988), 91.
91. Minus's essays "Cultural Contacts in Malaysia as Seen through Mythology" and "Weaving Techniques in the Peruvian Area" are part of the Robert Redfield Papers, Special Collections Research Center, University of Chicago.
92. Dorothy West to Rachel West, October 1938, DWP.
93. Alumni Directory information submitted by Marian Minus, September 25, 1969, Special Collections, Franklin Library, Fisk University.
94. Richard Wright, "Blueprint for Negro Writing," *New Challenge* 2, no. 2 (Fall 1937): 53.
95. Countee Cullen to Dorothy West, May 16, 1938, DWP.

96. Langston Hughes, September 7, 1934, in *West: Where the Wild Grape Grows*, 203–204.
97. Elmer Carter to Harry Shaw, April 11, 1938, DWP.
98. Dorothy West to Countee Cullen, January 26, 1945, in *West: Where the Wild Grape Grows*, 44.
99. Marian Minus, "Twice in His Lifetime," *Woman's Day*, December 1949, 40.
100. As quoted in Verner D. Mitchell, introduction to *This Waiting for Love*, 10.
101. Abigail McGrath, e-mail to the authors, October 22, 2001; and McGrath, "Afterword," 125.
102. Zora Neale Hurston, *Dust Tracks on a Road* (New York: Harper Perennial, 2006), 277.

Epilogue

1. Abigail McGrath, "Afterword: A Daughter Reminisces," in *This Waiting for Love: Helene Johnson, Poet of the Harlem Renaissance*, ed. Verner D. Mitchell (Amherst: University of Massachusetts Press, 2000), 125.
2. For more on the film, see Peter Donaldson, "Shakespeare on Stage: Liz White's *Othello*," *Shakespeare Quarterly* 38, no. 4 (Winter 1987): 482–495. The West quote is from James Saunders and Renae Shackelford, eds., *The Dorothy West Martha's Vineyard* (Jefferson, NC: McFarland, 2001), 118.
3. Adelaide M. Cromwell, afterword to *The Living Is Easy*, by Dorothy West (New York: Feminist Press, 1982), 349, 350.

Selected Bibliography

Manuscript Collections

Sybille Bedford Papers. Manuscript Division, Harry Ransom Humanities Research Center, University of Texas at Austin.

Countee Cullen Papers, 1900–1947 (CCP). Manuscript Division, Amistad Research Center, Tulane University, New Orleans.

Countee Cullen/Harold Jackman Memorial Collection, 1881–1995. Archives and Special Collections, Woodruff Library, Atlanta University Center.

Eugene Gordon Papers, 1927–1972. Manuscript Division, Schomburg Center for Research in Black Culture, New York Public Library.

Marian Minus Papers. Alumni Records, Special Collections, Franklin Library, Fisk University, Nashville, TN.

Robert Redfield Papers. Special Collections Research Center, University of Chicago.

Ruffin Family Papers, 1832–1936, and Edna Thomas vertical file, Manuscript Division, Moorland-Spingarn Research Center, Howard University, Washington, DC.

Wallace Thurman Papers. James Weldon Johnson Memorial Collection, Beinecke Rare Book and Manuscript Library, Yale University, New Haven.

Dorothy West Papers, 1914–1985 (DWP). Schlesinger Library, Radcliffe Institute for Advanced Study, Harvard University, Cambridge.

Dorothy West Collection. Howard Gotlieb Archival Research Center at Boston University.

WPA Federal Writers' Project Collection. Manuscript Division, Library of Congress, Washington, DC.

Interviews by the Authors

Cromwell, Adelaide M. Telephone interview: April 4, 2003.

Franklin, Barbara L. Personal interview, New Haven, CT: June 20, 2002. Telephone interviews: November 15 and 20, 2001, and April 8, 2002.

Franklin, K. Courtney. Personal interview, New Haven, CT: June 20, 2002.

Johnson, John. Telephone interviews: November 10 and 16, 2009.

McGrath, Abigail. Telephone interviews: August 1, 2002, and June 22, August 18, September 15, and October 8, 2008. E-mail interviews: October 22, 2001, and January 19 and August 30, 2010.

Powell, Isabel Washington. Telephone interviews: October 25, 2001, and January 22, 2003.

BOOKS AND ARTICLES

Alexander, Adele Logan. *Homelands and Waterways: The American Journey of the Bond Family, 1846–1926.* New York: Vintage, 2000.

Amory, Cleveland. *The Proper Bostonians.* New York: E. P. Dutton, 1947.

Annual Report of the School Committee of the City of Boston, 1865. Boston: J. E. Farwell, 1865.

Antin, Mary. *The Promised Land.* 1912. Reprint, New York: Penguin, 1997.

Beaton, Cecil. *The Glass of Fashion.* London: Weidenfeld and Nicolson, 1954.

Bennett, Gwendolyn. "The Ebony Flute." *Opportunity: A Journal of Negro Life,* September (1926): 292–293; October (1926): 322–323; December (1926): 391; January (1927): 29; July (1927): 212–213.

Benstock, Shari. *Women of the Left Bank.* Austin: University of Texas Press, 1986.

Bernard, Emily, ed. *Remember Me to Harlem: The Letters of Langston Hughes and Carl Van Vechten.* New York: Knopf, 2001.

"Black Entrepreneurs of the Eighteenth and Nineteenth Centuries." Boston: Federal Reserve Bank of Boston and the Museum of African American History, 2009–2010. http://www.economicadventure.org/visit/exhibits/black-entrepreneurs/brochure.pdf.

Bogle, Donald. *Bright Boulevards, Bold Dreams: The Story of Black Hollywood.* New York: Ballantine, 2005.

Boston Latin and High Schools Tercentenary Report, 1635–1935. City of Boston Printing Department, 1935.

Boyd, Valerie. *Wrapped in Rainbows: The Life of Zora Neale Hurston.* New York: Scribner, 2002.

Brown, Jayna. *Babylon Girls: Black Women Performers and the Shaping of the Modern.* Durham, NC: Duke University Press, 2008.

Brown, Lois. *Pauline Elizabeth Hopkins: Black Daughter of the Revolution.* Chapel Hill: University of North Carolina Press, 2008.

Bryan, T. J. "Helene Johnson." In *Notable Black American Women,* edited by Jessie Carney Smith, 587–591. Detroit: Gale, 1992.

Crawford, Cheryl. *One Naked Individual: My Fifty Years in the Theatre.* New York: Bobbs-Merrill, 1977.

Cromwell, Adelaide M. Afterword to *The Living Is Easy,* by Dorothy West, 349–364. New York: Feminist Press, 1982.

————. *The Other Brahmins: Boston's Black Upper Class, 1750–1950.* Fayetteville: University of Arkansas Press, 1994.

Cullen, Countee. "Poet on Poet." *Opportunity: A Journal of Negro Life* 4, no. 38 (February 1926): 73–74.

Dalsgård, Katrine. "Alive and Well and Living on the Island of Martha's Vineyard: An Interview with Dorothy West, October 29, 1988." *Langston Hughes Review* 12, no. 2 (Fall 1993): 28–44.

Daniels, John. *In Freedom's Birthplace.* Boston: Houghton Mifflin, 1914.

Davis, Cynthia, and Verner D. Mitchell. "Eugene Gordon, Dorothy West, and the Saturday Evening Quill Club." *CLA Journal* 52, no. 4 (June 2009): 393–408.

Deutsch, Sarah. "Boston as a Women's City." *Organization of American Historians Newsletter* 32, no. 1 (February 2004): A1, A8.

Donaldson, Peter. "Shakespeare on Stage: Liz White's *Othello*." *Shakespeare Quarterly* 38, no. 4 (Winter 1987): 482–495.

Dougan, Michael P. "Dorothy Scarborough." In *American National Biography*, edited by John Garraty and Mark Carnes, 19:345–346. New York: Oxford University Press, 1999.

Duberman, Martin. *Hidden from History: Reclaiming the Gay and Lesbian Past*. New York: Plume, 1990.

———. *Paul Robeson: A Biography*. New York: Ballantine, 1989.

Durham, Joyce. "Dorothy West and the Importance of Black 'Little' Magazines of the 1930s: *Challenge* and *New Challenge*." *Langston Hughes Review* 16, nos. 1 and 2 (Fall/Spring 1999–2001): 19–31.

Dworkin, Ira, ed. *Daughter of the Revolution: The Major Nonfiction Works of Pauline E. Hopkins*. New Brunswick: Rutgers University Press, 2007.

"Eugene Gordon and the Sunday *New York Times*." March 23, 2008; http://moscowthroughbrowneyes.blogspot.com.

Federal Bureau of Investigation. Interviews of Edythe Mae Chapman Gordon Kelley. Boston. March 16, and April 30, 1954. Documents obtained under the Freedom of Information Act.

Fitch, Noel Riley. *Anaïs: The Erotic Life of Anaïs Nin*. New York: Little Brown, 1993.

Franklin, Ruth. "A Life in Good Taste." *New Yorker,* September 27, 2004, 142–146.

Fikenbine, Roy E. "Boston's Black Churches: Institutional Centers of the Antislavery Movement." In *Courage and Conscience: Black and White Abolitionists in Boston*, edited by Donald M. Jacobs, 169–189. Bloomington: Indiana University Press, 1993.

French, Desiree. "Dorothy West: A Child of the Harlem Renaissance Remembers Those Exciting Times." *Boston Globe*, August 12, 1989, 20.

Gatewood, Willard B. *Aristocrats of Color: The Black Elite, 1880–1920*. Fayetteville: University of Arkansas Press, 2000.

George-Graves, Nadine. *The Royalty of Negro Vaudeville: The Whitman Sisters and the Negotiation of Race, Gender and Class in African American Theater, 1900–1940*. New York: St. Martin's Press, 2000.

Gill, Glenda E. *A Study of the Federal Theatre, 1935–1939*. New York: Peter Lang, 1989.

Gillespie, Fern. "The Life and Legacy of Lois Mailou Jones." *Howard Magazine* 8, no. 2 (Winter 1999): 8–13, 19.

Gordon, Eugene. "Massachusetts: Land of the Free and Home of the Brave Colored Man." *Messenger* 7, no. 6 (June 1925): 219–222, 243.

———. "Negro Fictionists in America." *Saturday Evening Quill* 2 (April 1929): 16–21.

———. "Negro Society." *Scribners Magazine* 88 (August 1930): 134–142.

———. "The Opportunity Dinner: An Impression." *Opportunity: A Journal of Negro Life* (July 1927): 208–209.

Gordon, Lois. *Nancy Cunard: Heiress, Muse, Political Idealist*. New York: Columbia University Press, 2007.

Gruesser, John Cullen, ed. *The Unruly Voice: Rediscovering Pauline Elizabeth Hopkins*. Urbana: University of Illinois Press, 1996.

Guinier, Genii. "Interview with Dorothy West, May 6, 1978." In *The Black Women Oral History Project*, edited by Ruth Edmonds Hill, 10:143–223. Westport, CT: Meckler, 1991.

Guzman, Yvonne. "Family and Friends Honor Dottie West in Memorial Service." *Vineyard Gazette*, August 25, 1998, 1, 11.

Harper, Frances Ellen Watkins. *Iola Leroy; or, Shadows Uplifted*. 1892. Reprint, New York: Oxford University Press, 1990.

Hayden, Karen E., and Robert C. Hayden. *African-Americans on Martha's Vineyard and Nantucket: A History of People, Places and Events*. Boston: Select Publications, 1999.

Henry, George W. *Sex Variants: A Study of Homosexual Patterns*. New York: Paul Hoebber, 1948.

Hill, Errol, and James Vernon Hatch. *A History of African American Theatre*. New York: Cambridge University Press, 2006.

Hill, Tony. "Where Do We Go from Here: The Politics of Black Education, 1780–1980." *Boston Review,* October (1981): 1.

Himes, Chester. *Pinktoes*. 1961. Reprint, Jackson, MS: Banner Books, 1996.

———. *The Quality of Hurt: The Early Years, the Autobiography of Chester Himes*. 1972. Reprint, New York: Paragon House, 1990.

Hopkins, Pauline E. "Autobiographical Sketch." *Colored American Magazine* 2, no. 3 (January 1901): 218–219.

———. *Contending Forces: A Romance Illustrative of Negro Life North and South*. 1900. Reprint, New York: Oxford University Press, 1988.

———. "The Mystery within Us." *Colored American Magazine* 1, no. 1 (May 1900): 14–18.

———. *Of One Blood: Or, the Hidden Self*. 1902–1903. In *The Magazine Novels of Pauline Hopkins*, edited by Henry Louis Gates, 441–621. New York: Oxford University Press, 1988.

———. *Peculiar Sam; or, The Underground Railroad*. 1879. In *The Roots of African American Drama: An Anthology of Early Plays, 1858–1938*, edited by Leo Hamalian and James V. Hatch, 101–123. Detroit: Wayne State University Press, 1991.

———. *Winona: A Tale of Negro Life in the South and Southwest*. 1902. In *The Magazine Novels of Pauline Hopkins*, edited by Henry Louis Gates, 285–437. New York: Oxford University Press, 1988.

———. "Women's Department." *Colored American Magazine* 1, no. 2 (June 1900): 118–123.

Horton, James Oliver, and Lois E. Horton. *Hard Road to Freedom: The Story of African America*. New Brunswick: Rutgers University Press, 2001.

Houseman, John. *Run-Through: A Memoir*. New York: Simon and Schuster, 1972.

Hughes, Langston. *The Big Sea*. 1940. Reprint, New York: Hill and Wang, 1998.

———. *I Wonder as I Wander*. New York: Hill and Wang, 1956.

———. "The Negro Artist and the Racial Mountain." *Nation* 122 (June 23, 1926): 692–694.

Hull, Gloria, ed. *Give Us Each Day: The Diary of Alice Dunbar Nelson*. New York: Norton, 1986.

Hurston, Zora Neale. *Dust Tracks on a Road*. 1942. Reprint, New York: Harper Perennial, 2006.

———. "Stories of Conflict." *Saturday Review of Literature* 17 (April 2, 1938): 32.

———. *Their Eyes Were Watching God*. 1937. Reprint, New York: Perennial, 1998.

Ione, Carole. *Pride of Family: Four Generations of American Women of Color.* New York: Harlem Moon, 2004.

Jacobs, Donald M., ed. *Courage and Conscience: Black and White Abolitionists in Boston.* Bloomington: Indiana University Press, 1993.

James, Henry. *The Bostonians.* 1886. Reprint, New York: Modern Library, 2003.

Johnson, Cherene Sherrard. "'This plague of their own locusts': Space, Property, and Identity in Dorothy West's *The Living Is Easy.*" *African American Review* 38, no. 4 (2004): 609–624.

Johnson, James Weldon. *Black Manhattan.* 1930. Reprint, New York: Da Capo, 1991.

Jones, Sharon. *Rereading the Harlem Renaissance: Race, Class, and Gender in the Fiction of Jessie Fauset, Zora Neale Hurston, and Dorothy West.* New York: Praeger, 2002.

Kaplan, Carla, ed. *Zora Neale Hurston: A Life in Letters.* New York: Doubleday, 2002.

Kavanagh, Julie. *Secret Muses: The Life of Frederick Ashton.* New York: Pantheon, 1997.

Kirka, Danica. "Dorothy West—A Voice of Harlem Renaissance Talks of Past—But Values the 'Now.'" *Los Angeles Times*, January 1, 1995.

Lewis, Alfred Allan. *Ladies and Not-So-Gentle Women: Elisabeth Marbury, Anne Morgan, Elsie de Wolfe, Anne Vanderbilt, and Their Times.* New York: Penguin, 2000.

Lewis, David Levering. *When Harlem Was in Vogue.* New York: Penguin, 1997.

Lynes, Katherine R. "'A real honest-to-cripe jungle': Contested Authenticities in Helene Johnson's 'Bottled.'" *Modernism/Modernity* 14, no. 3 (September 2007): 517–525.

———. "'Sprung from American Soil': The 'Nature' of Africa in the Poetry of Helene Johnson." *Interdisciplinary Studies in Literature and Environment* 16, no. 3 (2009): 525–549.

Marbury, Elisabeth. *My Crystal Ball.* New York: Boni and Liveright, 1923.

McCullough, Kate. "Slavery, Sexuality, and Genre: Pauline Hopkins and the Representation of Female Desire." In *The Unruly Voice: Rediscovering Pauline Elizabeth Hopkins*, edited by John Cullen Gruesser, 21–49. Urbana: University of Illinois Press, 1996.

McDowell, Deborah E. "Conversations with Dorothy West." In *Harlem Renaissance Re-examined: A Revised and Expanded Edition*, edited by Victor Kramer and Robert Russ, 285–303. Troy, NY: Whitston, 1997.

McGrath, Abigail. "Afterword: A Daughter Reminisces." In *This Waiting for Love: Helene Johnson, Poet of the Harlem Renaissance*, edited by Verner D. Mitchell, 123–130. Amherst: University of Massachusetts Press, 2000.

———. "Three Little Women: A Memoir Based on a Couple of Facts." Unpublished novel.

McKay, Nellie. "Foreword." In *Shadowed Dreams: Women's Poetry of the Harlem Renaissance*, 2nd ed. revised and expanded, edited by Maureen Honey, xxv–xxviii. New Brunswick: Rutgers University Press, 2006.

Miller, Nina. *Making Love Modern: The Intimate Public Worlds of New York's Literary Women.* New York: Oxford University Press, 1998.

Minus, Marian. "The Fine Line." *Opportunity: A Journal of Negro Life* 17, no. 11 (November 1939): 333–337, 351.

———. "The Negro as a Consumer." *Opportunity* 16, no. 9 (September 1938): 274–276.

————. "Twice in His Lifetime." *Woman's Day* (December 1949): 40, 72, 74, 78.

Mitchell, Verner D., ed. *This Waiting for Love: Helene Johnson, Poet of the Harlem Renaissance*. Amherst: University of Massachusetts Press, 2000.

Mitchell, Verner D., and Cynthia Davis, eds. *Dorothy West: Where the Wild Grape Grows, Selected Writings 1930–1950*. Amherst: University of Massachusetts Press, 2005.

Moon, Henry Lee. "Black Proper Bostonians: A Review of *The Living Is Easy*." *Crisis* 55, no. 10 (October 1948): 308.

Nelson, Jill. *Finding Martha's Vineyard: African Americans at Home on an Island*. New York: Doubleday, 2005.

Newson, Adele. "An Interview with Dorothy West." *Zora Neale Hurston Forum* 2 (1987): 19–24.

Nugent, Richard Bruce. *Gentleman Jigger*. Philadelphia: Da Capo, 2008.

Perry, Margaret, *Silence to the Drums: A Survey of the Literature of the Harlem Renaissance*. Westport, CT: Greenwood Press, 1976.

Proust, Marcel. *Remembrance of Things Past*. 1927. Translated by Terence Kilmartin and C. K. Scott Moncrief. New York: Random House, 1981.

Rampersad, Arnold. *The Life of Langston Hughes*. Vol. 1. New York: Oxford University Press, 1986.

Ridley, Florida Ruffin. "Other Bostonians." *Saturday Evening Quill* 1 (June 1928): 54–56.

Roses, Lorraine Elena. "Interviews with Black Women Writers: Dorothy West at Oak Bluffs, Massachusetts, July 1984." *SAGE* 2, no. 1 (Spring 1985): 47–49.

————, ed. *Selected Works of Edythe Mae Gordon*. New York: G. K. Hall, 1996.

Roses, Lorraine Elena, and Ruth E. Randolph, eds. *Harlem's Glory: Black Women Writing, 1900–1950*. Cambridge: Harvard University Press, 1996.

Rowley, Hazel. *Richard Wright: The Life and Times*. New York: Henry Holt, 2001.

Royster, Jacqueline Jones, ed. *Southern Horrors and Other Writings: The Anti-Lynching Campaign of Ida B. Wells, 1892–1900*. New York: Bedford, 1996.

Saunders, James, and Renae Shackelford, eds. *The Dorothy West Martha's Vineyard*. Jefferson, NC: McFarland, 2001.

See, Sam. " 'Spectacles in Color': The Primitive Drag of Langston Hughes." *PMLA* 124, no. 3 (May 2009): 798–816.

Sherman, Joan R. "James Monroe Whitfield, Poet and Emigrationist: A Voice of Protest and Despair." *Journal of Negro History* 57, no. 2 (April 1972): 169–176.

Singh, Amritjit, and Daniel M. Scott III, eds. *The Collected Writings of Wallace Thurman: A Harlem Renaissance Reader*. New Brunswick: Rutgers University Press, 2003.

Smith, Homer. *Black Man in Red Russia*. Chicago: Johnson Publishing, 1964.

Somerville, Siobhan. *Queering the Color Line: Race and the Invention of Homosexuality in American Culture*. Durham, NC: Duke University Press, 2000.

Spillers, Hortense J. "Cross-Currents, Discontinuities." Afterword to *Conjuring: Black Women, Fiction, and Literary Tradition*, edited by Hortense Spillers and Marjorie Pryse, 249–261. Bloomington: Indiana University Press, 1985.

Sterling, Dorothy. *Black Foremothers: Three Lives*. 2nd ed. New York: Feminist Press, 1988.

Stevens, Walter J. *Chip on My Shoulder*. Boston: Meador, 1946.

Stone, Lori. "Spirit of Resistance: A Study of the Effects of Compulsory Hetero-sexuality in Selected Novels by African-American Women." M.A. thesis, University of Illinois, 1994.

Tate, Claudia. "Allegories of Black Female Desire; or, Reading Nineteenth-Century Sentimental Narratives of Black Female Authority." In *Changing Our Own Words: Essays on Criticism, Theory, and Writing by Black Women*, edited by Cheryl A. Wall, 98–126. New Brunswick: Rutgers University Press, 1989.

Taylor, Frank C. *Alberta Hunter: A Celebration of the Blues*. New York: McGraw-Hill, 1987.

Teel, Leonard Ray. "W. A. Scott and the Atlanta *World.*" *American Journalism* 6, no. 3 (1989): 158–178.

Thurman, Wallace. *Infants of the Spring*. 1932. Reprint, Boston: Northeastern University Press, 1992.

Ullman, Victor. *Martin R. Delaney: The Beginnings of Black Nationalism*. Boston: Bedford, 1971.

Wald, Alan M. *Exiles from a Future Time: The Forging of the Mid-Twentieth Century Literary Left*. Chapel Hill: University of North Carolina Press, 2001.

Walker, Alice. *In Search of Our Mothers' Gardens*. New York: Harcourt Brace, 1983.

Walker, Margaret. *Richard Wright: Daemonic Genius*. New York: Amistad, 1988.

Wall, Cheryl A. " 'Chromatic Words': The Poetry of Helene Johnson." Foreword to *This Waiting for Love: Helene Johnson, Poet of the Harlem Renaissance*, edited by Verner D. Mitchell, ix–xiii. Amherst: University of Massachusetts Press, 2000.

———. *Worrying the Line: Black Women Writers, Lineage, and Literary Tradition*. Chapel Hill: University of North Carolina Press, 2005.

Wallinger, Hannah. *Pauline E. Hopkins: A Literary Biography*. Athens: University of Georgia Press, 2005.

Warner, Sam B., Jr. *Streetcar Suburbs: The Process of Growth in Boston, 1870–1900*. New York: Atheneum, 1972.

Weiss, Andrea. *Paris Was a Woman: Portraits from the Left Bank*. San Francisco: Harper, 1995.

West, Dorothy. "Anecdotes Interview with Mrs. Ella Johnson." October 26, 1938. WPA Federal Writers' Project, 1936–1940, Manuscript Division, Library of Congress. http://rs6.10c.gov/wpaintro/wpahome.html.

———. "Cocktail Party." 1939. In *A Renaissance in Harlem*, edited by Lionel C. Bascom, 271–279. New York: Amistad, 2001.

———. *The Living Is Easy*. 1948. Reprint, New York: Feminist Press, 1982.

———. "Mrs. Ella Johnson." October 20, 1938. WPA Federal Writers' Project, 1936–1940, Manuscript Division, Library of Congress. http://rs6.10c.gov/wpaintro/wpahome.html.

———. *The Richer, the Poorer: Stories, Sketches, and Reminiscences*. New York: Anchor, 1995.

———. [Mary Christopher]. "Room in Red Square." *Challenge* 1, no. 1 (March 1934): 10–15.

———. [Mary Christopher]. "Russian Correspondence." *Challenge* 1, no. 2 (September 1934): 14–20.

———. *The Wedding*. New York: Anchor, 1995.

Whitfield, James Monroe. *America and Other Poems*. Buffalo, NY: James S. Leavitt, 1853. http://www.classroomelectric.org/volume1/levine/amindex.html.

Wiggins, Lida Keck, ed. *The Life and Works of Paul Laurence Dunbar.* New York: Dodd, Mead, 1907.

Williams, Blanche Colton. Introduction to *O. Henry Memorial Award Prize Stories of 1926*, vii–xxvii. New York: Doubleday, 1928.

———. *Our Short Story Writers.* 1920. Reprint, Freeport, NY: Books for Libraries Press, 1969.

Williams, George W. *History of the Twelfth Baptist Church, Boston Mass., from 1840–1874.* Boston: James H. Earle, 1874.

Wirth, Thomas H., ed. *Gay Rebel of the Harlem Renaissance: Selections from the Work of Richard Bruce Nugent.* Durham, NC: Duke University Press, 2002.

———. Introduction to *Gentleman Jigger*, by Richard Bruce Nugent, x–xviii. Philadelphia: Da Capo, 2008.

Wright, Richard. "Blueprint for Negro Writing." *New Challenge* 2, no. 2 (Fall 1937): 53–64.

INDEX

About the Authors

VERNER D. MITCHELL is Associate Professor and Director of Graduate Studies in English at the University of Memphis. He is the editor of *This Waiting for Love: Helene Johnson, Poet of the Harlem Renaissance.*

CYNTHIA DAVIS is Professor of English and Director of Faculty and Curriculum at Barry University. She is the author of *Dynamic Communication for Engineers* and (with Verner Mitchell) *Dorothy West: Where the Wild Grape Grows* and *Western Echoes of the Harlem Renaissance: The Life and Writings of Anita Scott Coleman.*

810.9 M69   HALIW
Mitchell, Verner D.,
Literary sisters :Dorothy West and
her circle : a biography of the Har
 ALIEF
 05/12